# CETA

## Accomplishments
## Problems Solutions

### A Report by the Bureau of
### Social Science Research, Inc.

William Mirengoff * Lester Rindler
Harry Greenspan * Charles Harris

THE W. E. UPJOHN INSTITUTE FOR EMPLOYMENT RESEARCH

**Library of Congress Cataloging in Publication Data**
Main entry under title:

CETA, accomplishments, problems, solutions.

"BSSR: 562."
"BSSR report no. 0621-4."
1. Manpower policy—United States.    I.   Mirengoff,
William.    II.   Bureau of Social Science Research
(Washington, D.C.)    III.   Title:  C.E.T.A., accomplishments,
problems, solutions.
HD5724.C4            331.11'0973          82-2856
ISBN 0-911558-97-7
ISBN 0-911558-96-9 (pbk.)                 AACR2

THE INSTITUTE, a nonprofit research organization, was established
on July 1, 1945. It is an activity of the W. E. Upjohn Unemployment
Trustee Corporation, which was formed in 1932 to administer a fund
set aside by the late Dr. W. E. Upjohn for the purpose of carrying on
"research into the causes and effects of unemployment and measures
for the alleviation of unemployment."

iii

# Authors

William Mirengoff played a key role in the establishment of the Manpower Administration in the Department of Labor (1968) where his responsibilities included the development of plans and policies for the implementation of the Manpower Development and Training Act and the Neighborhood Youth Corps. He has also served as director of the Job Corps, director of the Public Employment Program, and manpower consultant to the governments of Brazil and Jamaica.

From 1974 to 1981, Mr. Mirengoff was associated with the National Academy of Sciences as study director of the CETA evaluation project. He is principal author of eight volumes analyzing the CETA programs. Mirengoff joined the Bureau of Social Science Research in 1981 as director of the Employment and Training Evaluation Project. He has a B.A. from Brooklyn College and M.A. from American University in economics.

Lester Rindler joined the Bureau of Social Science Research to continue with the CETA evaluation study with which he was associated at the National Academy of Sciences. Previously he had been a labor economist at the U.S. Department of Labor's Manpower Administration, serving in a number of posts including three years as an analyst in the Office of Program Research. He also served as head of the Area Labor Reports Branch of the U.S. Employment Service, assistant chief of the Automation and Manpower Skills Division, and before that, chief of the Farm Labor and Migration Studies Division. His most recent position, before joining the NAS, was chief of the Division of Program Data and Requirements in the Office of Public Employment Programs. Rindler has a B.A. from Harvard and an M.A. in sociology and public welfare from the American University. He is a member of the Montgomery County (Maryland) Employment Development Commission.

Prior to his association with the Bureau of Social Science Research, Harry Greenspan worked with William Mirengoff at the National Academy of Sciences. Previous to that, Mr. Greenspan was an economist at the National Planning Association (NPA) for three years where he headed the Manpower Group for the LEAA-supported nationwide survey of law enforcement and criminal justice personnel needs and resources, which BSSR conducted in collaboration with NPA and the American Institutes for Research. From 1968 to 1974 he headed the Division of Resource Allocation, Planning and Program Analysis of the Employment and Training Administration (ETA) of the Department of Labor. He was a labor economist for eight years at ETA, and chief of the Bureau of Labor Statistics' Branch of Occupational Structure Studies. Greenspan has a B.A. and M.A. in economics from the University of Minnesota.

Charles S. Harris, research associate with the Bureau of Social Science Research, was a member of the project staff of the study reported here. He is currently directing an investigation of how states have allocated federal monies for aging programs. Prior to joining the Bureau, Dr. Harris headed research and evaluation for the National Council on the Aging, where he directed an evaluation of employment and training programs for middle-aged and older adults, and a study of the impact of political, social, and economic changes on the elderly. In 1978 he edited *Fact Book on Aging: A Profile of America's Older Population.* He recently authored "Current Programs for the Retired" in Malcolm Morrison's *Economics of Aging* (Von Nostrand, 1981) and is co-author of a forthcoming book *Applied Research in Aging* (Little Brown, 1982). He has a Ph.D. in sociology from Duke University.

# Foreword

The W. E. Upjohn Institute is pleased to publish the latest in a series of evaluation studies on the programs funded under the Comprehensive Employment and Training Act (CETA). This series, directed by William Mirengoff, began in 1974 under the aegis of the National Academy of Sciences and was funded by a grant from the U.S. Department of Labor. This latest report was completed under the auspices of the Bureau of Social Science Research, Inc., with co-authors Lester Rindler, Harry Greenspan and Charles Harris.

*CETA: Accomplishments, Problems and Solutions* concludes that the overriding objectives of CETA to serve more fully those on the lower rung of the economic ladder and to increase their opportunities in the labor market have been achieved through the 1978 reauthorization act. Despite these achievements, however, major policy questions persist and are addressed by the authors.

This report was based largely on information obtained from on-site examinations of CETA operations completed by field research associates at 28 sites.

Findings of the study bear directly on the employment and training issues now being considered by the Administration and Congress.

Facts and observations presented in this study are the sole responsibility of the authors. Their viewpoints do not necessarily represent the positions of The W. E. Upjohn Institute for Employment Research.

E. Earl Wright
*Director*

*Kalamazoo, Michigan*
*March 1982*

# Preface

This report, dealing with the implementation and impact of the Comprehensive Employment and Training Act Amendments of 1978 (PL 95-524), is a followup of a study conducted in 1979 under the auspices of the National Academy of Sciences entitled *The New CETA: Effect on Public Service Employment Programs.* The present study was funded by a grant from the Employment and Training Administration, U.S. Department of Labor, and is part of the research program of the Bureau of Social Science Research.

The field survey was conducted in October-November 1980, at a time when the public service employment program was being cut back, but before steps were taken to phase out the program by the end of FY 1981. The report was written when Congress was considering the reauthorization of CETA which expires in September 1982. Its findings are expected to contribute to the deliberations on the design of a federally supported employment and training system.

CETA was enacted in 1973 to reform the employment and training system that had developed under the Manpower Development and Training Act of 1962 (MDTA), the Economic Opportunity Act of 1964 (EOA), and the Emergency Employment Act of 1971 (EEA). CETA consolidated the numerous categorical programs under these statutes and transferred control to local and state governments—prime sponsors—under general policy guidelines of the federal government.

Since that time, CETA has both expanded and contracted in size, new programs have been added and the original block grant design has been altered. Major changes included the addition of a large-scale countercyclical PSE program in 1974, a major expansion of PSE and the addition of new youth projects in 1977, and in 1978, the establishment of a "private sector initiative program." These legislative changes were accompanied by substantial fluctuations in funding. Outlays increased about three-fold from $3.2 billion in 1975 to a peak of $9.6 billion in 1978, then declined to about $7.6 billion in fiscal 1981.[1]

The management of employment and training programs became increasingly complex as local and state prime sponsors struggled with new programs, changes in policies, and shifts in funding levels. As an indication of the size and complexity of the task, the Department of Labor estimated that in 1980 there were more than 50,000 subcontractors providing employment, training, or other services for some 3.5 million CETA clients under the supervision of 471 prime sponsors.

The 1978 amendments, the latest in a series of legislative changes, reauthorized CETA for four years (through September 1982), and made a number of far-reaching changes intended to resolve problems that had plagued CETA, particularly its public service jobs program, since its beginning. The amendments changed eligibility requirements to focus more sharply on the disadvantaged, lowered wages for public service jobs, required training for public service employment enrollees, and limited the length of time par-

---

1. The Reagan Administration budget projects outlays for 1982 at $4.5 billion.

ticipants could remain in CETA. Also, significant changes were made to tighten administrative controls at the federal and local level.

The present report reviews developments in CETA two years after the reauthorization act. It is based largely on information obtained in the October 1980 on-site examination of a sample of 28 prime sponsors drawn from a universe of over 400, supplemented by national level data from the Department of Labor and other sources. This assessment is focused particularly, though not exclusively, on PSE programs and, as noted earlier, was undertaken at a time when some retrenchment was assumed but before the rapid phaseout of PSE. The report expands the information in a preliminary report published in April 1981 and adds new topics. Major subjects include: the effect of the amendments on local program management, the characteristics profile of clients, wages paid for PSE jobs, the types of jobs and services provided, and the training and employability development services provided to enrollees. The report also deals with changes in the systems used to deliver services, the role of unions in CETA programs, and the experience of prime sponsors in placing enrollees in unsubsidized jobs.

The report relies heavily on the findings and assessments of resident field associates who used a common study outline as a basis for examining and reporting on CETA developments. Most of them have been following the CETA programs in their areas for several years. We are grateful for their valuable contribution. We also wish to thank the CETA administrators and other local officials who patiently participated in lengthy discussions and provided statistical and program materials. Officials of the U.S. Department of Labor and of Westat, Inc. were particularly helpful in providing statistical data. We appreciate the assistance of Seymour Brandwein, director, Office of Program Evaluation, and his associates, John Elliott and Jaime G. Salgado, who contributed to the formulation of the study objectives, provided technical advice, and arranged for obtaining national statistical data. We are also indebted to Ruth P. Carroll for editorial review and to Helen Wynne who provided the administrative support. Michael E. Yancey was responsible for the graphic material.

William Mirengoff
*Project Director*

# Executive Summary

## *Introduction*

This report deals with CETA developments subsequent to the passage of the reauthorization act amendments of 1978. In addition to the changes in the public service employment (PSE) programs, the report examines CETA's management, clientele, program mix and delivery systems as well as the role of organized labor and the outcomes of the programs. The final section of the report presents an agenda of unresolved policy issues.

## *Principal Findings*

Some of the chronic difficulties that plagued the CETA programs have been largely overcome by the amendments of 1978. Considerable progress was reported in redressing the problems of:

- "Creaming," selecting persons most likely to succeed rather than those most in need.
- Substitution, the use of CETA funds for work that otherwise would be supported by local resources.
- Program abuses, including the enrollment of ineligible persons.

However, the cumulative effect of the amendments has been to increase administrative burdens on a system already heavily encumbered and to quicken the drift of CETA towards recentralization.

1. Management. The CETA changes after 1978 substantially achieved the Congressional objective of making program managers more sensitive to the need to protect the integrity of CETA. Compliance procedures were tightened; responsibility for misspent funds was clarified and the Department of Labor was given new powers to deal with abuses. In addition, monitoring and auditing received greater attention. The erratic appropriations and allocation cycles, however, kept CETA administrators on a roller-coaster and frustrated their efforts to conduct an orderly program.

2. Participants. The reauthorization act of 1978 succeeded in one of its primary objectives—to orient the program more fully to those who have the greatest difficulty in getting and keeping jobs. By 1980, low income persons were 92 percent of new PSE enrollees and 95 percent of the participants in training programs (17 and 22 percentage points, respectively, above the 1978 levels). In addition, larger proportions of welfare recipients (31 percent vs. 22 percent), members of minority groups (48 percent vs. 39 percent) and persons with less than a high school education (35 percent vs. 25 percent) had entered PSE programs. Youth were particularly prominent. In 1980, they comprised 60 percent of all CETA enrollees.

3. PSE Wages, Jobs and Services. The reduction in PSE wage levels had the intended effect of discouraging more qualified persons from competing for PSE jobs and discouraging local governments from using CETA participants in place of regular employees. However, the lowered wage rates also reduced the skill levels of PSE jobs and the usefulness of the PSE services to the community.

4. Organized Labor. Labor organizations played a significant role in local CETA programs in 20 percent of the areas studied, but involvement was very limited in a majority of

the areas, either by their own choice or because their position in the community was weak. Labor participation generally sought to protect employment standards of regular employees and to help improve the effectiveness of CETA programs.

5. Outcomes. CETA reorganization provisions affected job placements in two directions. Employability of participants was enhanced by the mandate to add a training component to PSE jobs and by an improved enrollee assessment process. However, the tighter eligibility requirements and the lowered wage levels resulted in the enrollment of individuals who were less competitive in the job market. Placement rates declined between 1978 and 1980, but this was attributed to softer labor markets and a less marketable clientele.

### Study Design

The study is based largely on field reviews of a sample of 28 prime sponsors conducted in October-November 1980, about 18 months after the CETA amendments became fully effective. The reviews were conducted by local analysts, mainly from academic or research organizations, who used a common set of survey instruments to examine and assess the CETA experiences in their areas. The study was directed by William Mirengoff under a grant from the Department of Labor to the Bureau of Social Science Research, Inc.

# Contents

# Tables

xxi

# Charts

# Figures

# 1 Overview

The Comprehensive Employment and Training Act Amendments of 1978 reauthorized CETA for four years, added new programs, and made sweeping changes in the continuing ones. The revisions were directed largely at problems associated with the public service employment (PSE) programs and, in the main, were successful in redressing them, but at a price.

Administrative controls were tightened, larger proportions of disadvantaged persons were enrolled, the tenure of participants was curtailed, supplementary training was provided to PSE enrollees, and wage levels for PSE positions were lowered. However, under the new provisions, CETA was more difficult to administer and PSE activities were less useful to communities and participants. Moreover, the new requirements quickened the drift of CETA to a more centralized and categorical employment and training system.

This report describes the experiences of the prime sponsors, through 1980, under the new programmatic and administrative provisions of the reauthorization act, examines the extent to which the objectives of the amendments have been realized, and assesses the consequences of pursuing these goals.

1

# Background

Congress enacted the Comprehensive Employment and Training Act in 1973 to reform the system of manpower programs that had evolved haphazardly since the early sixties. CETA shifted management responsibility from federal to state and local officials and replaced the numerous categorical programs with a block grant that permitted local officials to tailor employment and training programs to fit the needs of the unemployed population and the labor market setting of their areas. However, its central purpose—to improve the employability of persons handicapped by skill deficiencies or labor market barriers—remained the same as that of its predecessor programs.

CETA was barely launched when it was overtaken by the recession of 1974 and pressed into service as a countercyclical program. Congress passed and later expanded Title VI, its major public service employment program. By 1978, PSE, accounting for 60 percent of all CETA expenditures, had elbowed aside the original structurally oriented programs and became the centerpiece of CETA. In the eyes of many local officials, PSE was the CETA program. The reasons for this perception were not hard to discern. In March 1978, almost 5 percent of the 13 million state and local government employees were PSE enrollees. Further, PSE provided visible and useful services to most communities and fiscal relief to some hard pressed localities. However, the rapid expansion of PSE created a number of thorny problems that surfaced during the deliberations over the reauthorization of CETA.

## The 1978 Amendments

CETA came before Congress for reauthorization in 1978 amid a barrage of criticism and continuing concerns:

- "Creaming" - the selection of persons most likely to succeed rather than those most in need.
- Substitution - the use of PSE funds for work that otherwise would be supported by local resources.
- Program abuse - in the hasty pursuit of ambitious enrollment goals, ineligible persons were enrolled, and there were allegations that PSE programs were approved on the basis of expediency rather than effectiveness.
- High wage rates - in some cases, the attractiveness of PSE wages induced participants to remain in their federally subsidized jobs rather than to seek unsubsidized employment.
- Unrestricted tenure - although PSE was designed as a transitional program, many enrollees remained in the program for years.
- Lack of training - PSE employment often did not prepare enrollees adequately for regular jobs.

Most of the objections were leveled at PSE and almost led to its demise. It was rescued at the last moment only by the adoption of several far-reaching reforms (see Chart 1). The persistence of some of the problems reflected the difficulty, inherent in a decentalized system, of achieving congruence between national goals and the varied objectives of local officials who administer the programs. The problems had been made more intractable by the weakness of the federal and local monitoring systems, the failure of Congress to assign explicit liability and clear sanctions for program abuses, and the tendency of Congress to write ambiguous and overly ambitious legislation.

The weaknesses of the PSE programs had been identified in the Emergency Jobs Programs Extension Act of 1976 which attempted to constrain substitution and to sharpen the focus on the disadvantaged by mandating short-duration PSE projects and limiting enrollment to the low-income, long term unemployed. But the remedies adopted under that

## Chart 1
## Major Changes in the Comprehensive Employment and Training Act Resulting from the 1978 Amendments

| | Comprehensive Employment and Training Act of 1973 (PL 93-203) | | Comprehensive Employment and Training Act Amendments of 1978 (PL 95-524) |
|---|---|---|---|
| Title I | Training programs for the unemployed, under-employed, and economically disadvantaged. | Title IIB/C | Training programs for the economically disadvantaged unemployed and underemployed; upgrading and retraining. Tenure in CETA programs (except PSE) limited to 30 months. |
| Title II | Public service jobs for the unemployed and underemployed in areas of high unemployment. | Title IID | Public service jobs for the low-income, long term unemployed, and for welfare recipients. A portion of allotments reserved for training. Employability development plans required. Tenure limited to 18 months. Wages lowered. |
| Title III | National programs for Indians, migrant farm workers, youth and other special groups. Research, evaluation, and labor market information. | Title III | National programs for Indians, migrant farm workers, older workers, and other special groups. Research, evaluation, and labor market information. |
| Title IV | Job Corps. | Title IV | Job Corps. Summer youth programs. Other youth employment projects. |
| Title V | National Commission for Manpower Policy. | Title V | National Commission for Employment and Training Policy. |
| Title VI | Countercyclical public service jobs for the unemployed and underemployed. Part of funds reserved for short duration projects for the low-income, long term unemployed, and welfare recipients. | Title VI | Countercyclical public service jobs for the low-income, long term unemployed, and for welfare recipients. A portion of allotments reserved for training and employability counseling. Tenure limited to 18 months. Wages lowered. |

| Title I | Administrative provisions: designation of prime sponsors; planning. Requires sponsors to establish independent monitoring units. |
| Title VII | Experimental private sector initiative programs. |
| Title VIII | Youth conservation projects. |

| Title VII | Administrative provisions: designation of prime sponsors; planning. |

act were not equal to the task. The amendments of the 1978 reauthorization act, on the other hand, were considerably more successful. The reauthorization act reaffirmed the basic commitment to "provide job training and employment opportunities for economically disadvantaged unemployed or underemployed persons." However, it also responded to the adverse criticism by radical changes in several of the program and administrative features of PSE. Programmatically, the amendments sought to restrict PSE to the low-income, long term unemployed and to restrict eligibility in Title IIB/C programs to the economically disadvantaged. To accomplish this, Congress relied on two basic strategies: tighter eligibility criteria and lower permissible wage levels for PSE workers. The administrative measures to protect the integrity of the program called for the establishment of an Office of Management Assistance, independent monitoring units (IMUs) at the local level, rigorous procedures for verifying the eligibility of applicants, and prime sponsor liability for program abuses.

## The Balance Sheet

### Accomplishments

The survey findings indicate that, in large measure, the intent of the reauthorization amendments was realized. In particular, the program attacked the following difficulties which the legislation had identified:

- Targeting - the overriding objective of the CETA amendments—to serve more fully those on the lower rungs of the socioeconomic ladder—was achieved. Between 1978 and 1980, groups that typically experience high unemployment rates increased their share of CETA slots.
- Substitution - the survey did not attempt to measure the extent to which PSE replaced regular public sector

workers. However, with the shift to less qualified enrollees, with fewer opportunities to fill skilled positions, and with the limited tenure of PSE enrollees, the temptation to substitute was lessened.

- Program integrity - the vulnerability of the PSE program to abuses was reduced. By fixing the liability for improper expenditures on the prime sponsor and by prescribing strict monitoring and auditing procedures, program managers have become much more sensitive to the need to protect the integrity of CETA and have taken preventive measures.
- Participant employability - the two measures taken to direct more attention to participant development—individual employability development plans (EDPs), and the addition of a formal training component to PSE jobs—did help to improve the employability of CETA participants.

## *Shortfalls*

Other goals, however, were not readily attained.

- Planning and administration - one of the continuing complaints—indeed a constant refrain—of local sponsors has been the amount of red tape with which the CETA planning and grant processes are wrapped. In an effort to simplify the procedures, the reauthorization act consolidated some of the planning documents. In practice, however, planning was no easier than before. Moreover, the new titles, complicated eligibility and wage provisions, and stricter monitoring added new administrative tasks to a system already stretched to its limits.
- Transition - despite the reauthorization act's greater emphasis on the transition of CETA participants into unsubsidized employment, job entry rates declined between 1978 and 1980. The decline was attributed to the

lower skill level of the new enrollees and the softening of the labor markets in which they sought employment.

Although the primary objectives of the 1978 amendments were, in large measure, attained, there were unanticipated consequences that exacted a high price. Indeed, some of the objectives were achieved at the expense of other explicit and implicit goals.

1. The major tradeoff was targeting vs. community services—limiting PSE enrollment to disadvantaged persons at the cost of diminished usefulness of community services.

2. PSE jobs were also less useful to participants. The wage restrictions resulted in many positions with limited job content that did little to provide enrollees with the kind of job experience that would improve their prospects of obtaining unsubsidized employment. In effect, the eligibility and wage limits resulted in the creation of poor jobs for poor people.

3. Holding prime sponsors financially liable for expenditures found to be improper has made them extremely cautious in the operation of their programs and has discouraged innovations. In some functions, particularly eligibility determination, it has led to duplication of activities and enrollment delays as sponsors sought to make assurances doubly sure.

4. In a broader context, the reauthorization changes have constrained local sponsor flexibility. The new mandates have taken CETA a considerable distance back to a centralized program design.

5. Some government agencies concluded that the wage and eligibility restrictions created burdens that outweighed benefits and withdrew from PSE programs.

# Summing Up

## *Managing CETA Programs*

Since its inception, CETA has been buffeted by frequent changes in program direction, uncertain resource allocations, and a host of administrative problems. The 1978 reauthorization act, in its effort to reform the CETA system, has added significantly to these difficulties. However, as sponsors adjusted to the new prescriptions and proscriptions, the turbulence experienced in the first transitional year was somewhat less evident in the second.

*Compliance.* The 1978 amendments that had the most direct effect on program management were those that focused on compliance and tightened administrative controls. Both the Department of Labor (DOL) and prime sponsors were directed to strengthen their enforcement activities.

The DOL was required to:

- Take more positive steps in defining responsibility for improper expenditures or for other program abuses and for obtaining repayment of misspent funds.
- Establish an Office of Inspector General.[1]
- Establish an Office of Management Assistance to provide prime sponsors with technical assistance.
- Conduct timely audits.

Prime sponsors were directed to:

- Follow rigorous procedures for determining and verifying the eligibility of participants.
- Establish independent monitoring units (IMUs) to ensure local compliance and program effectiveness.

---

1. Created under the Inspector Generals Act of 1978 as part of a government-wide reform.

Although these measures were generally successful in achieving closer program compliance, there were some failings:

- The DOL did not meet its auditing goals despite the addition of more auditors. Although the quality of the department investigations improved, some audits were below GAO standards.
- IMUs were established in all prime sponsor jurisdictions, but there was duplication of monitoring, inadequate follow through on recommendations, and confusion as to staff responsibilities. Moreover, in some instances, the independence of the IMU was questioned.

*Planning and staffing.* Congress responded to the criticism that planning and grant management documents were overdrawn by simplifying the process. Separate full blown annual plans for each CETA title were replaced by a one-time master plan, supplemented yearly by annual plan subparts incorporated in a single document. Forty-three percent of the CETA planners saw no significant change in the degree of difficulty in preparing the new plans; 32 percent found them less burdensome and 25 percent said they required more work.

By far, the most frustrating problems that sponsors faced in trying to manage their programs were the uncertainties, delays, and changes in funding allocations. These constant shifts disrupted planning and operations and made the orderly management of PSE almost impossible. Other common complaints revolved around four problems: labor market information was inadequate and unreliable; planning for administrative costs was exceedingly complicated; contrary to expectations, the master plans did require revisions; and repetition and unnecessary detail in the planning documents persisted.

A majority of the prime sponsors in the survey reported that the plans contributed to the design and operations of programs, and regional offices indicated that they were useful in reviewing local program operations. More than a third, however, viewed them as a perfunctory exercise to turn on the federal funding spigot.

On the whole, there were few changes in the role of planning councils attributable to the reauthorization act. However, the establishment of the private industry councils and the continuation of youth councils tended to fragment the planning process.

With increased funding, more intensive monitoring, and more record keeping requirements, the size of the prime sponsors' and subcontractors' administrative staffs was estimated to have grown from 20,000 in 1976 to more than 30,000 in 1980. Despite the stress and strain on CETA personnel, staff turnover was comparable to that in like industries. However, substantial separations were expected in the wake of program reductions in fiscal 1981 and 1982.

*Decentralization.* The development of the CETA program since its enactment portrays a steady drift away from one of its principal precepts—decentralization. The original design of a flexible, locally managed system was compromised by legislative and administrative actions that reintroduced categorical programs and increased the federal presence at the expense of local prime sponsor control.

## Delivering Services to Participants

With reductions in PSE funding, even before its phaseout by the end of fiscal 1981, program emphasis began to shift to the training components, particularly classroom training.

One of the aims of CETA was to bring the many separate activities of the employment and training programs together through an integrated delivery system. The movement towards such a comprehensive system for Title I programs was discernible immediately after the enactment of CETA.[2] Some of the reauthorization amendments speeded this trend. For example, some sponsors, concerned about their liability under the 1978 amendments, performed intake functions themselves to minimize the risk of enrolling ineligible participants. On the other hand, the establishment of a private sector initiative program (Title VII), along with the youth programs, has tended to splinter the overall CETA delivery system.

The reauthorization act not only affected the methods for delivering services but also the institutions used to provide them. The post-reauthorization period saw a significant reduction in the employment service participation in CETA due, in part, to the amendments and to reduced PSE funding. The new provisions removed the liability exemption that sponsors had previously enjoyed if they used the employment service for applicant recruitment and screening. With it went the special incentive to make extensive use of the employment service.

Relationships between prime sponsors and the employment service have, from the outset, been very sensitive. In this survey, most of the CETA administrators and the employment service officials characterized their relationships as basically "good" or "fair," reflecting a gradual accommodation.

### Reaching the Target Groups

The reauthorization act succeeded in accomplishing the overriding but elusive objective of CETA—to serve only those who experience the greatest difficulties in getting and

---

2. Title I, comprehensive manpower programs, was redesignated Title IIB in 1978.

keeping jobs. By 1980, low-income persons were 92 percent of new PSE enrollees (17 points above the 1978 level) and 95 percent of those entering Title IIB training programs (22 points above the 1978 level). In addition, larger proportions of welfare recipients, members of minority groups, and persons with less than a high school education had entered CETA programs. Youth were particularly prominent in CETA. In 1980, 60 percent of all CETA enrollees were under 22 years of age and 40 percent of all CETA appropriations were for youth programs.

The reauthorization achieved its targeting objective by direct and indirect means—directly, by using a finer eligibility mesh to screen applicants for the PSE program, and indirectly, by lowering the level of PSE wages, thus discouraging applications from those more able to "make it" in the job market.

Most CETA administrators considered the tightened eligibility requirements the most effective of the new provisions in targeting the PSE program. To ensure that only persons meeting the new criteria are enrolled, a rigorous eligibility determination and verification process was prescribed, and prime sponsors were held financially liable for ineligible enrollments.

The eligibility and wage requirements were not the only factors that shaped the characteristics profile of PSE participants. Perceptions of prime sponsors as to the purposes of PSE and their recruitment techniques also played some role. Where the recruitment sources were client oriented, such as welfare agencies and community based organizations, larger percentages of disadvantaged persons were enrolled.

The framers of the reauthorization act envisioned a two-part PSE program: Title IID for the structurally unemployed and Title VI for victims of cyclical unemployment. However, the differences in the eligibility criteria of the two titles were minimal and tended to obscure rather than sharpen the differences between the programs. In the post-reauthorization period, the clientele in Title IID and VI were almost indistinguishable. The coalescing of participant characteristics suggest that the two programs were serving essentially the same clientele and that the justification for separate programs was dubious.

### Conducting Needs Assessment and Training

Congress recognized that the effect of the tighter eligibility and wage provisions of the reauthorization act would be to enroll persons with fewer labor market capabilities and greater needs for employability development. To provide this support, two new requirements were prescribed:

- Individual employability development plans (EDPs) to assess the needs of enrollees, evaluate their labor market prospects, and make appropriate referrals to services and programs.
- A specific training component as a supplement to PSE jobs.

The study found that all prime sponsors were preparing EDPs, not only for Title II enrollees as mandated but also for most Title VI participants. However, the sponsors' perceptions of the utility of the EDPs were mixed. Some were complying *pro forma* but were skeptical of the usefulness of EDPs for all enrollees. On balance, however, they felt that the requirement served to emphasize the need for better participant assessment.

Although prime sponsors had always been free to use their PSE funds for training or other CETA activities, very few had done so. Prior to the reauthorization, only 1 percent of PSE expenditures was used to train Title II or VI enrollees.

Following the 1978 amendments, all sponsors in the survey provided some form of PSE training. In 1980, more than 30 percent of PSE enrollees were receiving training in occupational skills, job search techniques, orientation to the labor market, or other forms of preparation for employment.

In their haste to comply with the expenditure requirements, many sponsors had not had time to develop and test training arrangements. Moreover, the efforts to mesh training with PSE jobs ran into resistance from participants who resented the interruption of their work and reduced earnings, from employing agencies whose work schedules were disrupted, and from training agencies who complained about lack of motivation and reluctance of PSE enrollees to participate in training. To avoid these problems, some sponsors chose the expedient of providing general work orientation or job search courses at the beginning or end of the employment period.

Despite the operational difficulties, the consensus of the CETA administrators was that the training helped participants to obtain and retain regular jobs, benefited PSE employers by improving job performance, and served the community by upgrading the skills of the hard-core unemployed. The placement data suggest that sponsors who emphasize training have higher placement rates for their Title IID enrollees than those who do not.

### Providing Wages, Jobs, and Services

The wage provisions of the reauthorization act were aimed at two of the most intractable problems of the PSE program: the failure to enroll adequate proportions of persons who were most in need, and the use of PSE to supplant rather than supplement existing positions.

Congress expected that the restrictive wage provisions would discourage the more qualified persons from competing for PSE jobs and that prime sponsors, faced with lesser skilled enrollees, would not be as inclined to use them in place of regular workers. These expectations were, in large part, realized.

The new provisions affected all aspects of PSE wage arrangements:

- The permissible national average wage level to be paid from CETA funds was lowered from $7,800 to $7,200 per year.
- The $10,000 maximum wage was retained except for high wage areas where it could be as high as $12,000.
- The authority of prime sponsors to supplement PSE wages with local funds was prohibited for Title IID participants and limited for Title VI enrollees.

Three strategies were used to accommodate PSE positions to the new requirements: some high-wage jobs were discontinued, some restructured, and in many instances, new low-wage jobs were created. By October 1980, about 40 percent of the sample areas indicated that more than half of their PSE jobs were new or restructured. Restructuring frequently was only cosmetic. Jobs were designated as trainees or aides, and little changed but salary and title.

The effect was to reduce the proportion of jobs requiring specialized skills in favor of jobs with more limited requirements. Professional, technical, and administrative jobs dropped from 20 percent of total PSE in 1978 to 14 percent in the last half of fiscal 1979. The share for craft jobs also declined. Offsetting increases occurred in the shares for clerical workers, laborers, and service workers.

Although the 1978 wage amendments succeeded in accomplishing their major objectives, they did exact a price. In half of the study areas, local officials said that the kinds of jobs created to conform to lower PSE wage requirements did not provide services as useful to their communities as those previously supplied. Further, respondents in 39 percent of the areas reported that the new low-wage jobs often did not provide the participants with the kinds of job experience that would improve their employability.

The extent to which PSE services are continued after federal funding is withdrawn provides some indication of the usefulness of PSE services to the community. In over half of the areas where PSE enrollment had declined by more than 20 percent, some services were continued with local funding. In those instances, most PSE workers were absorbed into the regular workforce.

The dissatisfaction of prime sponsors with the average wage provisions of the reauthorization act was reflected in a number of legislative proposals. In the waning days of the 96th Congress, the base for the national average wage was raised to $8,000 from $7,200. Since the new wage base was tied to 1979 and subject to annual wage adjustments, the effective national average for 1981 was $9,190.

## Assessing Organized Labor's Role in CETA

Organized labor's participation in CETA was motivated by two considerations: protecting the employment standards of union members and helping to improve the effectiveness of CETA's employment and training programs.

Opportunities for organized labor to influence CETA programs were available through membership on prime sponsor planning councils, formal review of the sponsors' plans, and informal access to CETA administrators. Organized labor was represented on all but one of the planning councils in the survey and constituted, on the average, 8 percent of council membership. In 13 of the 28 survey areas, prime sponsors received substantive comments on their plans from labor representatives. Unions expressed considerable dissatisfaction with their limited role in the early development of prime sponsors' plans and with the lack of adequate time to review the voluminous documents. In some areas, they pressed for increased representation on the councils.

Union representatives sought to affect CETA activities by preventing some practices and encouraging others. They objected to:

- The substitution of PSE participants for regular employees.
- Training in occupations in which there were surplus workers.
- Establishing PSE positions that paid less than the prevailing rates.

Unions expressed interest in enhancing training and employment programs in several ways. They proposed that prime sponsors:

- Tie CETA training to apprenticeship programs.
- Make greater use of other training institutions.
- Give civil service preference to PSE employees in filling vacancies for regular public sector jobs.
- Increase their efforts to hire PSE participants at the end of their 18 months tenure in PSE.

Although organized labor played a significant role in some instances, its involvement was very limited in a majority of the areas—either by its own choice or because its influence in the community was weak and its views disregarded.

Following the passage of the 1978 reauthorization act, collective bargaining agreements dealing with PSE issues were modified in one quarter of the areas where contracts were in effect. Most of the modifications were the result of the act's new wage provisions and involved the establishment of new positions and the protection of the existing wage structure.

## Promoting Unsubsidized Employment

The placement of participants in suitable unsubsidized employment has long been a major goal of employment and training programs. The objective was reaffirmed in the original CETA legislation which declared that the purpose of the programs was to assure "that training and other services lead to maximum employment opportunities and enhance self-sufficiency." The reauthorization act of 1978 enlarged the objective to include increasing "earned income." Thus the aim became not merely a job but stable employment and increased compensation.

In assessing the effects of the reauthorization act on job placement, the survey noted countervailing forces. The new PSE training provisions and the improved assessment process were viewed as enhancing employability. On the other hand, the stricter eligibility requirements and the lowered wage levels have tended to enroll persons with fewer qualifications with which to compete in the job market.

National office emphasis on placement was scarcely greater than in the past. Indeed, DOL regulations appear to be weaker since they no longer require specific transition goals, and grant instructions dealing with placements are only slightly more specific. The act requires the Secretary of Labor for the first time to establish performance standards, including placement goals. However, these are in the development stage and have been introduced only experimentally. Locally, there were few major changes in the organization or procedures for the transition of enrollees that are directly attributable to the reauthorization act.

Despite the intent of the reauthorization act, job entry rates were lower in 1980 than 1978. Respondents attributed the change to softer labor market conditions and less marketable enrollees. However, sponsors who adopted aggressive management practices directed at improving transition generally had higher job entry rates.[3]

Since the inception of CETA, more than one-third of the enrollees who terminated were reported by sponsors as entering employment immediately after leaving the program. Job entry rates were higher for Title IIB/C enrollees (Title I in 1973) than for those in the PSE programs (Titles IID and VI). Longitudinal studies[4] found improved labor market status and higher earnings for PSE participants over subsequent months (some of which would have occurred without program participation). When efforts to isolate program impact were made, it was found that earnings of enrollees were positively affected by their CETA experience when compared with earnings of a matched group of non-CETA individuals. The greatest gains were made by those with poor employment records and low earnings prior to entry. On the average, persons who had high earnings before entering CETA earned less after leaving the programs.

## A Policy Agenda

From the beginning, CETA has had to deal with a number of basic policy questions. Some have been addressed by the reauthorization amendments, and the elimination of PSE has responded to other issues. But major knotty questions remain. The nine issues listed below pose questions—not yet fully resolved by legislation or experience—about the fundamental purposes and practices of CETA.

---

3. It should be noted that the BSSR survey was conducted in late 1980, before the new Administration had begun to phase out PSE and had launched a drive to place laid off CETA enrollees in unsubsidized jobs.

4. *Continuous Longitudinal Manpower Survey* (CLMS) administered by the Bureau of the Census and Westat, Inc., supported by the Office of Program Evaluation, Employment and Training Administration, DOL.

- What are the limits of CETA? CETA has been an employment and training workhorse, driven in many directions at once. It was expected to: serve the structurally unemployed, create public sector jobs for the cyclically unemployed, provide essential community services, relieve the fiscal problems of hard pressed localities, and give special consideration to a host of target groups. At issue is whether CETA can be used as a program for all seasons. The phaseout of the PSE programs has, in part, reined in the reach of the system.
- Can the program continue to pursue multiple—sometimes contradictory—goals? The problem of which direction to take is compounded by CETA's liberal sprinkling of goals. Since some are competitive or contradictory, the pursuit of one may preclude the attainment of another. For example, CETA sets a high priority on placements, but limits enrollment to persons most difficult to place. CETA also expected PSE to provide essential community services, but prohibited the payment of wage levels necessary for the performance of these tasks. In short, CETA embraces a wide spectrum of national goals but has neither harmonized nor set priorities among them.
- How can local needs and national policies be made more compatible? One of the underlying premises of the decentralized block grant concept is that local program practices are congruent with national policies. There are in fact significant divergencies. CETA is a meld of local, state, and federal aspirations implemented by an army of federal, state, and local institutions. Each partner in the triad is motivated by its own interests and attempts to shape the program to those ends. The recentralization of CETA that began immediately after the implementation of the legislation had its roots in the effort to make local practices, particularly PSE practices, conform to federal objectives. Without PSE, the divergence be-

tween national and local interests may be mitigated.

- Is CETA a social or an economic program? After seven years there was still no clear perception as to whether CETA was to serve social or economic purposes, or both. As inheritor of the manpower programs of the sixties, CETA was concerned with the labor market problems of the disadvantaged and had a distinctly social orientation. The addition of Title VI and its subsequent expansion as a part of the 1977 economic stimulus package gave CETA a countercyclical cast. However, even though the job creation function of PSE remained unchanged, the continuous amendments to tighten eligibility underscored the perception of CETA as a social program. Thus, although born out of economic concerns, PSE was reared as a social program. With the elimination of PSE, the program composition of CETA reverts to its original configuration.

- Can the countercyclical trigger be made to work? The effectiveness of PSE as a countercyclical instrument depended, in part, upon the extent to which it could be fine tuned to expand and contract in tandem with unemployment rates. The 1978 amendments authorized a "trigger" to accomplish this conjunction, but it was not employed. Earlier studies indicate that although rapid expansion was possible, it exacted a toll in program abuses. In any event, the historical experience of PSE does not reveal that PSE enrollment levels match changes in the unemployment rate.

- Whom should CETA programs serve? How fine should the screening mesh be? With limited resources, should all but the most seriously disadvantaged be screened out? Or should there be enough flexibility to permit CETA to address the problems of the less disadvantaged who face structural difficulties such as job obsolescence, plant closings, and the need to relocate from chronically depressed areas?

- Can CETA be used more effectively for economic development? Although no longer a national counter-cyclical program, CETA has considerable potential as an instrument to promote local economic development. It could, by developing appropriate training programs, alleviate skill shortages, develop pools of trained workers that will attract industry, and help meet the needs of a changing economy.
- What kind of block grants? Closely related to the issues discussed above is the question of whether it is more ef-fective and efficient to deliver employment and training programs through the present federal-local block grant system, or whether the state should be the primary reci-pient and administrator of block grants for CETA pro-grams and perhaps for the employment service and vocational education systems as well. The issue was ad-dressed in 1973 when the legislation was enacted. It has resurfaced as part of the present Administration's com-mitment to the strategy of state block grants.
- Is CETA the answer? Finally, there remains the fun-damental question of whether federal funds are best used to support "repair shop" programs such as CETA—directed to those who have not been served adequately by the traditional institutions—or to rehabilitate and reform the basic institutions that are charged with development of human capital.

# 2 Management of CETA Programs

The Comprehensive Employment and Training Act of 1973 set out to improve the effectiveness of the employment and training programs that had evolved over a 12-year period. CETA proposed to accomplish this by shifting management responsibility from federal to state and local officials and by replacing the numerous categorical programs with a block grant that would permit local officials to select the blend of programs most suitable for the unemployed population and labor market setting of their areas. This decentralized and decategorized design, it was expected, would eliminate duplication, make the system more responsive to local needs, provide for grass roots participation, and improve the administration of the programs.

The CETA reform was directed more to improving the systems for delivering employment and training programs for the unemployed than to their substance. Prior to CETA, manpower programs generally were administered by the federal establishment dealing directly with state and local public and private organizations. Training programs were administered largely through state employment security and vocational education agencies, while work experience and other special programs were contracted directly with local public or private nonprofit agencies. The role of elected officials was minimal except for summer youth programs in major cities.

The direct line from local organizations to the federal establishment was cut. State and local officials were designated as "prime sponsors" and made responsible for the planning, management, and oversight of employment and training programs in their jurisdictions. They, in turn, were to contract with public or private agencies for specific services.

The administration of the employment and training programs that was to be facilitated under CETA has become increasingly complex. Program additions, modifications and uncertainties have kept administration in a state of flux. No sooner had CETA been enacted, than it became the vehicle for new categorical programs, such as the public service employment (PSE) programs and a variety of youth programs. These additions and accompanying regulations have tended to limit local management flexibility.

Moreover, prime sponsors faced with the task of building the institutional framework to manage the employment and training system were beset by a host of problems: constant need for staff training, control and coordination of subcontractors, balancing of different local interests, and frequent revisions of procedures. Overlaying—indeed overshadowing—these difficulties were problems stemming from federal actions or inactions: fluctuation in funding levels, delays in appropriations, changes in allocation of funds, and shifts in policies and emphases which left prime sponsors without a clear sense of direction. The administration of CETA was also affected by other federal laws dealing with such matters as veterans' preference, equal employment opportunity, and federal auditing procedures.

The reauthorization act of 1978 was the most far-reaching effort to redesign the CETA system. Enacted to protect the integrity of CETA and to achieve greater conformity of local programs with national purposes, the 1978 amendments added considerably to the burdens of program managers already sorely pressed.

This chapter reviews the experiences of prime sponsors during the 18 months after the implementation of the reauthorization act, with particular reference to the effect of the amendments on planning, staffing, monitoring, and other administrative aspects. The chapter is also concerned with the implications of the additional provisions for the original decentralization thrust of CETA; it examines the degree to which local decision making is constrained by detailed statutory mandates and departmental regulations.

## Effect of Reauthorization Act on Administrative Controls

### Measures to Improve Compliance

The CETA reauthorization act affected local administration of CETA in a number of ways. Provisions relating to eligibility, wages, tenure of participants, private sector initiatives, youth projects, and other programmatic changes affected overall management indirectly. Other changes related to planning, reporting, administrative costs, monitoring, and liability had a more direct effect. This section focuses on efforts to prevent program abuses by tougher compliance measures and the consequences of these efforts. The basic finding is that the strict monitoring and auditing provisions of the act helped to protect the integrity of the program, but the costs, in terms of administrative burdens and frustration of local officials, were considerable.

The emphasis on compliance activities evident throughout the reauthorization act reflected a widespread feeling in Congress and in the Administration that CETA was not being managed stringently enough. To deal with this, the Department of Labor proposed changes that would permit the Secretary of Labor to impose sanctions on CETA subcontractors as well as on sponsors.[1]

The House and Senate, however, went much further. Aroused by allegations of improper expenditures, use of CETA enrollees to supplant rather than supplement regular public service workers, and other abuses, Congress strengthened the compliance provisions of the act.[2] As finally enacted, the amendments defined more specifically the kinds of abuses that are prohibited, made explicit the enforcement authority of the DOL, added new powers that reinforced the Department's ability to control the system, and defined liability more clearly than in the earlier legislation.

The original legislation prohibited discrimination, use of CETA funds for political activities or for religious facilities, substitution of CETA participants for regular employees, and improper use of funds. The reauthorization act added many more proscriptions—against nepotism, conflict of interest, fees for placing CETA enrollees, kickbacks, inauditable records, and use of CETA funds for unionization or anti-unionization activities. Criminal provisions in the original act were extended to include obstruction of investigations and knowingly hiring an ineligible participant as well as embezzlement and improper inducement (Chart 2).

The act armed the Department with more effective means of preventing the misuse of funds or other irregularities and responded more forcefully in seeking corrective action or

1. See statement of Ernest G. Green, Assistant Secretary for Employment and Training, U.S. Department of Labor. *Hearings Before a Subcommittee of the Committee on Government Operations,* House of Representatives, August 17, 1978, p. 746.

2. U.S. Congress, House Committee on Education and Labor, *Comprehensive Employment and Training Act Amendments of 1978,* H.R. Rept. 95-1124, May 10, 1978, p. 13; U.S. Congress, Senate Committee on Human Resources, *Comprehensive Employment and Training Act Amendments of 1978,* S. Rept. 95-891, May 15, 1978, p. 42.

repayment.[3] The original act called for internal administrative controls, auditing, and accounting procedures and authorized the Secretary of Labor to withhold funds unless he could be assured that they would be used effectively. The 1978 amendments give the DOL new powers to subpoena records and witnesses for hearings and to recover funds directly from subcontractors as well as from prime sponsors. One of the controversial features is authorization to order repayment of misspent funds from sources other than CETA. The DOL must conduct timely audits and report to Congress annually on results. In addition to the investigative provisions of CETA, the Inspector Generals Act of 1978 required the establishment of an independent Office of Inspector General to strengthen the Department's compliance authority.[4]

Prime sponsors, for their part, were required to establish independent monitoring units (IMUs) to ensure compliance with CETA. They were obliged also to have an acceptable and proven method of determining and verifying the eligibility of participants.

Prime sponsors as well as subcontractors are held responsible for enrolling persons who were not eligible for CETA programs. Prior to the reauthorization act, CETA was not clear as to how liability was to be assigned. To facilitate the rapid buildup of Title VI PSE enrollments in 1977 and 1978, prime sponsors were urged to use the employment service to recruit enrollees and determine their eligibility. Where such arrangements were made, neither the Job Service nor the prime sponsor was liable for costs resulting from ineligible enrollments. The reauthorization act closed this loophole.

---

3. Ilona Rashkow, "Dealing with Fraud and Abuse Under the Comprehensive Employment and Training Act," Congressional Research Service, February 1981 (unpublished).

4. Prior to the establishment of the Office of Inspector General in October 1978, the Office of Special Investigations was responsible for the Department's auditing and investigative programs.

## Chart 2
### Provisions Relating to Administrative Controls, Monitoring, and Liability for Noncompliance Comprehensive Employment and Training Act of 1973 and Amendments of 1978

| | Reauthorization of CETA (1978 Amendments) | Original CETA (1973 Act as amended through 1976) |
|---|---|---|
| Records, audits | 1. The Secretary shall establish standards and procedures to assure against program abuses (Sec. 123(g)). Prime sponsor plans must include specific management and accounting procedures to assure adequate supervision and monitoring (Sec. 104(c) (2) and Sec. 103(a) (4)). Prime sponsors must keep appropriate records and make them available for review by the Department of Labor (Sec. 133(a)). The Secretary must make an annual report to Congress on the delays in making audits and personnel required to complete audits in a timely fashion (Sec. 133(b)). | 1. The prime sponsor must maintain records and make them available for auditing (Sec. 713). The Secretary shall not provide financial assistance unless the program has adequate administrative controls and accounting procedures (Sec. 703(12) and (14)). The Secretary shall prescribe regulations to assure adequate internal administrative controls and accounting procedures for public service employment programs (Sec. 208(d)). |
| Monitoring | 2. Prime sponsors and subrecipients must establish independent monitoring units. The Secretary shall annually assess the effectiveness of the units established (Sec. 121(q)). | |
| Eligibility verification | 3. Prime sponsors must have a recognizable and proven method of verifying eligibility of all participants (Sec. 104(c) (3)). | |
| Office of Management Assistance | 4. The Secretary shall establish an Office of Management Assistance to provide help to prime sponsors who request it or who are identified, based on complaints or audits, as not being in compliance with respect to some features of the Act (Sec. 135). | |

| | |
|---|---|
| Definition of abuses | 5. Defines abuses as nepotism, conflict of interest, charging fees to participants, excessive legal fees, improper commingling of funds, failure to keep auditable records, kickbacks, political patronage, violation of child labor laws, use of funds for religious, antireligious, unionization, anti-unionization, political activities, and lobbying (Sec. 123(g) and (j). Sec. 121(n), and Sec. 131); substitution of CETA for regular government or private organization funds (Sec. 121(e) and (g), and 122(c) and (e)); discrimination (Sec. 121(a), and Sec. 132). Embezzlement, improper inducement, knowingly hiring an ineligible person, or obstructing an investigation (Sec. 3). |
| | 5. Defines abuses as discrimination, use of funds for political activities, religious facilities, displacement of employed workers (Sec. 703, 710, 712; 205, 208). Also embezzlement and improper inducement (Sec. 711). |
| Liability provisions and sanctions | 6. The Secretary shall have the authority to revoke a prime sponsor's plan and terminate financial assistance, after a hearing, if the prime sponsor fails to carry out provisions of the Act (Sec. 106(c)). He has authority to require attendance of witnesses (Sec. 133(a) (3)). The Secretary may order repayment of misspent funds and take action if necessary against subcontractors (Sec. 106(d) (1) and Sec. 106(8)). He may require repayment of misspent funds from sources other than CETA funds (Sec. 106(d) (2)). He may take appropriate action in cases of discrimination (Sec. 106(f)). Criminal penalties apply for theft, embezzlement, improper inducement, for knowingly hiring an ineligible individual, or obstructing an investigation (Sec. 3). |
| | Prime sponsors are liable for the eligibility of those enrolled; they may delegate responsibility for determining eligibility under reasonable safeguards including provision for reimbursement of costs incurred because of erroneous determinations made with insufficient care (Sec. 123(i)). |
| | 6. The Secretary shall, after hearings, suspend payments under a plan or portions of a plan if he finds it is not in compliance with the Act (Sec. 108). Specifies criminal penalties for embezzlement and improper inducement (Sec. 711). |

Prime sponsors are responsible. Moreover—and this may have a greater deterring effect—criminal penalties apply for persons who knowingly hire ineligible persons under the act. Prime sponsors may delegate determination provided there are reasonable safeguards including provision for reimbursement of costs incurred because of "erroneous determinations made with insufficient care."

## Department of Labor Responses

The DOL developed several strategies to tighten its administration of CETA. It strengthened monitoring requirements, prescribed a rigorous eligibility determination and verification procedure, and spelled out liability provisions. In addition to establishing the Office of Inspector General to give more direction to the auditing and investigative actions, it set up an Office of Management Assistance to help sponsors resolve management difficulties before they became compliance problems.

However, a 1980 report of the General Accounting Office indicated that the DOL fell short of its goal of auditing, biennially, all organizations receiving CETA funds. The report also found that some audits that were performed did not conform to acceptable standards.[5] The Department responded by adding more auditors and improving the quality of its investigations. In addition to DOL auditors, the Office of Inspector General uses CPA firms and state and local government audit agencies. Despite these efforts, the

---

5. General Accounting Office, *More and Better Audits Needed of CETA Grant Recipients,* FGMSD-81-1 (Washington: General Accounting Office, November 6, 1980); U.S. Congress, House Committee on Government Operations, *Department of Labor's Administration of the Comprehensive Employment and Training Act,* 10th Report of the Committee on Government Operations, 96th Congress, H.R. Rept. 96-657, November 20, 1979, and *High-Level Emphasis on Accountability Needed in CETA,* 24th Report by the Committee on Government Operations, 96th Congress, H.R. Rept. 96-1426, September 1980; and U.S. Congress, House, *CETA's Vulnerability to Fraud and Abuse,* Hearings before a Subcommittee of the Committee on Government Operations, 96th Congress, May-July 1980.

number of DOL audits lagged. In the fiscal year ending September 1980, 113 audit reports of state and local CETA programs were conducted compared with 125 in fiscal year 1979 and 179 in 1978. To carry out a complete 2-year auditing cycle, the number of audits per year would have to be doubled.[6]

In the latest report period (October 1980-March 1981) auditors took exception to $80 million of $2.8 billion in grants audited. Exceptions include costs which were questioned because of insufficient documentation as well as costs recommended for disallowance. The Inspector General found that the enrollment of ineligible participants was the most prevalent problem area followed by poor financial management systems and inadequate monitoring of subgrantees.[7]

The emphasis on auditing and the manner in which audits were conducted aroused strong reactions among prime sponsors and subgrantees. Public interest groups representing sponsors point out that it is exceedingly difficult to comply with the regulations that are constantly being revised, particularly when there are differences among Department spokesmen in interpreting rules. Sponsors also complain that the auditors are often inexperienced and unfamiliar with the practical problems of documenting all transactions and with the regulations that were in effect prior to the period in which the audits were made.

The audit rules have been criticized for their rigidity and their failure to distinguish adequately between unintentional errors and deliberate fraudulent activities. Many sponsors

---

6. U.S. Department of Labor, Office of the Inspector General, *Semiannual Report of the Inspector General,* October 1979-March 1980 and April 1980-September 1980; U.S. Department of Labor and U.S. Department of Health and Human Resources, *Employment and Training Report of the President, 1980* (Washington: Government Printing Office, 1980), p. 201.

7. *Semiannual Report of the Inspector General,* October 1980-March 1981, pp. 2-3.

also believe that the procedures for resolving audit exceptions unfairly place the burden of proof on the sponsor. Finally, they point out that most social programs accept a small error rate, while CETA, which relies heavily on small community based organizations and training institutions that have limited accounting and managerial resources, is expected to be virtually error free. Department of Labor grant officers have some flexibility in dealing with small disallowed costs where good faith is demonstrated and a plan of action is agreed on. Nevertheless, some CETA contractors and PSE employers felt seriously threatened and declined to accept responsibility for the CETA programs in fiscal 1981.[8]

For their part, federal officials maintain that the steps involved in the total investigation and recovery process are too time-consuming and cumbersome. Issuing a report, negotiating questioned costs, conducting hearings, resolving appeals, and obtaining repayment can take years.[9]

## Independent Monitoring Units (IMUs)

The reauthorization act strengthened—and to some extent structured—the prime sponsor monitoring function. Department regulations had always required periodic monitoring of program activities and management practices through on-site visits and examination of program data. But under the reauthorization act the regulations are much more prescriptive and there is a much greater emphasis on monitoring. The

---

8. Karen R. Eastman, "Local Liability and CETA . . . Is the Price Too High?" *County Employment Reporter,* December 1980, p. 3; U.S.Conference of Mayors, Office of Urban Employment and Education, *The CETA Audit Dilemma,* November 1980. The four jurisdictions which withdrew from PSE are: Kennebec County, Maine; Johnson/Leavenworth Consortium, Kansas; Berrien County, Michigan; and San Jose, California. Some smaller jurisdictions have also withdrawn as program agents or subcontractors. For example 19 counties in the North Carolina balance-of-state have declined to operate Title IID programs because of tighter eligibility, wage restrictions, and training requirements.

9. See also General Accounting Office, *More Effective Action is Needed on Auditors' Findings—Millions Can be Collected or Saved,* FGMSD-79-3, October 1978.

clearest expression of this is the independent monitoring units (IMUs) mandated by the reauthorization act to monitor management practices and program activities of prime sponsors and their subcontractors.

By mid-1980, all sponsors in the study sample had established IMUs. Several accomplished this by reassigning existing personnel, but most added new staff. Of 20 local areas for which comparable figures are available, 14 increased their monitoring and evaluation staff between 1978 and 1980, 4 reported no change, and 2 registered declines. In addition to prescribing IMUs at the prime sponsor level, regulations require that subrecipients of CETA funds also have appropriate monitoring arrangements. However, only 2 of the 28 sponsors insisted that their subjurisdictions have such units.

*Independence of IMUs.* The independence of IMUs has been questioned from their inception. The degree of independence is influenced by several factors including its organizational locus and its access to a level of authority high enough to obtain necessary information and to ensure followup actions. In 25 of 28 survey areas, IMUs reported directly to the CETA director; in 2 of the remaining 3 areas, the IMU reported to an official in a higher administrative level.

The degree of independence is often related to management style. Eighteen of the 28 areas reported "completely" independent units, 8, "partially" independent, while 2 indicated little or no independence. However, field researchers found shades of differences in the degree of freedom in both the "completely" and "partially" independent classes. Those classified as "completely" independent were likely to have discretion in selecting the areas of investigation, the methods to be used, and in the preparation of reports. The administrators in such areas tended to reinforce the IMU's independence and use the units as an aid to management. There were, however, variations in the extent to which the CETA administrators used the IMU reports to identify and address problem situations. Variations were found also among IMUs classified as "partially" independent. Some were free to select areas to investigate; others were restricted. Differences were also reported in the amount of interference in the preparation of reports and recommendations.

In one of the two units classified as having "little or no independence," the sponsor complied with the formal requirements by assigning a PSE enrollee to the monitoring position. His role was undefined and most of the monitoring was carried out routinely by the CETA administrator's regular staff.

These findings suggest that the formal classification of IMUs may not fully characterize their status. While most were described as fully or partially independent, there were in fact informal controls over the subjects selected for review, procedures for presenting the results of investigations, and follow-through on recommendations.

*Scope of monitoring.* It is clear that the effects of the reauthorization act were to intensify program supervision, extend the scope of monitoring, improve record keeping and in general engender a greater sense of responsibility. Although nearly all of the sponsors in the sample reported some monitoring in the pre-reauthorization period, the effect of the amendments was to systematize and increase the scope of monitoring of both program performance and adherence to legal requirements.

Monitoring is done variously through on-site visits, interviews with participants, supervisors, and employers, as well as through review of records and reports. At the time of the survey in October 1980, the major activities of IMUs were eligibility verification and monitoring contracts.

Eligibility is verified by a detailed check of a sample of enrollees to confirm the unemployment history and family income information supplied at the time of application. Where feasible, this verification is documented. Contract monitoring is undertaken to ascertain whether contractual obligations are being fulfilled. IMUs reviewed accounting and reporting systems of contractors, visited work sites of summer youth programs, and checked on participant attendance in jobs and training programs.

In about one-half of the areas, IMUs were also responsible for reviewing the prime sponsors' administrative procedures including financial management, procurement, and management information systems. In a few cases, they also examined program activities, such as intake and placement services. Several were charged with administering equal employment opportunity, affirmative action, and complaint procedures. Only two field research associates reported that IMUs attempted to monitor maintenance-of-effort requirements, which prohibit the substitution of public service employment resources for local funding sources. Past studies have shown that PSE substitution is extremely difficult to trace.[10]

IMUs differed widely in the areas on which they focused. The Cleveland IMU, staffed with people who had law and accounting backgrounds, directed its attention to evaluating eligibility determination and verification, the management information system, and accounting procedures. In Cook County, Illinois and Middlesex County, New Jersey, IMUs regularly reviewed the program performance as well as the

10. William Mirengoff and Lester Rindler, *CETA: Manpower Programs Under Local Control* (Washington: National Academy of Sciences, 1978), pp. 176-89. See also Richard P. Nathan et al., *Monitoring the Public Service Employment Program: The Second Round,* Special Report No. 32, prepared by the Brookings Institution for the National Commission for Manpower Policy (Washington: National Commission for Manpower Policy, March 1979), pp. 3-19; Michael Borus and Daniel Hamermesh, "Study of the Net Employment Effects of Public Service Employment—Econometric Analyses," *Job Creation through Public Service Employment,* vol. III, Commissioned Papers, Report no. 6 (Washington: National Commission for Manpower Policy, March 1978), pp. 89-150.

fiscal management system of each subrecipient. In Pasco County, Florida, the IMU reviewed all activities of subrecipients against their contracts, conducted the quarterly review of eligibility, checked on participant attendance at jobs and training, and investigated other concerns such as the use of youth in hazardous activities.

The most significant increases in monitoring activity from 1978 to 1980 were in eligibility determination and verification, PSE wage requirements, enrollee training, provision of services, and supervision of enrollees. In addition, records and reports and fraudulent activities received greater emphasis.

*Problems in IMUs.* The survey conducted immediately after the implementation of the reauthorization act (1979) identified several problems in establishing and providing ground rules for IMUs: finding specialists to staff the IMUs, defining responsibilities, developing approaches to monitoring maintenance-of-effort, and lack of guidance in distinguishing between "fraudulent" activity and non-compliance due to unintentional errors or misunderstandings.

The major problem identified in the followup survey (October 1980) was confusion over the responsibilities of IMUs. Other problems were: duplication of activities with regular staff and with DOL auditors, lack of guidance on corrective actions, and lack of follow-through. About one-half of the areas reported insufficient or inadequately trained staff. In a number of areas, the regular staff resented the IMU and failed to support its activities. Similarly, there was tension between IMU staffs and subcontractors who viewed the IMUs as a threat.

*Effect of IMUs.* Observers do not agree on the effect of IMUs on program administration and operations. One field research associate concluded:

IMU is basically a joke. They go through motions,
but findings are not taken seriously enough to affect program management or design of the delivery
system. No corrective action [is taken] by the
CETA administrator's staff to implement
changes. . . . IMU believes it is helping insure pro-
per regulation interpretations, but other CETA administrator staff find they only muddy the waters.

A sharply different view was expressed by another
observer who found that:

Setting up the IMU, getting it operational and iron-
ing out the bugs did cause administrative burdens
and created more problems than it solved. Now,
with a track record and an experienced serious IMU
staff, things have changed. Many serious cases of
abuse, fraud, conflict of interest, etc. have surfaced
and [have] substantially [been corrected] that simply would have gone undetected without the IMU
effort . . . and, the IMU has the Director's ear; he
is anxious to head off any scandal before it blows
up.

On balance, most of the persons interviewed and most of
the field research associates felt that IMUs were having the
intended effect of strengthening program administration—eligibility determination and verification, supervision
of subcontractors, and record keeping and documentation.
Over one-third noted improvements in accounting and in
allowance and wage payment systems. However, more than
half found less effect on the substance of training and
employment programs. A few stated that there may be some
indirect benefit from feedback to the CETA administrator
and from making contractors more aware of their responsibilities. In one case, the IMU recommended that some
training contracts be reduced or not renewed. In another,
changes were made in youth work sites based on IMU findings.

Among those who felt that the effect of IMUs was negligible were several CETA administrators who reported having had satisfactory monitoring systems before the reauthorization. In their view, the IMU contributed little to quality control. As one PSE administrator stated:

> I am confused about their purpose. We do our own monitoring. There is a lot of repetition with us, the IMU, and the regional office all hitting the service units. I question whether the IMU can do it better.

Several IMUs were authorized to report to elected officials rather than to the CETA administrator if their findings warranted it, but there is no information that this has actually occurred.

In sum, the effectiveness of the IMU depends on the status of the IMU and willingness of the CETA officials to accept its findings and follow through with corrective action. This, in turn, depends in part on the relationships with regular administrative and operating units, and in part on the level of detail with which the IMU is concerned. While there are problems, the presence of IMUs tends to underscore the importance of monitoring and evaluation and contributes to tighter administration. Sixteen of 28 field research associates concluded that the independent monitoring units generated a greater sense of responsibility on the part of sponsors and subagents, 6 found that they had not improved accountability, and the remaining 6 did not express an opinion.

Monitoring by sponsors and auditing by the DOL or other agencies are only part of the administrative control mechanism. A comprehensive compliance system includes other control procedures. At the local level, sponsors supervise the progress of contractors through reports, financial management systems, and on-site visits. At the federal level, intervention is possible before, during, or after the annual cycle of activity. The system has a built-in structure of plan reviews, quarterly progress reports, visits by regional office representatives, and performance assessments by federal officials.

The problem is not a lack of control instruments but rather a lack of trained staff to apply the instruments. Moreover, the limited available staff resources often have not been focused on the most serious situations. It is also necessary to tackle a fundamental problem that underlies many of the compliance difficulties—the unending stream of complex and changing rules and regulations.

The emphasis on auditing and compliance activities, which Congress deemed necessary to assure the integrity of the CETA programs, added burdens at all levels of administration and may have stifled initiative. The intensive surveillance has strengthened federal oversight and made sponsors more cautious. As one field research associate notes: "Obviously, the tendency is to retrench to more of the old-line institutions rather than to act as a free wheeling, creative agency addressing local needs." In other instances, the time and attention directed to efforts to keep CETA programs in compliance with the provisions of the legislation detracted from substantive program activities. This, plus the added administrative burden, represents the costs of protecting the integrity of CETA.

## Effect of Reauthorization Act on the Planning System

In a decentralized system, planning assumes major importance. Congress focused on this aspect of CETA and sought to change the planning system from the maze of documents it had become to a functioning management tool.

## Federal Intent and Actions

Congress was sensitive to the criticism that the planning and grant management processes were excessively complicated and set out to streamline them. The reauthorization act replaced separate plans and grant applications for each CETA title with a single, one-time master plan supplemented by an annual plan covering all titles. However, the relief obtained by the consolidation of plans was negated, in part, by the requirement for greater detail in the new planning documents.

Specifications for the 1981 plans were changed in a number of ways. The detailed occupational summary, a listing of PSE positions to be filled, was replaced by a narrative statement. In addition, the separate estimates of the eligible population for each CETA title were consolidated into one table. The workload savings from these changes, however, were offset by the effort required to prepare more refined cost estimates. A number of narrative items, both in the master and annual plans, that were revised to make them more useful for review purposes may also have increased workload. And there is still excessive and repetitious detail in the plans and subplans.

The evidence suggests that, on the whole, the consolidation of plans under the reauthorization has had little effect on the burden of preparing plans for Titles IIB, IID and VI. Many sponsors find plans useful for some purposes, but it is not clear that they are now more relevant as a guide for program operations than formerly. The major planning difficulty continues to be the uncertainty of funding levels and timing along with national policy shifts.

## Prime Sponsors' Experiences

The early reactions of CETA planners to the new design was mixed. During the 1979 survey, more than half of the planners thought that the new plans were more difficult to prepare and more time-consuming than the pre-reauthorization plans. The remaining planners reported little effect or noted that, with the accumulation of data, the job would become easier. In the followup survey, conducted in October 1980, only one-fourth of the planners thought that the plans were more exacting. Most found the preparation of plans about as difficult or less difficult than before the reauthorization.

| | Percent of Reporting Areas | |
| Preparation of Plans | 1979 Survey | 1980 Survey |
| --- | --- | --- |
| More difficult than | | |
| before reauthorization . . . . . . . | 57 | 25 |
| About the same . . . . . . . . . . . . . . | 29 | 43 |
| Less difficult . . . . . . . . . . . . . . . | 14 | 32 |
| | 100 | 100 |

There were four major complaints: (1) current demographic and labor market data are not available in the detail necessary to prepare the required plans; (2) preparing a consolidated administrative cost schedule covering all titles is especially complex, particularly since revisions in projected expenditures for any one title requires changes in the combined schedule; (3) the master plans, which were expected to be non-recurring, do have to be revised; (4) the required plans and subplans call for unnecessary and redundant detail.

There were scattered reports of difficulties in preparing the youth sections of plans, the average wage information, and the listing of service deliverers before program funding levels were firm and contracts negotiated. A number of planners reported that the budget information summaries were particularly time-consuming and difficult because of the multiplicity of programs. The requirement for detailed projections of expenditures for each separate program was considered unrealistic in view of the funding uncertainties and of the contractual arrangements that are made months ahead of the planning year.[11]

While the volume of planning documents may be cut, new paperwork requirements for other purposes have multiplied: documentation of financial transactions for audit purposes, maintaining files for eligibility verification, record keeping, and tracking the length of stay of participants. Reporting requirements have also increased. The change from quarterly to monthly and, more recently, semimonthly reporting of PSE enrollments was seen as particularly burdensome in areas with many jurisdictions.

### Usefulness of Plans

Planning documents are one element in the CETA planning process, which begins with an estimate of expected funds and their use under various titles of the act and includes consultations with service deliverers, clients, and advisory groups. The extent to which plans are used is contingent, in part, on local political situations and the management style of the prime sponsor. Depending upon such considerations, the plans may be merely a formality to qualify for a grant, a reflection of decisions already made on some other basis, or, more constructively, a guide for operations based upon an analysis of the community's employment and training needs and the use of CETA resources to meet those needs.

Many prime sponsors found the plans useful in providing a systematic overview of the various CETA programs.

---

11. Further revisions in instructions for planning documents have been made for the 1982 planning cycle. The principal changes deleted the annual plans for Title IID and for Title VI which were not to be funded in fiscal 1982 and limited plans for Youth Employment and Training Programs (YETP) and Youth Community Conservation and Improvement Projects (YCCIP) under Title IV to phase out projects. See Field Memorandum 171-81, May 11, 1981, and Field Memorandum 174-81, May 15, 1981.

About 60 percent of the CETA administrators in the sample said that the plans helped them with overall planning and more immediate operating decisions. They were used to orient the staff, gauge the size and timing of operations, identify target groups, and provide general program guidance. The plans have an added usefulness for consortia and balance of states where the process of compiling and integrating the individual plans of their component areas permit sponsors to review the operations of the subjurisdictions. Generally, the planning system was judged more relevant for the comprehensive training and other services under Title IIB than for the PSE programs, but sponsors were able to use the monthly PSE planning schedule in controlling PSE outlays.

On the other hand, the remaining 40 percent of the CETA administrators did not use the plans for operating decisions. According to these officials, plans tend to reflect decisions made independently of the planning process and to follow, rather than guide, operations. They regard plans as a ritual necessary to comply with federal funding requirements. Some sponsors found it impossible to plan realistically in the face of changes during the course of a year in funding levels, enrollment goals, and guidelines as well as shifts in labor market conditions.

While the usefulness of the planning documents is limited, nearly all agreed that the other element in the planning process—consultation with service deliverers in the preparation of plans, both at the prime sponsor and subjurisdictional levels—is essential. Feedback from operators is useful for fine-tuning employment and training programs. In one case, for example, welfare agencies were consulted in planning for the enrollment of public assistance clients, educational agencies in developing training programs, and public housing agencies on training possibilities in weatherization projects.

Regional offices use planning documents as a framework for assessing systems and program operations. They were interested, for example, in the systems used for eligibility determination, management information, tracking the length of stay of enrollees, participant selection, as well as for program outcomes.

Development of performance benchmarks, introduced informally for the 1982 planning cycle, may add a new dimension to the planning system. The performance standards attempt to quantify the expected placements and unit costs for each prime sponsor, based on past performance, the mix of programs, the clientele, and the local economy as compared with national norms. Whether these additional analytical requirements will simplify the planning system, aid or hinder local goal setting, or tie plans more closely to operations remains to be determined.[12]

## Role of Planning Councils

The reauthorization act made a number of changes which affect the role of local advisory councils. However, a review of developments since 1978 indicates that local conditions had more effect on the influence of councils than the act's provisions.

One of the goals of the original CETA was to provide for grass roots participation in planning and decision making. Prime sponsors were to establish advisory councils to participate in determining the needs for employment and training in their local communities, in monitoring and evaluating existing programs, and in making recommendations regarding program plans. The growing complexity of the act and regulations and turnover of council members made it more and more difficult for council members to participate actively in the CETA decision making process.

---

12. Field Memorandum 175-81, *CETA Grant Review Guidelines for Fiscal Year 1982*, May 15, 1981.

The reauthorization act attempted to make planning councils more effective in several ways: (1) Membership was broadened to include more client groups and agencies with close ties with CETA. Under the original act, members were drawn from the client community, community based organizations, the employment service, educational agencies, business, labor, and agriculture. On the average about one-fourth of council members were service deliverers. The 1978 amendments expanded membership to include "unorganized labor," agricultural workers, veterans, and the handicapped. Representation of public welfare and vocational education agencies was also mandated. (2) The council chairman must be chosen from among the public members of the council. Previously the chairman was often an elected or administrative official. (3) The language of the act makes it clear that the sponsor must give consideration to recommendations of the council. It is more explicit in spelling out procedures for review of plans, and requires written justification by the CETA administrator if council recommendations are not accepted.

Other provisions of the reauthorization act have a bearing on the council's role. The most important is the establishment, under a new Title VII, of a separately chartered private industry council (PIC) consisting of representatives of business, labor, community based organizations, and educational institutions. The regular planning council must take into account comments and recommendations of the PIC in reviewing plans. Similarly, a youth employment council, established under Title IV of the act, is also responsible for making recommendations. The effect of these provisions is to fragment the planning process among several groups with overlapping memberships.[13]

---

13. Youth councils were originally established under the Youth Employment and Demonstration Projects Act of 1977. That act was consolidated with CETA by the 1978 amendments.

*Influence of planning councils.* Whether councils have become more influential or more active as a result of the reauthorization changes is dubious. Of 28 study areas, only 3 reported greater influence or activity of local advisory councils attributable to changes in the act. One of these is New York where the act's clearer requirement for consultation has brought the planning council and CETA administration into a closer relationship. In Cook County, Illinois, the appointment of a public member as chairman has given the local council more voice in decision making. On the other hand, the CETA administrator in the Capital consortium (Texas) relies less than formerly on the planning council for advice in selection of service deliverers because of the prime sponsor liability provisions of the act.

Elsewhere, changes have been taking place that are not necessarily related to any of the act's provisions. In Cleveland, for example, the planning council was reactivated by an incoming mayor, while in Philadelphia a change in administration resulted in the council being temporarily suspended. The advisory council in the San Joaquin consortium has become more forceful due to a decision to exclude members of the consortium board; consequently, other council members feel less constrained in expressing their views. In other cases, the council's participation was believed to be greater than in the past because of a change in the committee structure or greater support by the prime sponsor's staff. In areas where the council role appeared to be in decline, it was felt that the business of the council had become repetitive, momentum was difficult to maintain, attendance at meetings declined, or members, unable to keep up with a myriad of changes in regulations, were content to rely on the administrators' staffs.

For the most part, observers noted little change either in council activity or influence since the CETA reauthorization. As one pointed out, broadening the composition was merely tinkering at the edges with little effect on the council's role.

*Effect of private industry councils.* Congress expected that establishing private industry councils (PICs) under Title VII would mobilize industry efforts on behalf of local employment and training programs. At the time of the survey, PICs were established in 95 percent of the prime sponsor areas. The PICs were established as separate entities to emphasize their role and importance. They are, however, under the formal authority of the prime sponsor, and their plans are coordinated with those of the planning council.

To assure cross-fertilization and joint planning, the act provides for the chairperson (or designee) of each council to be a nonvoting member of the other.[14] Aside from the cross-membership on the councils, there is little evidence that the establishment of private industry councils is having a significant effect on the role and activities of the CETA planning councils in the 28 study areas. Moreover, there is some confusion as to the appropriate role of each council in a comprehensive planning effort.[15] A few cases of duplication or lack of understanding or communication were reported. In other areas the responsibilities of the two groups were separate. There were two instances where the involvement of PIC members in the advisory council resulted in greater emphasis on the linking of CETA programs with the private sector.

## Funding and Enrollment Shifts

The major problem in CETA planning, as well as operations, continues to be the perennial uncertainty of the

---

14. U.S. Congress, Senate, *Comprehensive Employment and Training Act Amendments of 1978,* S.Rept. 95-891, May 15, 1978, pp. 40-41.

15. See also Randall B. Ripley, et al., *A Formative Evaluation of the Private Sector Initiative Program,* prepared for Office of Program Evaluation, Employment and Training Administration by the Mershon Center of The Ohio State University, Report 5, January 1981, pp. 29-30 and Report 6, June 1981, pp. 24-32; and *Private Sector Initiatives Program, CETA Title VII Implementation in Seventeen Study Sites,* Third Year Interim Report (Philadelphia: Public/Private Ventures, 1981).

amount of funds to be made available because of changes in the level of appropriations, delays in funding, the influence of changes in variables, such as the unemployment rate, and the allocation formulas.

To afford adequate notice of funding, CETA authorized appropriations to be made a year in advance of the year to which they apply. But the forward funding provision has never actually been used except in 1977 when the economic stimulus appropriation covered public service employment funds for 1978 as well. The more common situation is to enact appropriations at the last possible moment or after the new year has begun.

## Changes in Appropriations and Allocations

Appropriations through the normal budget process have varied considerably from year to year. The amount appropriated for all titles rose from $3.7 billion in 1975 to $10.3 billion in 1979; it dropped again to $8.1 billion in 1980 and to $7.7 billion in 1981 (table 1). The public service employment share was even more volatile, rising from $1.3 billion in 1975 to $5.9 billion in 1979 and being reduced nearly one-half to $3.1 billion in 1980. In the face of pressures for federal budget constraints, PSE funding was further reduced in 1981 to $2.9 billion by the outgoing Administration. The 1981 PSE appropriation was cut to $2.4 billion by the new Administration, and no new funds have been appropriated for either Title IID or Title VI for fiscal year 1982.[16]

For prime sponsors, the controlling figures are the allocations, and these fluctuate widely for individual areas depending upon the allocation formulas for each title, the amount

---

16. On March 2, 1981 the Labor Department ordered a freeze on hiring of Title IID and Title VI workers. This was done pursuant to the new Administration's policy to phase out over 300,000 Title IID and Title VI jobs by the end of the 1981 fiscal year, to reduce the 1981 PSE budget authority by $841 million and outlays by $600 million.

of unexpended funds that may be carried forward from one fiscal year to the next, as well as the level of the appropriations. The DOL issues "planning estimates" in May of each year for use in preparing plans for each title, but the amounts which an area finally receives some months later, when appropriations are enacted and more timely unemployment data are available for use in allocation formulas, may be quite different. All but one of the prime sponsors in the sample lost funds in 1980 compared with 1979. Declines ranged from 10 to 45 percent; the median decrease was 25 percent. The shifts in the amount of funds available to prime sponsors create unusual planning and operating difficulties that make the orderly management of CETA almost impossible.

What this means for individual areas is illustrated by two of the prime sponsors in the survey sample. The Title IID and Title VI allocation for Orange County, California, was cut from $35 million in 1979 to $16 million in 1980. The first planning estimate for 1981, released in May 1980, was $12 million; the allotment was reduced in October to $10 million and cut again in December to $8.6 million. The latest revision in March 1981 lowered the figure to $5.2 million. Philadelphia's PSE allotment, which was cut from $72 million in 1979 to $62 million in 1980 and to $45 million in the initial planning estimates issued for 1981, rose in the second 1981 allotment to $57 million. As of December, the figure was reduced to $48 million, and, in March 1981, it was lowered again to $32 million. No funds have been allotted to continue the program in these areas in 1982.

### Shifts in Enrollment Goals

The seesaw funding in the PSE programs is reflected in the DOL enrollment goals. The Department's aim was to maintain enrollment at levels authorized by the funds available. The difficulty, of course, is that the funding levels were

## Table 1
### CETA Appropriations, Fiscal 1975-1982
(millions of dollars)

| Title[a] | 1975 | 1976 | July-Sept. 1976[b] | 1977 | 1978 | 1979 | 1980 | 1981 Original | 1981 Revised | 1982 Original[c] | 1982 Proposed[d] |
|---|---|---|---|---|---|---|---|---|---|---|---|
| Total | 3,743 | 5,742 | 598 | 8,053 | 8,125 | 10,290 | 8,128 | 7,975 | 7,740[e] | 3,895 | 3,138 |
| **Comprehensive programs** | 1,819 | 1,848 | 454 | 2,481 | 2,268 | 2,361 | 2,922 | 2,572 | 2,821 | 1,925 | 1,697 |
| I (IIA, B, C) | 1,580 | 1,580 | 395 | 1,880 | 1,880 | 1,914 | 2,061 | 2,117 | 2,117 | 1,431[f] | 1,226[f] |
| III | 239 | 268 | 58 | 601[g] | 388 | 372 | 536 | 305 | 554[h] | 219[i] | 183[i] |
| VII[j] | - | - | - | - | - | 75 | 325 | 150 | 150 | 275 | 288 |
| **Youth programs** | 648 | 668 | 44 | 1,869 | 1,173 | 2,023 | 2,101 | 2,475 | 2,475 | 1,970 | 1,441 |
| IV[k] | 175 | 140 | 44 | 1,274 | 417 | 1,238 | 1,492 | 1,636 | 1,636 | 1,204 | 767 |
| Summer youth | 473 | 528 | - | 595 | 756 | 785 | 609 | 839 | 839 | 766[l] | 674[l] |
| **Public service employment programs** | 1,275 | 3,225 | 100 | 3,703 | 4,684[m] | 5,905 | 3,105 | 2,928 | 2,444 | - | - |
| II (IID) | 400 | 1,600 | 100 | 524 | 1,016[m] | 2,501 | 1,478 | 2,199 | 1,950 | - | - |
| VI | 875 | 1,625 | - | 3,179 | 3,668[m] | 3,404 | 1,627 | 729 | 494 | - | - |

SOURCE: Employment and Training Administration, U.S. Department of Labor data.

a. Beginning in fiscal 1979, titles redesignated as shown in parentheses.
b. Transition quarter.
c. Omnibus Reconciliation Act, August 1981.
d. Administration's proposed revision of 1982 appropriation, October 1982.
e. Includes $705 million deferred until fiscal 1982; excludes $234 million rescinded from Title VI.
f. Excludes $606 million deferred from fiscal 1981.
g. Includes funds for veterans programs (HIRE), Skill Training Improvement Programs (STIP).

h. Includes $234 million transferred from Title IID for unemployment insurance payments for PSE enrollees.

i. Excludes $47 million deferred from fiscal 1981.

j. Private sector initiative, begins in fiscal 1979.

k. Includes Job Corps; Youth Employment and Training Programs (YETP); Youth Community Conservation and Improvement Projects (YCCIP); and Young Adult Conservation Corps (YACC) (Title VII). In fiscal 1977 youth projects were authorized under Title III.

l. Excludes $39 million deferred from fiscal 1981.

m. Fiscal year 1978 budget authority of 1977 Economic Stimulus Appropriations Act amount.

uncertain. The DOL's original plan for fiscal year 1980 called for an enrollment level of 450,000 by September 1980, about 100,000 below the previous year's level. But actual enrollments in the first half of fiscal 1980 fell considerably below planned levels (table 2). In January 1980, the Department attempted to spur enrollments by threatening to reallocate funds from lagging areas to prime sponsors able to meet goals. By April 1980, however, the picture changed again. With President Carter's emphasis on balancing the federal budget, the DOL revised its planned level down to 400,000 and froze new hires. In August, with only one more month left in the fiscal year, the hiring freeze was lifted, but only up to on-board enrollment as of July. At the end of fiscal 1980, enrollments had fallen to 328,000 reflecting local sponsors' expectations of further congressional cuts in 1981.

These short-range "stop-and-go" signals are more disruptive of program operations than year-to-year changes. The system is geared to an annual planning cycle with five months' advance notice of anticipated allocation changes to give local officials time to plan operations and arrange for subcontracts. However, if funding levels are changed close to the start of the program year, or after the year has actually begun, prime sponsors cannot plan an orderly program that takes into account the targeting, training, and public service employment objectives of the CETA legislation.

Shifts in enrollment goals play havoc with both plans and operations. When enrollment goals are raised, it is likely to result in poorly developed PSE projects and hasty improvisation to fill positions. When planned levels are cut back, employer work schedules are disrupted, commitments to employers and workers are abrogated and hurried arrangements must be made to deal with the transition problems of the terminated participants.

The problem is especially acute when substantial lead time is required to arrange for training services and public service jobs. One consequence of the cancellations and cutbacks in programs has been the loss of credibility with training institutions, employers, and other subrecipients. In addition, there is a continuing problem of staff morale; sensing a lack of policy direction, the staff commitment to the program often has given way to a growing sense of frustration and insecurity. Sudden turns were particularly difficult for multijurisdictional sponsors where communications pass through several layers to subareas and program agents.

Serious operational problems occurred in September 1979 when large numbers of PSE enrollees reached the end of their 18-month limit. In some cases, waivers granted by the DOL eased the adjustment problem by stretching out the layoff period. In New York, some 5,000 PSE enrollees were separated in September 1979, and waivers of 10,000 others enabled the city to spread the terminations over a 9-month period. About 2,000 of the 15,000 terminees were placed in regular public service positions. Philadelphia was granted waivers for 3,300 enrollees in October 1979, and about one-third were still in PSE slots a year later. However, the city made plans to absorb them. In both cities, possibilities for employment in the private sector were unfavorable because of high unemployment rates.

About one-half of the sponsors devised strategies to mitigate the adverse effect of funding and enrollment shifts. The device most commonly used was underenrollment and underspending. Some sponsors were able to anticipate and prepare for increases or decreases in program size by obtaining advance information. Others resorted to "foot dragging"—delay in acting on Department of Labor directives with the expectation that they may be changed.

### Phaseout of PSE in 1981

In the CETA reauthorization, Congress sought to make the Title VI public service jobs more responsive to cyclical

## Table 2
## Participants in CETA Title II (IID) and Title VI
## and U.S. Unemployment Rates, Fiscal 1975-1981
(numbers in thousands)

| Year and month | Title II (IID)[a] | Title VI | Total | U.S. unemployment rate[b] (percent) |
|---|---|---|---|---|
| **FY 1975** | | | | |
| September (1974) ........... | 12 | - | 12 | 5.9 |
| December ................. | 55 | - | 55 | 7.2 |
| March (1975) .............. | 140 | 102 | 242 | 8.6 |
| June .................... | 154 | 124 | 278 | 8.7 |
| Average ................. | 90 | 57 | 147 | 7.6 |
| **FY 1976** | | | | |
| September ................ | 87 | 213 | 300 | 8.5 |
| December ................. | 62 | 267 | 329 | 8.2 |
| March (1976) .............. | 58 | 287 | 345 | 7.6 |
| June .................... | 95 | 206 | 301 | 7.5 |
| Average ................. | 76 | 243 | 319 | 8.0 |
| **Transition Quarter** | | | | |
| September (1976) ........... | 245 | 44 | 289 | 7.7 |
| **FY 1977** | | | | |
| December ................. | 243 | 29 | 272 | 7.8 |
| March (1977) .............. | 62 | 245 | 307 | 7.4 |
| June .................... | 71 | 292 | 363 | 7.1 |
| September ................ | 94 | 449 | 543 | 6.8 |
| Average ................. | 117 | 254 | 371 | 7.3 |
| **FY 1978** | | | | |
| December ................. | 110 | 517 | 627 | 6.4 |
| March (1978) .............. | 128 | 624 | 752 | 6.2 |
| June .................... | 126 | 603 | 729 | 5.9 |
| September ................ | 112 | 496 | 608 | 5.9 |
| Average ................. | 119 | 560 | 679 | 6.1 |
| **FY 1979** | | | | |
| December ................. | 118 | 416 | 534 | 5.7 |
| March (1979) .............. | 210 | 336 | 546 | 5.7 |
| June .................... | 266 | 326 | 592 | 5.8 |
| September ................ | 257 | 297 | 554 | 5.9 |
| Average ................. | 213 | 344 | 557 | 5.8 |
| **FY 1980** | | | | |
| December ................. | 194 | 204 | 398 | 6.0 |
| March (1980) .............. | 190 | 200 | 390 | 6.3 |
| June .................... | 198 | 176 | 374 | 7.5 |
| September ................ | 206 | 122 | 328 | 7.4 |
| Average ................. | 197 | 176 | 373 | 6.8 |

| FY 1981 | | | | |
|---|---|---|---|---|
| December .................. | 192 | 114 | 306 | 7.4 |
| March (1981) .............. | 192 | 85 | 277 | 7.3 |
| June .................... | 65 | 31 | 96 | 7.3 |
| September (estimate)........ | 19 | 11 | 30 | 7.5 |
| Average (estimate).......... | 117 | 60 | 177 | 7.4 |

SOURCE: Employment and Training Administration, U.S. Department of Labor (unpublished), and *Employment and Earnings,* Bureau of Labor Statistics, U.S. Department of Labor.

a. Fiscal 1975 through the first 2 quarters of fiscal 1979 data are for Title II; data from June 1979 through September 1981 are for Title IID.

b. Seasonally adjusted.

shifts in unemployment by building in a trigger mechanism which would permit PSE funds to move in tandem with the level of unemployment. However, the trigger was not automatic: it depended upon recommendations of the Administration and action by the congressional appropriations committees. Despite changes in unemployment rates, the trigger was never used, and the level of Title VI PSE employment has not been in phase with unemployment (figure 1).

From 1975, when Title VI was originally passed, to 1978, enrollments in public service employment rose, the biggest increase occurring in the nine months following the passage of the Economic Stimulus Appropriations Act in 1977. Enrollments were curtailed in late 1978 and in 1979. As the national unemployment rate rose between 1979 and 1980, the number of participants in public service employment declined—the opposite of what Congress had intended.

At the time of the October 1980 survey, some downward adjustment in Title VI enrollments in fiscal 1981 was taken for granted. Survey respondents were asked to indicate the probable effects of a public service jobs program reduction. For those sponsors who were below authorized strength, serious adjustment problems were not expected. However, most did foresee program and staff problems.

Besides loss of public services, reduced enrollment levels were expected to disrupt existing projects and make it difficult to ensure service to target groups, maintain permissible wage levels, provide training, and retain the cooperation of public agencies and community organizations that employ CETA workers. Respondents anticipated that these layoffs would take place in a slack labor market with limited opportunity for transition of participants into private or regular public sector jobs. In the event of a PSE cutback, sponsors planned to trim back PSE enrollment in nonprofit agencies, transfer qualified enrollees to other CETA titles, and step up transition efforts. Several agencies, facing staff cuts, would reorganize and reassign their remaining staff.

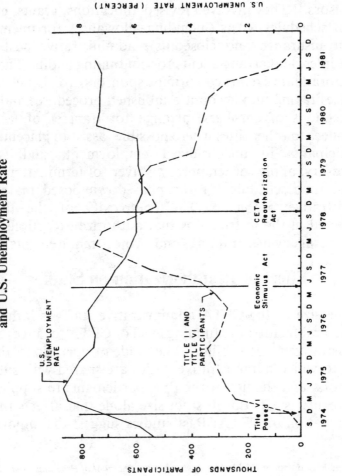

Figure 1
Participants in Title II/IID and Title VI
and U.S. Unemployment Rate

SOURCE: Based on data from Employment and Training Administration and Bureau of Labor Statistics.

In March 1981, the new Administration announced its decision to phase out the Title IID and Title VI programs in the remaining seven months of the fiscal year. Procedures for managing the phaseout and separation of over 300,000 enrollees were sent by the Department of Labor to all prime sponsors.[17] They involved revised allocations, grants, enrollment schedules, costs (including allowances for unemployment insurance and closeouts), administrative cost pool schedules, and arrangements for continuing audits. The field memorandum required prime sponsors to issue layoff notices taking into account established procedures and legal protections of enrollees, arrange for transfer of laid off enrollees to other titles where possible, assist in placement of participants in unsubsidized employment, and, where necessary, apply for temporary waivers of terminations. The rapid time schedule for the phasedown posed major administrative problems. The complexity of the task is reflected in the instructions that authorize exceptions from the average wage, training, and project requirements.[18]

## Effect of Reauthorization on Staffing

The size of the CETA administrative staffs is influenced by several factors: the funding level of CETA, changes in administrative responsibilities, the mode of operations, the extent to which administrative duties are shared with subcontractors, and the use of the PSE participants to supplement the regular staff. But it is not size alone that affects the administration of CETA. Past studies suggest the importance

---

17. Field Memorandum 133-81, *Management of the Phaseout of Programs Funded Under Title IID and VI of the Comprehensive Employment and Training Act by September 30, 1981,* March 13, 1981.

18. As of June 30, 1981, 175,000 had been terminated. Of these, 43 percent were placed, mostly in public sector jobs; 37 percent were either transferred to other CETA titles or were drawing unemployment compensation; and 5 percent were in school or the armed forces. The remaining 15 percent were unaccounted for. Among the remaining PSE enrollees, some were off the payroll but were held in enrolled status pending possible placement.

of the quality of the staff and its stability.[19] This section examines the effect of the reauthorization on staff requirements, turnover, and training.

For purposes of this report, CETA staff are classified as administrative—those assigned to "overhead" tasks such as planning, contract supervision, monitoring, reporting, and accounting; and operating—those who provide services to clients, such as intake, counseling, instruction, job development, and placement.

## Staff Size

In 1976, approximately 20,000 persons were estimated as employed by sponsors or subcontractors for administrative duties. Since then, with the addition of youth programs, growth of countercyclical public service employment and other programs, both staff and administrative cost ratios have increased sharply. With a 50 percent increase of CETA funds between 1976 and 1980, the size of administrative staff has probably risen above 30,000, excluding PSE enrollees employed on CETA staffs.

The growth of the prime sponsors' operating staffs over the years was associated not only with the expansion of CETA programs, but also with an increasing role as service deliverers. Many sponsors undertook to operate intake centers and handle the placement of enrollees. Some operated training or other programs directly (see chapter 3). At the inception of CETA, these operating tasks were almost always performed under contract by other public or private nonprofit agencies.

---

19. Mirengoff and Rindler, *CETA: Under Local Control,* pp. 104-105; Ripley et al., *CETA Prime Sponsor Management Decisions and Program Goal Achievement,* R&D Monograph 56, prepared for the Employment and Training Administration by the Mershon Center of The Ohio State University (Washington: U.S. Department of Labor, 1978), pp. 86-87.

In 1978, prior to the reauthorization, the average size of staff for 24 prime sponsors in the survey sample was 67, of whom 46 were engaged in administrative duties and 21 in operating functions (table 3). Since the reauthorization, despite a sharp decline in funds in all but one area, the average staff size rose to 81 in 1980. Most of the increase was in the administrative staff. These estimates include public service employment enrollees assigned to CETA administrator staffs, but do not include staffs of subjurisdictions or subcontractors. Seventeen of 24 areas with comparable data reported increases in administrative staffs ranging from 15 to 70 percent. The seven with decreases had more moderate changes, with declines ranging from 7 to 21 percent.

**Table 3**
**Average Size of CETA Administrative and Operating Staffs**
**Sample Prime Sponsor Areas, Fiscal 1978-1980**

| Type of staff and type of prime sponsor | Average number of positions authorized[a] | | |
|---|---|---|---|
| | 1978 | 1979 | 1980 |
| Average total staff ................. | 67 | 70 | 81 |
| Administrative staff ................ | 46 | 49 | 57 |
|    Cities, counties, consortia ......... | 41 | 45 | 51 |
|    Balance of states ................ | 71 | 70 | 82 |
| Operating staff .................... | 21 | 21 | 24 |
|    Cities, counties, consortia ......... | 26 | 26 | 29 |
|    Balance of states ................ | 0 | 0 | 0 |

SOURCE: Reports from 24 prime sponsors with comparable jurisdictions for 3 years. Of the 24 areas, 15 had operating as well as administrative staff.

a. Unweighted average.

Administrative staff increases were attributed, in the main, to heavier workload resulting from the reauthorization act; decreases, to reductions in funds. The largest gains were registered in the monitoring and record keeping staffs needed to document eligibility, track the length of stay of enrollees, tighten monitoring, and prepare reports (table 4).

**Table 4**
**Average Size of CETA Administrative and Operating Staffs**
**by Activity, Sample Prime Sponsor Areas, Fiscal 1978-1980**

| Type of activity | Average number of positions authorized[a] | | |
|---|---|---|---|
| | 1978 | 1979 | 1980 |
| Average total staff .................. | 67 | 70 | 81 |
| Average administrative staff ......... | 46 | 49 | 57 |
| Planning ...................... | 6 | 6 | 7 |
| Monitoring and evaluation ........ | 7 | 8 | 9 |
| Record keeping ................. | 7 | 7 | 9 |
| Fiscal services .................. | 9 | 9 | 10 |
| Contract supervision ............. | 4 | 4 | 5 |
| Overall supervision............... | 9 | 10 | 12 |
| Other ........................ | 5 | 5 | 5 |
| Average operating staff ............. | 21 | 21 | 24 |
| Intake services................... | 5 | 5 | 5 |
| Job development and placement.... | 4 | 4 | 5 |
| Training...................... | 3 | 3 | 4 |
| Other ........................ | 9 | 9 | 11 |

SOURCE: Reports from 24 prime sponsors with comparable jurisdictions for 3 years. Of the 24, 15 had operating as well as administrative staff.

NOTE: Details may not add to totals because of rounding.

a. Unweighted averages.

Operating staff of prime sponsors, on balance, changed little since the reauthorization act with increases in some areas offset by decreases in others. Gains were in job development, placement, training and such new responsibilities as preparing employability development plans and determining eligibility. It should be noted that one-third of the areas subcontract all operating activities; others, such as consortia and balance-of-states delegate them to subjurisdictions. In these cases, overall operating staff changes would not be reflected in the prime sponsor staff.

About half of the prime sponsors in the survey sample used PSE participants in their administrative units and, to a lesser extent, in their operating functions (table 5). Respondents reported almost unanimously that PSE enrollees filled these positions satisfactorily.

### Table 5
### Employment of CETA Public Service Employment Enrollees on Prime Sponsor Staff, Sample Prime Sponsor Areas

| Percent PSE to total staff | Administrative staff | Operating staff |
|---|---|---|
| Total ..................... | 28 | 28 |
| 0 ......................... | 14 | 19 |
| 1 - 9 ...................... | 6 | 3 |
| 10 - 29 .................... | 6 | 5 |
| 30 and above ............... | 2 | 1 |

SOURCE: Reports from 28 areas.

## Staff Turnover

Although the stresses and strains in the volatile CETA system were thought to cause heavy employee turnover, a review of prime sponsor experience during 1980 indicates that accession and separation rates were not as high as expected.[20] Accession rates for 27 areas for which data were available ranged from zero to 69 per hundred employees in a 12-month period. The average was 33, or 2.7 a month. Separation rates ranged from 7 to almost 70 per 100 employees, averaging 25 for a full year or just over 2 per month.

There is no turnover data series for regular state and local government employment. However, a recent study of turnover rates in selected industries, based on social security data, shows "new hire" rates of about 10 per 100 per quarter in banking and 12.3 in educational services—nonmanufacturing industries which may be comparable to state and local

---

20. "Accession rates" are the number of new hires and recalls per month divided by the average number of employees on prime sponsor staffs and multiplied by 100. "Separation rates" are the number of terminations per month, including quits and layoffs, divided by the average number of employees and multiplied by 100.

government. Expressed on a monthly basis, these new hire rates are 3.3 and 4.1 respectively. The separation rates in banking and educational services are 3.0 and 4.2 per month. These rates are higher than the turnover rates for the CETA prime sponsors studied.[21]

One-third of the 27 reporting areas had relatively high separation rates (over 24 per 100 employees per year). Both clerical and professional employees were involved, and in half of the areas reporting high turnover, top management was affected. Nearly all terminations were quits. CETA administrators blamed insecurity, lack of advancement opportunity, job dissatisfaction, or more favorable opportunities elsewhere. Several sponsors attributed the job dissatisfaction to frustration, ambiguous regulations or the negative public image of CETA. In one case, key employees were expected to resign with a change of local administration. Separated employees include some PSE participants who were terminated when their tenure expired. In the areas that reported high accession rates, program expansion was largely responsible.

Although overall turnover rates were not found to be unduly high in 1980, their effects are particularly harmful in a program like CETA that has been undergoing constant change. New employees must become familiar with a vast accumulation of regulations and procedures. The loss of top staff is especially disruptive since it not only affects adversely program operations and the quality of services, but also leadership and continuity of management.

Turnover problems are expected to be much more severe in 1981 and 1982 with the phaseout of the public service jobs

---

21. Malcolm S. Cohen and Arthur R. Schwartz, "U.S. Labor Turnover: Analysis of a New Measure," *Monthly Labor Review,* November 1980, p. 9. Figures are for the second quarter of 1976. "New hires" are usually lower than accessions. According to ETA the 25 per year separation rate is comparable to other federal grant programs, but is lower than that shown by unpublished internal data for CETA.

program, anticipated cutbacks in youth programs, and the general uncertainty as to the future of CETA when the act expires in 1982.

## Quality of Staff

The problem of staff turnover points up a broader question—the ability of CETA sponsors to attract, develop, and retain qualified staff. The rapid changes in programs and processes that have characterized CETA over the years militate against staff development. In addition to compensation levels, quality of staff is often associated with two processes—selection on the basis of merit and the training of those selected.

*Merit systems.* DOL regulations require that public agencies administering CETA programs must comply with merit standards of the U.S. Office of Personnel Management. The purpose of these regulations is to assure that sponsors hire and retain qualified staff. Merit standards incorporate six principles: (1) recruitment, selection, and advancement based on ability; (2) equitable and adequate compensation; (3) staff training; (4) retention on the basis of merit; (5) nondiscrimination in all aspects of personnel administration; and (6) restrictions on political activities.

Nationally, about half the sponsors had or were planning to adopt an acceptable merit system in 1980. Many of the others were in local governments which have not had formal personnel structures. Among the sponsors in the study sample, 22 hired through competitive merit systems, and 6 did not. Of the 22, several met federal standards but were not part of a local civil service system either because the local government did not have civil service or because the CETA staff pattern did not correspond with the classification structure. Of the 6 without acceptable merit systems, 2 were in the process of developing them, 3 selected employees by less formal interview and rating procedures, and 1 hired CETA employees as "temporaries" to avoid civil service entanglements.

Most sponsors believed that the merit system does assure qualified personnel. Others felt that although it eliminates political influence and assures that candidates have minimal qualifications, it did not guarantee that the best qualified will be hired. Several preferred the hiring flexibility afforded by their own system.

*Staff training.* More than one-half of the sponsors believed that the administration of their programs was impeded by inadequately trained staff. While there was no consensus about the kinds of training needed, most sponsors agreed that staff should improve their knowledge of regulations, planning, fiscal management, contract development and supervision, record keeping, and evaluation. They also identified training needs in client services, job development, and linkages with other programs.

Most sponsors in the study sample arranged for some formal or informal staff training. Two patterns emerged: (1) training in administrative processes—monitoring, planning, subcontracting, fiscal management, equal employment opportunity, and data processing; and (2) program training—intake, counseling, preparation of EDPs, and job development. Eleven of the areas reported that staff members were either given tuition credits for professional development courses or permitted to attend regional office courses. Seven of the 28 areas were reported to have little or no formal training except for general orientation in new regulations and procedures.

The new requirements of the 1978 amendments resulted in a greater recognition of the need for staff development and an increased commitment on the part of federal officials to provide it. Two-thirds of the study areas reported an increase in the training funded by the Department of Labor and made available to their staffs. In addition to those given at regional training centers, courses were being offered in colleges with DOL institutional grants, such as the Rutgers Center for Human Resources, the University of Kansas Human Resources Program, and the University of Texas. Training programs were also available through such state-funded institutions as the Ohio Training Institute, the Michigan Training Institute, and the Illinois Management Training Institute.

Opinions of sponsors and regional office staff on the usefulness of federal training varied. Half the respondents felt that federal training was useful in transmitting "hard" information on such matters as interpretation of regulations or on grant closeout procedures. There was less positive reaction to training in broad program areas or in management skills. One respondent observed: "There is a distinction between training and telling a person how to fill out a form." Another commented: "It does little good to bring together 10 to 15 primes and read the regs to them. The problem is they won't commit themselves to the tough questions. . . ."

Another way of gauging the usefulness of federally sponsored training is to ascertain its effect on operations. Most respondents felt that it was useful in specific activities such as determining eligibility or monitoring. Others noted that the training only benefited the few persons who attended; in balance-of-states, for example, training seldom reached the subjurisdiction levels where actual operations take place.

*DOL management assistance.* The training limitations identified in the study areas are one reflection of the more widespread deficiencies in the technical assistance provided to CETA prime sponsors. A 1979 report of a Department of Labor Technical Assistance and Training Committee found that, despite a great flow of information, the system was not providing adequate training and assistance to grant recipients: regional office staff were busy with other assignments and were not equipped to provide technical training; there were not sufficient specialists either in the national or regional offices in key functional areas to meet the need; training was being provided variously by national office staff, regional training centers, state employment and training councils, state training institutions, national community based organizations, public interest groups, and outside consultants. The major problem identified by the committee report is that the entire system was uncoordinated, fragmented, and without policy direction. The report also pointed out that since contractors rely on prime sponsors for training, there is a particular need for training that extends to the subgrantee level.

In an effort to improve the use of training resources and the quality of technical assistance, the Department of Labor established an Office of Management and Training. That office set out, in consultation with local sponsors and advisory groups, to identify training needs, formulate plans to meet those needs, increase capacity for training at all levels, and evaluate the training provided. Among the more visible accomplishments was the establishment of a national training center near Washington to provide, on a continuing basis, intensive training for federal representatives, and to develop a series of training guides. Additionally, a management assistance unit was set up in each regional office to concentrate specifically on training activities.

In sum, for most of the sponsors in the sample, turnover has not been unduly high. However, because of the many changes that have taken place in CETA, staff losses, especially among key personnel, have been injurious. Heavy turnover is likely to follow program reductions in 1981 and 1982. Staff development training has been meager and fragmented. But efforts to increase, improve, and coordinate such training are underway. The reauthorization act had little direct effect on staff turnover; but the new provisions of the legislation and the accompanying regulations served to underscore the need for staff training.

# Decentralization and Federal-Local Relationships

The framers of CETA envisioned an employment and training system in which program management decisions would be made by state and local officials within a framework of broad federal policy. However, from the outset, this decentralized design was diluted. Much of this nibbling away at local control stems from the act's ambiguity, the divergence between the policies and priorities of the principals in the federal-state-local partnership, and the strains that are inherent in a poorly defined relationship.

The 1978 amendments, intended to tighten the administration of CETA and make local programs and practices conform more closely with national policies, resulted in greater specificity in the act which, in turn, further constrained the freedom of local authorities. Decisions as to who may be served in employment and training programs, how long they may remain in the programs, how their needs are to be assessed, what wages they are to be paid, and other detailed program matters are prescribed in the statute. Despite the erosion of local control, most sponsors appeared to be adjusting to the more centralized and monitored operation.

One significant aspect of the decentralization issue involves the relationship between federal and local personnel who share responsibility for the CETA program. This relationship is shaped by objective and subjective factors: the statute, federal regulations, the relations between regional offices and prime sponsors, as well as operational styles and personalities.

Prime sponsors base their view of their relationships with the federal establishment on the communications they receive, the regional office review of their plans, the assessment of their programs, as well as site visits and other meetings. In individual situations, these relationships are colored by the rapport between local staff and federal representatives and, of course, there are wide variations among regions and prime sponsors.

In the October 1980 survey, prime sponsors were asked to identify the activities in which the degree of federal presence changed. Their responses indicate that, for most standard forms of federal involvement—plan review, interpretation of regulations, technical assistance, performance assessment, and followup of reporting—federal contact was about the same or greater in 1980 than in 1979. The most significant change was in compliance review where increased federal activity was expected in view of the changes in the act. Several stated there was too little technical assistance while others felt that new requirements constrained local initiative. For the most part, respondents felt that in the light of the new amendments the federal presence was appropriate.

There were, however, significant local-federal differences on policy issues. Forty percent of the sponsors interviewed disagreed with federal policies on auditing, liability, the role of IMUs, underexpenditures, average wages, and placement goals. There were also scattered reports of problems relating to waivers of the 18-month limit on enrollment, technical assistance to subrecipients, meeting the fixed percentage of funds to be spent for PSE training, and conflicting interpretations of rules by federal officials.

The field research associates noted that federal surveillance had increased as a consequence of the reauthorization act's emphasis on tightening administrative control and fiscal management. They characterized the activities of regional office representatives as being centered on processes and numbers rather than on program quality and outcome. Several, however, did note increased attention to placement results.

## Summary

Although some of the shock felt by prime sponsors in the first year after the reauthorization wore off by the second year, a number of areas were still feeling its effects. Sponsors continued to struggle with the volume of rules and regulations promulgated to implement an increasingly complex employment and training system. The major administrative developments during fiscal year 1980 are summarized below:

- Monitoring and auditing occupied a great deal of attention. All sponsors in the sample had installed IMUs and most had increased the size of monitoring staffs. The scope of monitoring activities was broadened considerably and the monitoring focused largely on eligibility verification and monitoring contracts.

- Monitoring, along with stepped-up auditing activities and prime sponsor liability, had the intended effect of increasing accountability and responsibility at all levels of government. Although the DOL was not able to meet its beefed-up auditing schedules, the expectation of being audited stimulated sponsors to take preventive measures to avoid liability problems. However, prime sponsors' organizations have criticized the auditing process as being too stringent.

- The reauthorization act intended to simplify the CETA plans by separating them into a non-recurring master plan and an annual plan. However, since more detail was added in the process, sponsors found little change in workload. Problems relating to data sources persisted, as did the local view that too much repetition was still required in some sections of the plans. With the proliferation of special programs, plans became essentially a collection of grant applications.

- Nevertheless, 60 percent of the sponsors agreed that the planning process is useful for program development, identification of target groups, orientation of staff, reviewing activities of subjurisdictions, and for evaluating progress toward achieving goals. Those who did not find plans useful pointed out that operating decisions are subject to shifts in priorities and other considerations that are independent of the formal planning system.

- The act attempted to strengthen the role of local planning councils, but results were not discernible. Where changes occurred, they were generally due to circumstances not related to the reauthorization. The establishment of private industry councils and youth councils tended to fragment local planning.

- Abrupt changes in funding allocations and enrollment goals made orderly planning impossible and the restrictive wage, eligibility, and other provisions of the reauthorization act made it much more difficult to manage the CETA programs.

- Increases in monitoring, auditing, documentation, and record keeping enlarged both the administrative workload and administrative staffs. Turnover rates of CETA employees are comparable to other like industries. However, separations were expected to be considerably higher in 1981 and 1982 with the phasing out of public service employment programs and uncertainties as to the future of CETA beyond its expiration date of September 1982.

- The original thrust of CETA—decentralization—has been weakened. The increasingly detailed prescriptions and proscriptions mandated by the 1978 amendments to achieve greater congruence between local and federal objectives and to prevent program abuses have had the effect of increasing the federal presence and narrowing the decision making role of state and local officials. Differences between local and federal officials surfaced, particularly with respect to views on auditing, liability, the role of independent monitoring units, unexpended funds, wage provisions, and placement goals.

In short, increased administrative difficulties and greater centralization was the price paid to tighten administration of the employment and training system and protect its integrity. The cumulative effect of the 1978 amendments has been to complicate CETA's administration greatly. Practically all respondents identified administrative overload problems. One of the most common complaints was that the strain of implementing regulations not only overburdens local officials, but also limits prime sponsor flexibility, the cornerstone of a decentralized system.

# 3 Program Mix and Delivery of Services

The Comprehensive Employment and Training Act of 1973 gave state and local officials some flexibility in choosing employment and training programs and the organizations to deliver these programs. This chapter traces changes over the years in the mix of programs and in delivery systems, with particular attention to the effects of the 1978 reauthorization amendments on Title IIB/C.[1] The last part of the chapter reviews recent developments in the relationships between CETA and the public employment service system.

## The Composition of CETA Programs

### *Recategorization of CETA*

Despite the intent of CETA to consolidate manpower programs, the original legislation embodied elements of both block grant and categorical designs. Of the five substantive titles, only Title I permitted state and local officials latitude in selecting employment and training programs best suited to

---

1. Title IIB/C, under the amendments of 1978, provides for comprehensive training and employment services (IIB), and upgrading and retraining (IIC). It replaces Title I of the 1973 act.

the needs of their communities. The other four titles authorized categorical programs for specific purposes: Title II was intended to create additional public sector jobs in areas of substantial unemployment; Title III provided for nationally administered programs for Indians, migrant farm workers, and other special groups; Title IV continued the Job Corps; and Title VI, which was added shortly after CETA was enacted, authorized countercyclical public service employment programs. Thus, only under Title I could sponsors choose from a range of programs and activities—skill training, basic education, on-the-job training, work experience, public service employment, or manpower services such as counseling and job placement. They were permitted to continue programs established under earlier legislation—the Manpower Development and Training Act (MDTA) and the Economic Opportunity Act (EOA)—or to develop other activities according to their own perceptions of what is most responsive to their needs.

Between 1975 and 1978, with the expansion of public service employment programs (PSE) and the addition of special youth programs,[2] the configuration of employment and training programs became more categorized. Even though funds for Title I increased, proportionately more was added for other titles, and the "decategorized" portion of CETA declined from 42 to 23 percent of total CETA appropriations by 1978 (table 6). The 1978 reauthorization act continued the earlier categorical programs and added a new one—the private sector initiative program (Title VII). Each of these is a separate program with specific funding formulas, eligibility requirements, and operating rules. The decategorized portion—Title IIB/C—declined further to 18 percent in 1979. After 1979, with the curtailment and complete phaseout of PSE, the proportionate share of Title IIB/C rose; by fiscal

---

2. Authorized by the Youth Employment and Demonstration Projects Act of 1977, Pub. L. 95-93.

Table 6
CETA Appropriations, by Title, Fiscal 1975-1982

| Title[a] | 1975 | 1976[b] | 1977 | 1978 | 1979 | 1980 | 1981 | 1982 (est.) |
|---|---|---|---|---|---|---|---|---|
| Total (millions)......... | $3,743 | $6,339 | $8,053 | $8,125 | $10,290 | $8,128 | $7,035[c] | $3,917[d] |
| | | | | (Percent distribution) | | | | |
| **Total** | 100 | 100 | 100 | 100 | 100 | 100 | 100 | 100 |
| **Employability development** ....... | 48 | 36 | 30 | 28 | 23 | 36 | 36 | 62 |
| Title I (IIB/C) ......... | 42 | 31 | 23 | 23 | 18 | 25 | 30 | 47 |
| Title III ............... | 6 | 5 | 7 | 5 | 4 | 7 | 4 | 8 |
| Title VII[e] .............. | - | - | - | - | 1 | 4 | 2 | 7 |
| **Youth programs** ....... | 18 | 11 | 22 | 14 | 20 | 25 | 33 | 37 |
| Title IV Job Corps .... | 5 | 3 | 3 | 5 | 3 | 5 | 8 | 14 |
| Title IV other youth[f] .. | - | - | 12 | - | 9 | 13 | 14 | 5 |
| Summer youth ........ | 13 | 8 | 7 | 9 | 8 | 7 | 11 | 18 |
| **Public service employment** ....... | 34 | 53 | 46 | 58[g] | 57 | 38 | 30 | 0 |
| Title II (IID)......... | 11 | 27[h] | 7 | 13 | 24 | 18 | 23[i] | 0 |
| Title VI ............. | 23 | 26 | 39 | 45 | 33 | 20 | 7 | 0 |

SOURCE: Employment and Training Administration, U.S. Department of Labor, and Office of Management and Budget data.
NOTE: Details may not add to 100 percent due to rounding.
a. Beginning in fiscal 1979, titles redesignated as shown in parentheses.
b. Includes transition quarter, July-September 1976.
c. Excludes $234 million rescinded from Title VI and $705 million deferred from Title IID ($607 million), Title IV Summer Youth ($40 million), and Title IV other youth ($58 million).
d. Includes amounts deferred from fiscal 1981: Title IIB/C ($607 million); Title III ($47 million); and Title IV Summer Youth ($40 million).
e. Private sector initiative program beginning in fiscal 1979.
f. In fiscal 1977 $1 billion in youth programs funded in Title III under the 1977 Economic Stimulus Appropriation. Beginning in fiscal 1979 Young Adult Conservation Corps (YACC), Youth Employment and Training Programs (YETP), Youth Community Conservation and Improvement Projects (YCCIP).
g. Budget authority for fiscal 1978 from 1977 Economic Stimulus Appropriation.
h. Includes funds authorized for both Title II and VI.
i. Includes $248 million transferred to Title III to pay unemployment compensation to PSE workers ($245 million) and for other purposes ($3 million).

1982 it is expected to be back up to 47 percent, and the total funds available to be approximately the same as the first year.

## Service Mix

*Appropriations by title.* Another way of analyzing program trends is to divide CETA titles into those which essentially provide employability development services (Title IIB/C, Title III, Title IV other than the summer youth programs, and Title VII) and those whose major purpose is to provide experience and income maintenance (PSE and summer youth employment programs). The share of appropriations for employability development titles declined during the first 3 years of CETA while the share of funds for public service employment and summer youth employment rose (figure 2). By 1978, the latter accounted for two-thirds of the total. Emphasis on PSE during this period reflected the credence that Congress and the Administration gave to the efficacy of job creation in the public sector as a counter-cyclical strategy.

After 1978, however, the pattern was reversed: by 1980, employability development accounted for a major share, 54 percent. This was due to the introduction of youth projects and private sector initiative programs, as well as to the curtailment of PSE funds. Further relative increases of employability development titles occurred in 1981, and by 1982, with the elimination of PSE, employability titles were expected to increase to 82 percent.

| | CETA appropriations (percent) | | | |
| --- | --- | --- | --- | --- |
| | FY 1975 | FY 1978 | FY 1980 | FY 1982 (est.) |
| Employability development titles............. | 53 | 33 | 54 | 82 |
| PSE and summer youth titles ............ | 47 | 67 | 45 | 18 |

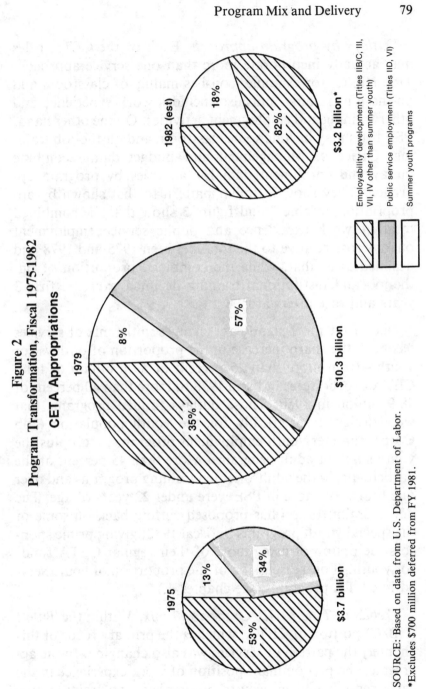

Figure 2
Program Transformation, Fiscal 1975-1982
CETA Appropriations

1982 (est)

18%

82%

$3.2 billion*

1979

8%

35%

57%

$10.3 billion

1975

13%

53%

34%

$3.7 billion

Employability development (Titles IIB/C, III, VII, IV other than summer youth)

Public service employment (Titles IID, VI)

Summer youth programs

SOURCE: Based on data from U.S. Department of Labor.
*Excludes $700 million deferred from FY 1981.

*Outlays by program approach.* Each of the CETA titles may actually incorporate more than one service approach. Title IIB/C, for example, consists mainly of classroom and on-the-job training, but also includes work experience and other training and employment activities. On the other hand, PSE titles may include some classroom and on-the-job training. Office of Management and Budget data recombine outlay and enrollment data for all titles by program approach. They show a similar pattern to that shown by appropriations. Table 7 and figure 3 show that the combined total of work experience and public service employment outlays rose relative to the total between 1975 and 1978 and declined after that, while the combined proportion of on-the-job and institutional training declined over the first 3 years and rose afterwards.

One of the more significant changes in the mix of services has been the sharp increase in the proportion of outlays for youth—from more than 25 percent of $9.6 billion of total CETA expenditures in fiscal 1978 to more than 40 percent of $8.9 billion in 1980. Those outlays funded programs that were designed specifically for the youth population (Job Corps, summer youth employment programs, etc.) plus the youth share of adult programs. More than 45 percent of the participants in the adult-oriented training programs and over one-fourth of those in PSE were under 22 years of age. The new Administration has proposed cutting back on some of the special youth programs in fiscal 1982, giving prime sponsors the option of using more of their regular CETA funds for youth. (For a discussion of the proportion of youth served in CETA programs, see chapter 4.)

*Trends in Title I (IIB/C) program mix.* Within the Title I (IIB/C) portion of CETA, which is the primary focus of this chapter, the pattern of services was also changing. In the aggregate, the predominant position of work experience in the early years has given way to an emphasis on training pro-

Table 7
CETA Outlays by Program Approach, Fiscal 1975-1981[a]

| Program approach | 1975 | 1976[b] | 1977 | 1978 | 1979 | 1980 | 1981 |
|---|---|---|---|---|---|---|---|
| Total outlays (millions) ........... | $3,175 | $5,045 | $5,631 | $9,584 | $9,425 | $8,862 | $7,641 |
| | | | | (Percent) | | | |
| Total ................ | 100 | 100 | 100 | 100 | 100 | 100 | 100 |
| On-the-job training.......... | 4 | 4 | 4 | 3 | 3 | 3 | 4 |
| Institutional training......... | 20 | 16 | 16 | 13 | 16 | 21 | 24 |
| Work experience[c].......... | 35 | 29 | 25 | 20 | 23 | 28 | 33 |
| Public service employment...... | 37 | 48 | 51 | 60 | 53 | 41 | 29 |
| Labor market services and program direction ..... | 5 | 4 | 4 | 4 | 5 | 7 | 9 |

SOURCE: Office of Management and Budget data.

NOTE: Details may not add to totals because of rounding.

a. Includes expenditures under all CETA training and employment accounts.

b. Transition quarter (July-September 1976) not included.

c. Includes in-school and out-of-school youth, summer youth, and adult work experience programs.

**Figure 3**
**CETA Outlays by Program Approach**

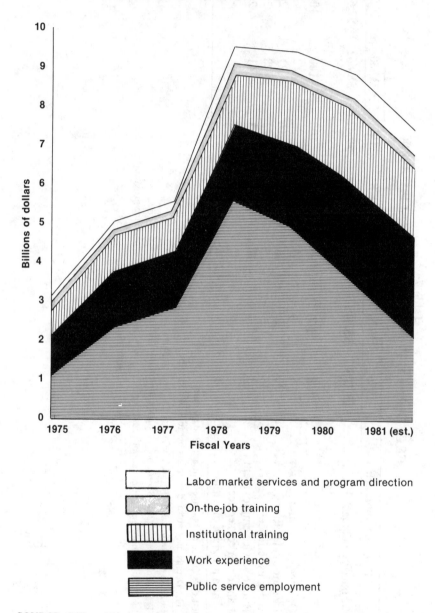

SOURCE: Office of Management and Budget data.

grams. Between 1975 and 1978, outlays for classroom and on-the-job training, as a proportion of total outlays, rose from 43 to 62 percent (table 8). The shift in emphasis from work experience and income support programs to substantive training activities was a practical recognition that funds for PSE and youth work experience were available under other CETA titles. Consequently more of Title I (IIB/C) funds could be concentrated on training. Since 1978, these trends have continued: the combined total of classroom and on-the-job training rose moderately to 67 percent of Title IIB/C outlays in 1980 (although the share of on-the-job training decreased). Increased training funds under special governors' grants and elimination of PSE help account for this trend.

In sum, it is useful to divide the seven years of CETA into two time frames: from 1975 to 1978 and from 1978 to 1981. During the first period, with the build-up of countercyclical PSE, activities which essentially provide experience and income maintenance became predominant. During the second period, due partly to the reauthorization act and partly to national policy decisions, the trend began to change; there has been more emphasis on training and employability development activities. Within Title IIB/C, the CETA title in which local officials have most decision making influence, there was a steady increase in resources devoted to training and employability development throughout both periods.

### Effect of the Reauthorization Act on Program Mix

Provisions of the 1978 reauthorization act influenced the Title IIB/C program mix directly and indirectly. Those which had a direct effect were: the prohibition on use of Title IIB/C funds for public service employment; the limit on the number of hours trainees could spend in work experience; the limit on duration of participation in all CETA programs;

Table 8

CETA Prime Sponsor Outlays by Activity, CETA Title I (IIB/C), Fiscal 1975-1980

| Activity | 1975 | 1976[a] | 1977 | 1978 | 1979 | 1980 |
|---|---|---|---|---|---|---|
| Total outlays (millions) ..... | $876 | $2,035 | $1,674 | $1,777 | $1,723[b] | $2,050[b] |
| | | | (Percent) | | | |
| Total ..................... | 100 | 100 | 100 | 100 | 100 | 100 |
| Classroom training[c] ....... | 34 | 35 | 43 | 48 | 53 | 57 |
| On-the-job training ...... | 9 | 10 | 12 | 14 | 13 | 10 |
| Public service employment ............. | 7 | 11 | 6 | 4 | 1 | - |
| Work experience .......... | 48 | 43 | 39 | 34 | 32 | 31 |
| Other ................... | 2 | 1 | 1 | 1 | 1 | 2 |

SOURCE: Employment and Training Administration, U.S. Department of Labor (unpublished).

NOTE: Details may not add to 100 percent due to rounding.

a. Includes transition quarter, July-September 1976.

b. Administrative expenditures, reported as a combined figure, prorated by activity.

c. Includes outlays for governors' vocational education programs operated by prime sponsors.

and allowing use of CETA funds for upgrading and retraining of employed workers under some circumstances.

Title IIB programs were affected indirectly by the enactment of the private sector initiative program (Title VII); the eligibility restrictions in Title IIB/C; and the requirement that sponsors set aside a portion of Title IID and Title VI funds for training PSE participants.

Of the various measures influencing the pattern of Title IIB/C activities, the requirement that some Title IID and Title VI enrollees must receive training was mentioned most frequently by the survey respondents. Funds for training PSE enrollees were used in some cases to bolster classroom training. In others, job search courses for PSE enrollees were extended to Title IIB enrollees as well. In two-thirds of the cases in the BSSR sample, the share of Title IIB expenditures for classroom training rose after 1978.

| Reauthorization act requirement | Effect on pattern of activities under Title IIB/C |
|---|---|
| | (Rank order by frequency of response) |
| Title IID and Title VI training . . . . . . . . . . . . | 1 |
| Separate title for private sector initiative programs. . . . . . . . . . . . . . . . . . . | 2 |
| Limits on hours of work experience. . . . . . . . | 3 |
| Changes in eligibility for Title IIB . . . . . . . . . | 4 |
| Prohibition on use of Title IIB funds for public service jobs . . . . . . . . . . . . . . . . | 5 |
| Other legislative changes . . . . . . . . . . . . . . . . | 6 |

The establishment of private industry programs under Title VII, which rely heavily on on-the-job (OJT) training, was beginning to have an effect on the Title IIB/C program mix by late 1980. Nationally, the proportion of Title IIB/C funds spent for OJT dropped from 14 percent in 1978 to 10 percent in 1980. In two-thirds of the study areas, the proportion of Title IIB/C funds spent for OJT programs was lower in 1980 than in 1978. Softness in the labor market was a factor, but there are indications that Title IIB projects were shifted to Title VII in some cases. In others, promising OJT training candidates were referred to Title VII openings instead of to Title IIB.[3]

The 1,000-hour per year limit on length of stay in adult work experience programs also affected the allocation of Title IIB resources. Work experience projects were curtailed in some areas because the time limit made it more difficult to arrange for work sites.

The mix of programs and activities offered under Title IIB was influenced also by management decisions unrelated to the reauthorization—cost and placement considerations, sifting out occupations with the best prospects of employment, and regional office pressure to expand job search programs for all enrollees.

## Opinions on the Allocation of Funds Among Titles

Against a backdrop of declining resources, restrictions on eligibility, wages and length of service, increased emphasis on private sector training and youth projects, and expected decreases in public service employment,[4] survey respondents were asked about their preferences in the distribution of funds among CETA titles. Opinions varied by type of respondent, but in general there was a preference for programs which are designed to provide training and other

3. Between fiscal 1979 and 1980 the number of individuals in Title IIB/C on-the-job training programs declined from 157,000 to 132,000; for the United States the number of individuals in Title VII on-the-job training programs was 16,000 in fiscal 1980. Corresponding Title VII participant figures are not available for fiscal 1979.
4. At the time of the survey some cutbacks in PSE were considered likely, but a complete phaseout was not announced until several months later.

employability development services rather than those which primarily provide employment experience.

Among manpower professionals, there was a decided preference for Title IIB and private sector initiatives. More than one-half of the CETA administrators interviewed believed that relatively more funds should be allotted for titles which emphasize employability development. One-third would give more weight to PSE. Respondents who favored training programs perceived the lack of skills and education as the main deficiency among enrollees. Public service employment, it was believed, was less useful than Title IIB for preparing enrollees for private or public sector openings.

The views of planning council chairmen were generally similar except that they showed more concern for youth unemployment and more interest in expanding youth programs. The pattern was less clear among elected officials and community based organizations. They supported PSE, as well as Title IIB/C, to provide supplemental jobs for the unemployed.

## Delivery of Services

The framers of the original CETA legislation expected that, with local decision making and control, prime sponsors would organize the pattern of service delivery to eliminate duplication among service deliverers and replace the fragmented arrangements with a coordinated system. Since CETA was enacted, however, two opposite developments have been in evidence. One moved the program in the direction of an integrated system for delivery of comprehensive training services to adult participants. The other weakened the patterns of integration as new programs were added with different institutional arrangements that were not completely compatible with the existing systems.

Under the reauthorization act, CETA has continued to move in both directions. The compliance provisions of the CETA reauthorization act reinforce the trend toward a more integrated service pattern. Emphasis on tighter administrative controls and liability makes it more likely that sponsors will take over eligibility determination and other intake functions to avoid the risks of enrolling ineligible participants. On the other hand, the reauthorization act has added more program categories and greater specificity in existing titles, and these tend to subdivide the entire delivery system.[5]

### Title IIB Service Delivery Systems

Before the enactment of CETA in 1973, there was no central local administrative mechanism through which the many MDTA and EOA training programs could be coordinated. A loose arrangement did exist—the Cooperative Area Manpower Planning System (CAMPS)—which provided a forum for the exchange of information but lacked authority to make decisions, eliminate duplication, or provide for needed services. In areas with skills centers or Concentrated Employment Programs, established under MDTA or EOA to provide a range of service options, applicants could be referred to one of many programs or from one service component to another. In most cases, however, clients had access only to the programs operated by the specific agency to which they had applied.

Following the enactment of CETA there was a gradual movement towards comprehensive delivery systems. Many

---

5. There are also many employment and training programs outside of local CETA agency control. These include programs for welfare recipients (such as WIN), older workers, the handicapped, offenders, and other special groups. A 1979 report of the General Accounting Office enumerated 44 federally assisted programs in the Tidewater area of Virginia, only 5 of which were administered by the local CETA agency. See General Accounting Office, *Federally Assisted Employment and Training: A Myriad of Programs Should be Simplified,* HRD79-11, May 8, 1979.

sponsors moved all the way to a comprehensive arrangement for delivering services, others retained arrangements with independent subcontractors, and some organized a mixed delivery system.

The term "delivery system" refers to the interrelationship of agencies which provide intake and exit services for clients, as well as substantive training or employment activities. In a "comprehensive" delivery system, the entry and exit services are centralized for all clients in the community. This can be done by designating a single agency to handle all intake and placement for all other organizations or by coordinating the activities of several organizations that perform these functions. In a typical arrangement, applicants enter through a single intake center (or network of coordinated centers) where eligibility is determined, clients' needs assessed, and referrals made to appropriate employment or training programs from a full range of options. On completion of the program, clients are assisted in finding unsubsidized employment either by specialists at the intake centers or by a designated placement agency such as the employment service.

In an "independent" model, each service deliverer is responsible for its own intake and placement activities as well as for a substantive program. Each agency or organization offers to applicants only the kind of service or training programs it is equipped to provide.

There are, of course, many variations of these models. A "mixed" system combines the features of both types. Intake may be coordinated or centralized, but placement may be delegated to each individual contractor; or some training or service components may be integrated while others are handled separately by independent agencies.

Opinions differ as to the advantages of the various models and the appropriateness of a particular system in a local situation. Several advantages for prime sponsors and clients have been attributed to the comprehensive model:

- The sponsor has more control over the selection process.
- Duplication of services is minimized.
- Economies of scale permit the hiring of specialized personnel.
- Clients are exposed to a wider range of program options.
- Competition among contractors for applicants and job openings is reduced.

Under an independent system, on the other hand, accountability for all the components of the delivery system can be assigned more readily. Moreover, there is less danger of losing clients as they are shuttled among the intake, program, and placement operations. In sparsely populated areas that lack training facilities, are distant from urban centers, and are without adequate public transportation, an independent system may be the only practical way of providing services.

*Comprehensive system.* One-third of the 24 local prime sponsors (cities, counties, and consortia) in the study group had basically comprehensive Title IIB/C systems, although there were variations in the extent of coordination. The Topeka-Shawnee Consortium, Kansas, is an example of this model.

The delivery system in Topeka-Shawnee evolved into a comprehensive system after going through several stages. The sponsor phased out all subcontractors and operated all programs directly including an intake center co-located with a state employment service office. It had its own training facility, but also arranged for classroom training by referring participants to private or public institutions.[6]

---

6. For an earlier and more complete description, see Charles E. Krider, "Topeka-Shawnee County Consortium, Kansas," in *Employment and Training Programs: The Local View,* ed. William Mirengoff (Washington: National Academy of Sciences, 1978), pp. 93-98.

The other local sponsors in the BSSR study group which are classified as comprehensive include three cities, three counties, and one consortium. Generally intake was unified, but there were variations in the extent to which subcontractors were used and in arrangements for counseling, placement, and other services.

*Mixed system.* The largest group—over one-half of the study areas—had mixed systems. In Gary, for example, the city operated manpower centers which provide intake services, but subcontractors shared placement and counseling services. The Capital Area Consortium in Texas is split between urban and rural components. In the urban sector, the prime sponsor handled intake, assessment, and referral for services; counseling was done by service deliverers; and placement was handled by either a community based organization or the prime sponsor. In the rural sector a community based organization handled all CETA services.

*Independent system.* Three sample areas, including the two largest cities (New York and Philadelphia), operated basically independent systems. The Lansing Consortium contracted for all services, using a competitive, performance-based rating system to select and evaluate contractors.[7] Each service deliverer handled the client from intake through training to placement.

In balance-of-states the patterns vary, but two major designs are discernible. In one, there is a common institution through which services are delivered. In the other arrangement, local jurisdictions or councils of governments (COGs) arrange for services through numerous different organizations. Arizona illustrates a design in which one institution, the employment service, provides intake for all CETA and

7. For an earlier and more complete description, see Steven M. Director, "Lansing Tri-County Regional Consortium, Michigan," in *Employment and Training Programs: The Local View*, pp. 130-34.

state welfare programs. In the other design, illustrated by Maine, a community action agency is usually designated as the delivery agent for Title IIB programs while county governments operate PSE programs. COG staff provide intake and assessment services in a typical Texas region.

The variety of local operations in a balance-of-state is best illustrated by North Carolina. Delivery systems and infrastructures vary from one region of the state to another. Each has its own arrangements with employment service, community college, or community based organizations. Depending on regional preferences, programs may be operated by any or all of these organizations independently, or one may be designated to contract for all services. The rural areas are generally not conducive to coordinated delivery systems.

### Effects of Reauthorization Act on Delivery Systems

The reauthorization act influenced the Title IIB employment and training delivery systems in two ways: in the choice of institutions used by prime sponsors to deliver services, and in the manner in which the services were delivered.

*Title IIB delivery systems.* Of 24 local prime sponsors, six have made significant changes in their delivery systems since 1978 attributable to both the influence of the reauthorization act and management considerations. The new eligibility determination process, the financial liability of the prime sponsor, and the new assessment procedure (employability development plans) made prime sponsor control of intake more vital. The experience of several of the prime sponsors illustrates the different ways in which they have modified their delivery systems.

The shift in Kansas City, Kansas towards a greater assumption of activities by the prime sponsor staff was attributed directly to the eligibility and liability provisions of the 1978 amendments. The CETA administrator established a central intake system to provide services formerly supplied by subcontractors. The CETA staff assumed responsibility for eligibility determination, counseling, preparation of employability development plans, referral to programs, monitoring of participants' progress, as well as job development and placement. And an employment service specialist was stationed at the central intake office to coordinate job development and placement.

The interplay of the reauthorization act provisions and management decisions affected the delivery system in Stanislaus County. Before reauthorization, each of several service deliverers took care of its own recruitment and intake. After 1978, the CETA administrator set up a central intake office to give him more control over eligibility determination and client assessment activities. Applicants enrolled at the manpower center are afforded a full range of training and employment options, provided, of course, there are available openings. Counseling is still delegated to individual service deliverers responsible also for placing enrollees in permanent positions. In addition, the central intake office has job developers to back up contractors in finding jobs for participants who complete their CETA programs. The change in Stanislaus County, designed to improve the effectiveness of service, was planned before the reauthorization, but was given added impetus by the new legislation.

The effect of the reauthorization act, especially the provisions dealing with client assessment and liability, is also evidenced in areas that did not reshuffle their basic delivery structures. Phoenix strengthened assessment functions by adding two new intake centers. Chester County, Pennsylvania and Orange County and the San Joaquin Consortium in California reported more intensive counseling and assessment. Pasco County, Florida strengthened its counseling operation by moving the employment service counselors into its own manpower office. The Capital Consortium, Texas reorganized its intake activities along defensive lines. It retained direct control over functions specifically mandated by the act, i.e., eligibility determination, tracking the length of stay of enrollees, and preparation of employability development plans. And it shifted to subcontractors other services such as counseling, job development, and placement.

The desirability of centralizing intake and placement depends upon a number of local factors including the size of the area, accessibility of intake centers, and managerial competence, as well as considerations related to the reauthorization act. In at least one instance, local factors (inadequate performance) led to a reversal of a centralized intake arrangement. In 1979, Philadelphia attempted to standardize its intake process and improve client assessment by consolidating most intake centers under the management of a single subcontractor. The following year, however—partly to carry out the Employability Development Plan (EDP) requirements of the 1978 amendments—it replaced the centralized design with 10 centers operated by several subcontractors. The sponsor in 1981 was considering a new arrangement with an "umbrella" agency to supervise and coordinate intake at these centers.

CETA administrators also took over client intake services in Cleveland and in Ramsey County, Minnesota. New York had planned to improve intake services prior to the reauthorization act and recently established a coordinated network of training, appraisal, and placement (TAP) centers, operated by community based organizations. Twenty percent of clients were processed through the TAP centers in late 1980; the remainder were recruited through individual program sponsors.

An examination of the basic delivery systems in the study sample's four balance-of-state prime sponsor areas showed no major changes, although counseling activity had been stimulated by new EDP requirements.

*Delivery systems for all titles.* As prime sponsors became more sophisticated in the management of their programs, there was a noticeable trend, quickened by the reauthorization act, toward more integration of Title IIB delivery systems. But there was also a discernible tendency away from integration in the overall delivery system for all titles because the reauthorization provisions, along with previous amendments, had made the total CETA operation more complex. In particular, the addition of public service employment and youth programs—each with its own "categorical" set of eligibility rules and design elements—has acted to make the system more diffuse.

Most sponsors in the study sample use some or all of the same organizations to provide program services to both youth and adults, but with separate contracts and often under the purview of different staff members. Even within the youth programs, varying rules and features for each sub-component call for specialization on the part of CETA staff. The establishment of a new title for private sector initiatives, with private industry councils (PICs) as its own separate planning body and in some cases, its own service apparatus, may create additional strains in the overall system.

## Effect of Reauthorization Act on Selection of Service Deliverers

The reauthorization has had an effect on the choice of service deliverers as well as on delivery systems. For about a year after CETA began, prime sponsors, lacking experience and under severe time pressures, were inclined to retain the service deliverers that had been operating programs under MDTA and EOA. In the second and succeeding years, however, as sponsors gained experience and confidence, the pattern began to change. New vendors were used, responsibilities of existing service deliverers were changed, and, in a significant proportion of cases, the prime sponsors themselves took over some of the activities formerly performed by subcontractors.

While the new eligibility determination, monitoring, and liability rules encouraged more prime sponsors to take over CETA intake functions, most CETA operations are still conducted by subcontractors. The 1978 amendments are more direct than the previous legislation in prescribing how program deliverers are to be selected. The original act required assurances that (1) consideration be given to service deliverers of proven capability, (2) appropriate arrangements be made with community based organizations (CBOs) serving the poverty community, and (3) to the extent deemed appropriate, facilities of existing employment service, education, and rehabilitation agencies be utilized. The new language is more specific: it requires sponsors to describe the methods used to involve CBOs, educational agencies, and others, and the criteria used for selecting service deliverers of demonstrated effectiveness.

There were five factors influencing the extent of contracting between 1978 and 1980: (1) widespread declines in the number of agencies employing Title VI participants as funds shrank; (2) increased contracts with training agencies due to the requirement to train Title IID participants; (3) increased use of nonprofit agencies as PSE employers because of their ability to accommodate to lower wages; (4) a rise in the number of Title VII contracts for new private sector projects; and (5) an increase in Title IV youth contracts. The number of Title IIB/C contractors remained about the same in most of the survey areas. The choice of service vendors was heavily influenced by liability concerns. Sponsors were careful to select contractors with sound fiscal systems.

## CETA/Employment Service Relations

The relationship between the CETA and the employment service systems continues to be a special concern. Prior to the enactment of CETA, the employment service had been the linchpin in the manpower program system. Under CETA, this role has been assigned to prime sponsors. Since then, relationships between employment service offices and the prime sponsors have been uneven.

Soon after the enactment of CETA, some prime sponsors began to reassign functions previously provided by employment service offices. As CETA administrators gained experience, many took over entry and exit functions—assessment, referral to training, counseling, job development, and placement. Others transferred those tasks to community based organizations or other contractors. In most cases, the employment service continued to provide labor market information for planning, and on a more limited scale, handled intake and placement activities. While the functions assigned to the employment service varied from area to area and among segments of large areas, generally its role on the employment and training scene dwindled.

The decline in the early years was partly offset by responsibilities related to the expanding public service employment program—advance listing of PSE openings for veterans, referral of applicants for PSE slots, and job development and placement services for trainees. In the rapid public service employment build-up of 1977-78, the Department of Labor urged prime sponsors to use employment service agencies to establish pools of eligible applicants. As an inducement, sponsors were absolved from liability for ineligible participants if employment service offices had determined eligibility. The "carrot" for the employment service was the placement credit they received for persons hired in PSE jobs.

The post-reauthorization period saw a notable drop in employment service involvement in CETA activities due to declining enrollments and the act's stricter liability provisions that removed the prime sponsor exemption for ineligible participants. Sponsors in 10 of the 28 study areas either discontinued or reduced reliance on the employment service for eligibility determination. To a lesser degree declines occurred in advance listing of PSE openings for veterans' recruitment, assessment, testing and counseling, and job development and placement.

There were two activities in which the participation of local employment service offices increased: preparation of employability development plans and payment of allowances to enrollees. Perhaps the most dramatic example of the increased role of the employment service occurred in the North Carolina balance-of-state program where 19 counties withdrew from the Title IID program and responsibility for these programs was delegated to the employment service (Chart 3).

## Chart 3
### Changes in Activities Performed by the Employment Service
### Fiscal 1978-1980

| Increased use | Little change | Decline |
|---|---|---|
| Preparation of employability development plans | Labor market information | Advance listing of PSE openings for veterans |
| | Recruitment | |
| Payment of allowances | | Applicant screening, interviewing and eligibility determination |
| | Referral of applicants to training or PSE | |
| | Assessment, testing, counseling | Eligibility verification |
| | Selection of CETA participants | |
| | Job development | |
| | Placement | |

Despite some setbacks, the employment service has had a significant, although declining piece of the action. The 653,000 employment service referrals to CETA programs in fiscal 1980 were 45 percent fewer than the 1978 figure due largely to declining enrollments. Nevertheless, they represented about one-fourth of the 2.6 million new 1980 CETA entrants (including some duplication among titles). Moreover, the 547,000 placed by employment service offices in CETA on-the-job training, work experience, and public service employment programs represented 13 percent of all employment service placements compared with 25 percent in 1978 (table 9 and figures 4 and 5).

The ties between ES and CETA are not limited to referral of enrollees. Job service representatives serve on planning councils and provide labor market information. In two-thirds or more of the study areas, the job service lists PSE openings for veterans and helps recruit and place CETA enrollees. In nearly one-half of the areas they provide assessment services. Through the WIN program, the employment service helps to enroll welfare recipients. Since early 1979, ES staff have worked with CETA prime sponsors in implementing the Targeted Jobs Tax Credit program.[8]

Despite a decline in activities, in most of the areas studied CETA funds contracted with employment service agencies remained virtually unchanged between 1978 and 1980.[9] In some instances, this was attributed to shifts in responsibilities among titles. In one area, for example, where total funding remained about the same, the responsibilities of the employment service increased in Title IID programs and

---

8. See Randall B. Ripley et al., *The Implementation of the Targeted Jobs Tax Credit,* prepared for the Office of Program Evaluation, Employment and Training Administration, by the Mershon Center of The Ohio State University, Report 3, May 1981.

9. In fiscal year 1979 state employment service agencies received $193 million through contractual agreements with prime sponsors—approximately 16 percent of all funds available to the employment service. See U.S. Department of Labor, "Report to Congress on Wagner-Peyser," Washington, June 1980, p. 36 (unpublished).

Table 9
Employment Service Placements in CETA Programs, Fiscal 1976-1980
(numbers in thousands)

| Fiscal year | Total individuals placed by ES | ES placements in CETA programs[a] | | | | Enrolled in CETA institutional training programs[b] |
|---|---|---|---|---|---|---|
| | | Total | On-the-job | Public service employment | Work experience | |
| | | (Number of individuals) | | | | |
| 1976[c] | 3,367 | 388 | 38 | 201 | 149 | 80 |
| 1977 | 4,138 | 722 | 54 | 334 | 384 | 77 |
| 1978 | 4,623 | 1,108 | 63 | 579 | 466 | 89 |
| 1979 | 4,537 | 849 | 48 | 393 | 408 | 92 |
| 1980 | 4,088 | 547 | 25 | 169 | 353 | 106 |
| | | (Percent of total placed) | | | | |
| 1976 | 100 | 11 | 1 | 6 | 4 | - |
| 1977 | 100 | 18 | 1 | 8 | 9 | - |
| 1978 | 100 | 25 | 1 | 13 | 10 | - |
| 1979 | 100 | 20 | 1 | 9 | 9 | - |
| 1980 | 100 | 13 | 1 | 4 | 9 | - |

SOURCE: Employment and Training Administration, U.S. Department of Labor (unpublished data).

NOTE: Details may not add to totals due to rounding.

a. May include some multiple placements of individuals.

b. ES applicants enrolled in institutional training programs are not counted as placements.

c. Excludes the transition quarter, July-September 1976.

## Figure 4
## Persons Placed in CETA Programs Through the Employment Service*
## as Percent of All Employment Service Placements

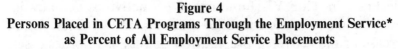
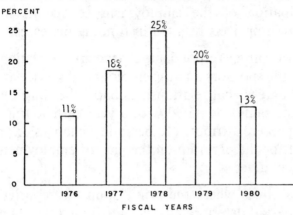

SOURCE: Employment and Training Administration, U.S. Department of Labor data.

*ES placements in CETA on-the-job training, work experience, and public service employment programs.

## Figure 5
## Persons Enrolled in CETA Programs Through the Employment Service*
## as a Percent of New CETA Enrollments

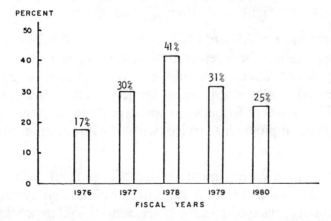

SOURCE: Employment and Training Administration, U.S. Department of Labor data.

*ES referrals enrolled in CETA institutional and on-the-job training, work experience, and public service employment programs.

declined in Title VI. Funding of ES activities actually increased in about one-fourth of the areas. In two cases, the increased funds covered preparation of EDPs. In other cases, the participation of the employment service in welfare demonstration projects resulted in funding increases.

Most of the survey respondents characterized relationships between prime sponsors and the employment service as good to fair and agreed that relationships had either improved or remained the same compared with a year earlier. Improved relationships were attributed to personnel changes or greater enthusiasm for the program on the part of employment service representatives.

In several areas where the prime sponsors reported that relationships had deteriorated, they attributed the change to dissatisfaction with eligibity determinations performed by the employment service or to the prime sponsor's interest in controlling this activity more directly because of the potential risks of improper enrollments. In some instances, employment service placement efforts were considered to be ineffective. A difference in basic orientation was cited by respondents: the employment service was considered to be less attuned to client needs than CETA agencies.

*Coordination of ES and CETA.* Within the 28 BSSR sample areas, relations between employment service agencies and prime sponsors ranged from minimal contact to almost complete dependence on employment service offices. Most sponsors fell somewhere in between with specified services provided by the employment services with or without reimbursement.

The ability of employment service offices to provide services is circumscribed by a funding formula that rewards employment service offices for placement of jobless workers in CETA on-the-job training, public service employment, or work experience activities, but not for other activities such as intake counseling or preparing employability development plans. Consequently, the employment service office may not be able to provide those services unless the prime sponsor can reimburse it for the staff time required. Several prime sponsors in the study sample recommended that consideration be given to providing incentives in the Wagner-Peyser funding formulas for activities other than placements.[10]

Some areas have improved coordination and the utilization of specialized staff by co-locating employment service and CETA offices, outstationing prime sponsor staff in ES offices, or arranging for ES personnel to be assigned to CETA intake centers. However, these solutions are not without problems. The personnel involved complain of dual lines of communication. And where ES staff are assigned to CETA offices they may not have access to complete and timely information on job openings.

*Underlying problems.* The accommodations of CETA and employment service agencies mask underlying tensions with roots in the origins of human resource development programs in the 1960s. The basic issue is the coexistence of two national manpower systems with the competition and duplication that result. CETA must concentrate on expanding employment opportunities for the segments of the labor force who are least qualified or disadvantaged in other respects. Although the employment service since the mid-1960s has assisted in placing the hard-to-employ, it must also perform its basic labor exchange function—matching job orders and qualified applicants.[11] Institutional fac-

10. The DOL resource allocation formula was changed in fiscal 1980 and 1981 and suspended in 1982. In fiscal 1980, each state employment service agency received 98 percent of its fiscal 1979 grant. Only 2 percent was awarded on the basis of performance measured by placements.

11. Art Besse, "CETA Prime Sponsors vs. the Employment Service: Why the Conflict," Department of Industry, Labor, and Human Relations, Balance-of-State, Wisconsin, October 1979 (unpublished).

tors—differences in planning cycles, service areas, location of offices, and funding mechanisms—also impede coordination.[12]

DOL regulations implementing the 1978 CETA amendments require, for the first time, a written agreement between each prime sponsor and the state employment security agency (SESA). The items to be included are: coordination in contacts with employers, allowance payments systems, certifications and referrals under the Targeted Jobs Tax Credit program, listing of PSE openings for unemployment insurance recipients and other applicants, cooperation in services to veterans and welfare recipients, and other local arrangements. The requirement for a formal agreement, with or without reimbursement, was expected to encourage close coordination. However, the question remains as to whether it is possible to mandate cooperation "because the requirement to have an agreement may not, in itself, lead to more efficient, better quality service to the unemployed."[13]

## Summary

The early years of CETA were marked by two major trends in the mix of programs: one was a trend toward more categorization, as specialized programs were enacted to meet special needs. The other was a proportionate increase in activities which essentially provide work experience and income maintenance.

Since fiscal year 1978, categorization has continued with the addition of youth and private sector programs. However, the pattern of service has shifted toward programs that contribute to employability development. The relative share of funds for adult and youth training programs has increased,

---

12. "Report to Congress on Wagner-Peyser," p. 5.
13. Ibid., p. 6.

while the share of appropriations for public service employment and summer youth programs has declined. Within Title IIB/C, the basic training component of CETA, the proportion of outlays for classroom training has gone up at the expense of work experience programs. The proportion for on-the-job training declined, with some indications of shifts of OJT to Title VII, the new private sector initiative program.

The reduction in public service employment was an obvious factor in the decline of work experience programs. But provisions of the 1978 amendments of CETA—the requirement that PSE enrollees must receive training, the establishment of private industry programs, and limitation on hours of work in work experience projects—also had some effect. CETA professionals interviewed favored employability development activities over public service employment. Elected officials, however, were equally supportive of both programs.

The CETA reauthorization act has affected the patterns for delivery of services to CETA participants. On the one hand, the act has tended to fragment service delivery by adding arrangements for youth programs and private sector initiatives under separate titles. But on the other hand, stricter liability provisions for ineligible participants (both for Title IIB and for PSE) and greater emphasis on assessment activities have tended to integrate the comprehensive services for adult Title IIB clients. Several of the sponsors surveyed have set up their own intake centers or arranged to centralize intake through contractors. Others have strengthened assessment and counseling services.

The reauthorization act has also affected the choice of deliverers. This is most clearly seen in relationships with employment service agencies. Because of the act's liability provisions, there is less reliance on employment service agencies for eligibility determination and verification. Other factors, such as the decline in PSE enrollments, are also affecting the role of employment service agencies in assessment, referral, and job development and placement.

# 4 Participants

The 1978 CETA amendments succeeded in their major objective of restricting public service employment (PSE) more narrowly to persons at a disadvantage in the job market. After 1978, appreciably larger proportions of PSE enrollees were women, youth, poorly educated persons, and members of minority groups. Over 90 percent were economically disadvantaged.[1]

The types of persons to be served in PSE programs, given limited resources, has been a central issue since the enactment of CETA in 1973. Decisions on whom to enroll in PSE should be related to program purposes. A countercyclical program might authorize the enrollment of any unemployed person. If program objectives also include assistance to financially distressed families, enrollment could be limited to the unemployed in families with low incomes. A program that is expected to improve the employment prospects of the structurally unemployed—those whose educational or other limitations make it hard for them to find jobs in good times

---

1. Data in this chapter are based, in part, on the special and regular tabulations of the *Continuous Longitudinal Manpower Survey* (Rockville, MD: Westat, Inc.), a national survey of a sample of new enrollees in 147 prime sponsor areas. The survey, supported by the Office of Program Evaluation of the Employment and Training Administration, was designed and administered by Westat, Inc. Data are collected by the U.S. Bureau of the Census.

as well as bad—should seek to enroll persons with employment impediments and exclude experienced workers who can expect to be reemployed when business conditions improve. If, however, providing essential public services is a major objective, a PSE program would be expected to enroll persons with skills adequate to the tasks proposed.

"Effectiveness" or what works best is another consideration in deciding on program clients. If improving the employability of the structurally unemployed is a central objective, the effectiveness criterion asks: which groups will benefit most from PSE—persons looking for their first jobs, the long term unemployed, the poorly educated, or persons with at least a high school education? An effectiveness criterion for selecting enrollees for CETA training programs suggested by one writer is the enrollment of persons who would show the greatest increase in earnings for each dollar of program expenditures.[2]

The multiple and changing purposes and priorities of PSE programs since CETA was enacted have made it difficult to develop a clear basis for decisions on the types of persons to enroll.[3]

The purpose of the initial PSE program (Title II, now IID) was to serve the structurally unemployed in areas of substantial unemployment.[4] Its authorizing language required prime sponsors to provide assurances that "special consideration in filling transitional public service jobs will be given to

---

2. See Michael Borus, "Assessing the Impact of Training Programs" in *Employing the Unemployed,* ed. Eli Ginzberg (New York: Basic Books, 1980), p. 29.

3. For a comprehensive discussion of CETA eligibility issues see William Barnes, "Target Groups" in *CETA: An Analysis of the Issues* (Washington: National Commission for Manpower Policy, 1978).

4. The CETA Title II PSE program for areas of substantial unemployment was changed under the 1978 reauthorization act to Title IID and the participants limited to the low-income, long term unemployed. The countercyclical PSE program remained in Title VI (see chart 1).

unemployed persons who are most severely disadvantaged in terms of the length of time they have been unemployed and their prospects of finding employment without assistance."[5] However, the reality of the operative legislative provisions did not match the rhetoric. The specific eligibility criteria, which, if violated, could result in financial penalties for prime sponsors, merely limited enrollment in Title II to persons who had been unemployed 30 days or more or were underemployed.[6]

In response to the onset of the recession in 1974, Congress added a countercyclical public service employment program—Title VI—to CETA. Eligibility for this title was similar to the original Title II PSE except that, in areas with an unemployment rate of 7 percent of more, persons could be enrolled if they had been unemployed as few as 15 days. "Preferred consideration" in the new PSE title was to be given to the long term unemployed with previous employment experience.[7]

The congressional intent was to design a double-barrelled program: Title II for the structurally unemployed in areas of "substantial" unemployment; and Title VI for the cyclically unemployed—persons out of work due to fluctuations of the economy. This distinction, however, was not reflected in the eligibility requirements, and program operators had little reason to differentiate between the structural and countercyclical objectives of the two PSE programs when selecting the clients to be served.

---

5. Pub. L. 93-203, 93rd Congress, December 28, 1973, Sec. 205(c) (7).

6. The Department of Labor regulations defined the unemployed and the underemployed as including part-time or full-time workers whose earnings in relation to family size were below the poverty level, persons from families receiving Aid for Families with Dependent Children (AFDC) or Supplemental Security Income (SSI), and persons working part time and seeking full-time work, as well as those unemployed for 30 days.

7. I.e., persons who had exhausted unemployment insurance benefits, or were ineligible for such benefits (except for those lacking work experience), and those who had been unemployed for 15 or more weeks (Pub. L. 93-203, Sec. 602(d)).

The socioeconomic characteristics of persons enrolled in PSE during the first two years of CETA indicate that the seriously disadvantaged were not sufficiently represented. Groups which typically experience above average unemployment, such as the poorly educated, women, youth, and older workers, were not enrolled in PSE in proportion to their share of the unemployed population. The only disadvantaged group served in greater proportion in PSE were blacks and other nonwhites.

The participation of disadvantaged persons in PSE programs was also much smaller than their proportion in the Title I (now Title IIB) CETA training program for adults. In effect, a two tier system had evolved. The most disadvantaged were enrolled in the CETA training programs which, except for the small OJT program, paid relatively low training allowances. The less disadvantaged obtained higher earnings by enrolling in PSE (table 10).

### Table 10
### Characteristics of Enrollees in Public Service Employment and Adult Training Programs, and of the Unemployed and Long Term Unemployed, 1976

| Characteristic | Enrollees in | | All unemployed | Long term unemployed[a] |
|---|---|---|---|---|
| | PSE | Title I adult training | | |
| | (Percent of total) | | | |
| Female ........... | 33 | 47 | 46 | 40 |
| Black and other nonwhite......... | 23 | 36 | 20 | 20 |
| Less than high school education .. | 25 | 37 | 42[b] | 39[b] |
| Age: | | | | |
| 16 to 21 .......... | 22 | 31 | 34[b] | 34[b] |
| 45 and over ....... | 12 | 28 | 18 | 28 |

SOURCE: Data on unemployed and long term unemployed from Bureau of Labor Statistics, *Employment and Earnings,* January 1977. PSE enrollee data from U.S. Department of Labor, Employment and Training Administration, special tabulations of the *Continuous Longitudinal Manpower Survey*, Westat, Inc. The latter data are on the October 1975 through September 1976 fiscal year basis.

a. Unemployed 15 weeks or more.

b. Includes youth still in school who may be seeking part-time or full-time jobs.

Congressional concern with the types of persons enrolled in PSE was reflected in legislative changes in 1976 and 1978. This chapter examines the influence of the changes and other factors on the socioeconomic profile of PSE enrollees, especially after the CETA amendments of 1978.

# Legislative Efforts to Target PSE

## The 1976 Amendments; Emergency Jobs Programs Extension Act

In 1976, Congress took its first serious steps to deal with two intractable problems of PSE: "creaming," the enrollment of persons able to compete in the regular job market; and "substitution," the use of PSE enrollees in jobs that would have been supported by local funds in the absence of PSE. The Emergency Jobs Programs Extension Act attempted to restrain substitution by requiring that all of the Title VI funds in excess of the amount needed to sustain the then current PSE enrollments were to be used for special projects that were limited to 12-months' duration and involved activities that would not otherwise be performed. To ensure greater participation of the disadvantaged in PSE programs, the 1976 amendments required that all expansion of Title VI enrollment, plus one-half of the vacancies occurring in the remainder of Title VI, were to be filled by the low-income, long term unemployed.[8] Thus, for the first time, an income

8. Eligibility for these programs was limited to those who had been unemployed for 15 weeks and whose family income was not above the OMB poverty level or 70 percent of the BLS lower living standard. Persons in families receiving AFDC were eligible without regard to their unemployment status.

criterion, usually associated with programs for the structurally unemployed, was added to the countercyclical Title VI PSE program and the distinction between the "countercyclical" Title VI PSE and the "counterstructural" Title II became even less clear.

The eligibility provisions assumed particular significance with the enactment of the Carter economic stimulus program that expanded Title VI enrollments from 245,000 in May 1977 to 613,000 in March 1978. Since about 70 percent of the participants in March 1978 were subject to the new eligibility criteria,[9] there were sharp increases between 1976 and 1978 in the percent of new enrollees who were from families with low incomes and who had been unemployed 15 weeks or more (table 11).

## The Reauthorization Act of 1978

PSE came under close scrutiny during the CETA reauthorization deliberations in 1978. Persons most in need were still perceived to be underrepresented, and Congress used the occasion of the reauthorization to press its targeting objectives. It relied most heavily on two legislative strategies: tighter enrollment requirements, and reductions in permissible wages. More rigorous methods for determining eligibility and monitoring to assure compliance with the legislation were also mandated.

- *Eligibility: Title II/IID PSE.* Prior to the reauthorization, participation in Title II was permitted regardless of family income, if the applicant had been unemployed for 30 days. The 1978 amendments limited enrollment in the new Title IID to: (a) persons from a family receiving public assistance, or (b) persons from families with income not above the poverty level, or not above 70 per-

9. William Mirengoff, Lester Rindler, Harry Greenspan, Scott Seablom, *CETA: Assessment of Public Service Employment Programs* (Washington: National Academy of Sciences, 1980), p. 105.

cent of the BLS lower living standard,[10] provided that the applicant had been unemployed at least 15 weeks.[11]

- *Title VI PSE.* As noted previously, there were two sets of eligibility criteria for Title VI prior to the reauthorization. After the reauthorization, eligibility for all Title VI enrollees was limited to persons who had been unemployed for 10 of the previous 12 weeks, and whose family income did not exceed 100 percent of the BLS lower living standard income level, or whose family was receiving public assistance.[12] Thus, the new eligibility requirements were marginally less restrictive for about half of the new enrollees in Title VI, but appreciably more restrictive for the other half.

- *Eligibility determination and liability.* To ensure that the new eligibility requirements were implemented stringently, the 1978 amendments prescribed a rigorous eligibility determination and verification process and made prime sponsors financially liable for ineligible participants.

- *Wages.* To deter applicants with marketable skills from competing for PSE jobs and to encourage PSE enrollees to seek unsubsidized employment, the national average wage for PSE jobs was reduced from $7,800 to $7,200. Supplementation of CETA wages with local funds was not permitted for Title IID jobs and was limited for Title VI positions. (The effects of the wage changes are discussed more fully in chapter 6.)

---

10. In the fall of 1978 the urban poverty level for a family of four was $6,200; 70 percent of the BLS lower living standard was $7,337. These levels had changed to $7,450 and $8,810 respectively by the fall of 1980.

11. DOL regulations loosened the 15 continuous weeks of unemployment requirement to permit enrollment of persons who had been unemplyed for 15 of the 20 weeks prior to application.

12. DOL regulations loosened the requirements to permit enrollment without regard to unemployment status of persons in families that had been receiving public assistance for 10 of the previous 12 weeks.

- *Monitoring.* Finally, to reinforce the measures to improve targeting, prime sponsors were required to establish independent monitoring units to review local compliance with the eligibility criteria and other requirements of the act.

Table 11
Characteristics of New Enrollees in CETA Title VI
Public Service Employment
Fiscal 1976 and 1978

| Characteristic | Percent of total | | Percentage point change |
| --- | --- | --- | --- |
| | 1976 | 1978 | |
| Female................... | 33 | 37 | + 4 |
| Age: 16 to 21.............. | 24 | 23 | -1 |
| Less than high school education .............. | 23 | 27 | + 4 |
| Member of a minority group[a] ................ | 29 | 40 | +11 |
| Unemployed 15 weeks or more ............... | 33 | 47 | +14 |
| Family receiving public assistance[b]............. | 15 | 22 | + 7 |
| Family receiving cash welfare or has income below OMB poverty level[c].. | 46 | 75 | +29 |

SOURCE: Special tabulations of the *Continuous Longitudinal Manpower Survey,* Westat, Inc. Data for 1976 as well as 1978 are on the October through September fiscal year basis.

a. Hispanics, blacks, and other nonwhite.

b. Includes cash and noncash public assistance.

c. The OMB poverty level for an urban family of four was $5,500 in 1976 and $6,200 in 1978.

# Effects of the 1978 Amendments
## on Participant Characteristics

The 1978 amendments turned the PSE program sharply toward the seriously disadvantaged. By fiscal 1980, 92 percent of new enrollees came from families with incomes no greater than 70 percent of the BLS lower living standard income level. New participants with less than a high school education increased their share of PSE jobs from 25 percent in 1978 to 35 percent in 1980. Large increases were also recorded for persons on welfare, members of minority groups, women, and youth (table 12).

Table 12
Characteristics of New Public Service
Employment Enrollees, Fiscal 1978 and 1980

| | Percent of total enrollment | | Percentage point change |
|---|---|---|---|
| Characteristic | 1978 | 1980 | |
| Female................... | 38 | 46 | + 8 |
| Age: 16 to 21.............. | 23 | 28 | + 5 |
| Less than high school education .............. | 25 | 35 | +10 |
| Member of a minority group[a] ................ | 39 | 48 | + 9 |
| Family receiving public assistance[b].............. | 22 | 31 | + 9 |
| Family income at or below 70 percent of lower living standard ........... | 75 | 92 | +17 |
| Unemployed 15 weeks or more ................ | 45 | 45 | - |

SOURCE: Special tabulations of the *Continuous Longitudinal Manpower Survey,* Westat, Inc.

a. Hispanics, blacks, and other nonwhite.

b. Includes cash and noncash public assistance.

A change in the job readiness of the PSE population accompanied the demographic shifts. Research associates in about three-fourths of the study areas emphasized that enrollees after 1978 had fewer job skills than their predecessors. One commented, "There has been only a modest change in demographic characteristics but skill levels are much reduced compared to those of earlier enrollees." Others described the new enrollees in such terms as "a difficult work force," "the hard-core unemployed," "less motivated," "in need of basic training" and "more difficult to transfer to a regular job." However, even in these areas, not all enrollees were seriously deficient in job skills or potential. In three areas, enrollees were reported to be not much different from earlier participants, probably because persistent high unemployment had created a pool of applicants not greatly affected by the new eligibility criteria.

### Characteristics of Persons in PSE, Training Programs, and the Unemployed Population

Between 1976 and 1980 PSE was increasingly successful in serving the disadvantaged. The improved performance—especially after the 1978 amendments—is evident in comparisons of the more recent PSE enrollees with those entering CETA training programs (Title IIB), and with the total unemployed population. In 1976, the proportion of disadvantaged persons enrolled in PSE ranged from 50 to about 70 percent of those in CETA training programs. By 1980, the difference for each of the disadvantaged groups had been eliminated or sharply reduced. For example, in 1976 enrollees from welfare families were 15 percent of new PSE enrollees and 31 percent of enrollees in CETA training programs. By 1980, welfare enrollees in both programs were 31 percent of total. For most groups—women, youth, the poorly educated, and welfare recipients—most of the increases occurred after the 1978 amendments (table 13 and figure 6).

**Table 13**
**Characteristics of New Enrollees**
**in Public Service Employment and Training Programs[a]**
**Fiscal 1976-1980**

| | Percent of total enrollment | | | | |
|---|---|---|---|---|---|
| Characteristic and program | 1976 | 1977 | 1978 | 1979 | 1980 |
| **Female:** | | | | | |
| Training programs ........ | 47 | 49 | 53 | 55 | 52 |
| PSE .................. | 33 | 36 | 38 | 47 | 46 |
| **Age: 16 to 21:** | | | | | |
| Training programs ........ | 31 | 32 | 34 | 30 | 29 |
| PSE .................. | 22 | 21 | 23 | 25 | 28 |
| **Less than high school education:** | | | | | |
| Training programs ........ | 37 | 36 | 35 | 36 | 39 |
| PSE .................. | 25 | 26 | 25 | 26 | 35 |
| **Member of a minority group:** | | | | | |
| Training program ........ | 49 | 45 | 45 | 47 | 48 |
| PSE .................. | 29 | 38 | 39 | 44 | 48 |
| **Family receiving public assistance[b]:** | | | | | |
| Training programs ........ | 31 | 30 | 28 | 35 | 31 |
| PSE .................. | 15 | 20 | 22 | 32 | 31 |
| **Family income at or below 70 percent of lower living standard[c]:** | | | | | |
| Training programs ........ | 63 | 70 | 73 | 80 | 95 |
| PSE .................. | 44 | 73 | 75 | 80 | 92 |

SOURCE: Special tabulations, *Continuous Longitudinal Manpower Survey,* Westat, Inc. Data for 1980 are from a sample of prime sponsor records, in place of interviews of a sample of enrollees, and must be considered preliminary.

a. Training programs include adults in classroom and on-the-job training and adult work experience (Title IIB).

b. Includes cash and noncash public assistance.

c. For 1976 and 1977 this included persons in families receiving cash welfare or having income below the OMB poverty level.

## Figure 6
## Changes in Characteristics of New Enrollees,
## Public Service Employment and Training Programs
## Fiscal 1976, 1978 and 1980

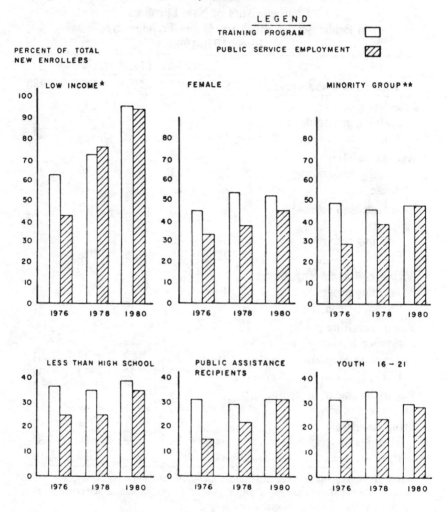

SOURCE: *Continuous Longitudinal Manpower Survey,* Westat, Inc.

  *See footnote c, table 13, p. 117.

**Hispanics, blacks and other nonwhite.

# Factors that Influenced Changes in Participants' Characteristics

The effects of the various factors that influenced the types of persons enrolled in PSE were explored with officials in the study areas.[13] In addition to being questioned about the major eligibility and wage changes in the 1978 amendments, officials were asked their views on the objectives of the local PSE programs and the kinds of persons who should be served. Information was also solicited about their recruiting methods, eligibility determination process, targeting efforts, basis for assigning applicants to PSE or the training programs, and the selection practices of PSE employers.

## Eligibility Criteria

Almost all the CETA directors interviewed credited the new eligibility requirements as a major factor in moving PSE toward the goal of serving the seriously disadvantaged. The central fact about eligibility for PSE after the 1978 amendments was that it was limited to persons from low income families. With minor exceptions, no one from a family with income above the BLS lower living standard was eligible for PSE regardless of the length of unemployment. Title IID enrollees, a majority of new PSE entrants in 1980, had to meet more stringent income requirements—receiving public assistance or family income not above the poverty level nor above 70 percent of the BLS lower living standard. PSE had become a poor peoples' program.

*Effect on the eligible population.* One of the ways in which the new criteria influenced the characteristics profile of PSE participants was by shrinking the size of the population eligible for PSE by 69 percent, from 18.3 to 5.7 million (see ap-

---

13. The shifts in enrollee characteristics reported in the survey areas were generally consistent with the evidence available from national program statistics (see Appendix).

pendix). This reduction had a particularly strong effect on the proportion of the eligible population that came from families receiving Aid to Families with Dependent Children (AFDC) who were registered with the Work Incentive (WIN) Program. The 2.1 million persons available for work from that group constituted a much larger proportion of the smaller eligible pool; the AFDC share increased from 12 percent of the eligible Title II and Title VI sustainment[14] populations before the amendments to 38 percent of Title VI and 55 percent of the IID eligibles after the reauthorization. The AFDC group differs markedly from other eligible groups. They are much more likely to be women, in the prime working ages of 22 to 44, members of a minority group, and high school dropouts. These features of the AFDC group are reflected in the changes in characteristics of the eligible populations following the 1978 amendments.

*Effects on pre-reauthorization enrollees.* The 1978 eligibility changes (effective in fiscal year 1979) removed a substantial portion of the "cream" from the earlier pool of eligible persons who accepted PSE jobs. If the new criteria had been applied to the enrollees of fiscal 1978, one-fourth would not have been eligible. The effect of the eligibility changes is shown most sharply by comparing the fiscal year 1978 enrollees, who were eligible under the old but not the new criteria, with the fiscal year 1978 enrollees who would have been eligible under both. Relatively high proportions of the group which would have been ineligible under the new criteria were non-Hispanic whites, had a high school or better education, had no dependents, earned about $4,000 in the year before enrollment, had family incomes above the lower living standard, and were classified as not in the labor force or had relatively short periods of unemployment prior to enrollment. On the other hand, a higher proportion of men than of women would have been eligible for PSE jobs if the

14. Title VI "sustainment" refers to the non-project part of Title VI PSE. See p. 111.

new eligibility rules had been applied to those who were hired for PSE in 1978 (table 17).

## Wages

The lower wage provisions of the 1978 amendments affected, indirectly, the kinds of persons enrolled in PSE programs. Many who could meet the eligibility requirements but possessed the qualifications to obtain unsubsidized employment were deterred from taking low paying PSE jobs. CETA administrators reported that the lower PSE wages turned away mature white males and workers with good job skills, leaving greater enrollment opportunities for persons with few skills, women, youth, and nonwhites. Moreover, the new wage provisions resulted in the establishment of lower skill jobs that more closely matched the limited qualifications of participants. As a consequence, employing agencies were less insistent upon the referral of better qualified applicants. Low wages also increased the use of entry level clerical and service worker jobs most often filled by women.

### Relative Influence of Eligibility and Wage Changes on Participant Characteristics

*Adjusting for the eligibility changes.* The relative influence on enrollee characteristics of the eligibility changes vs. wage and other changes in the reauthorization act was estimated by applying the new eligibility criteria to enrollees who entered PSE in fiscal 1978 under the old wage provisions, and comparing the characteristics of the adjusted 1978 entrants with those who actually enrolled in 1978 and 1980. The "adjusted" set of 1978 enrollees differed from the actual 1978 enrollees only with respect to the eligibility criteria, and, in theory, differed from the actual 1980 enrollees with respect to the new wage limits and all other factors except the changes in eligibility.

### Table 17
### Characteristics of Fiscal 1978 PSE Enrollees
### Eligible and Ineligible by the Post-1978 Eligibility Criteria[a]

| Characteristic | Not eligible under 1978 amendments | Eligible under 1978 amendments |
|---|---|---|
| | (Percent of total) | |
| Sex | | |
| Male | 56 | 61 |
| Female | 44 | 39 |
| Age | | |
| 21 and under | 21 | 20 |
| 22 to 44 | 63 | 67 |
| 45 and over | 16 | 13 |
| Minority status | | |
| White (not Hispanic) | 73 | 56 |
| Black, Hispanic, and other minority | 27 | 44 |
| Education | | |
| 0 to 11 years | 20 | 28 |
| 12 or more years | 80 | 72 |
| No dependents | 57 | 44 |
| Earnings in prior year | | |
| None | 27 | 43 |
| $1 to $3,999 | 42 | 45 |
| $4,000 to $5,999 | 18 | 8 |
| $6,000 to $9,999 | 10 | 4 |
| $10,000 and over | 3 | b |
| Economic status | | |
| Family receiving cash public assistance | 0 | 25 |
| Family income less than 70 percent of the lower living standard | 64 | 91 |
| 71 to 100 percent of lower living standard | 8 | 5 |
| More than 100 percent of lower living standard | 29 | 4 |
| Labor force status at entry | | |
| Employed | 2 | 5 |
| In school | b | 1 |
| Unemployed | 59 | 86 |
| Not in the labor force[c] | 38 | 7 |
| Weeks unemployed | | |
| None[c] | 40 | 14 |
| 1 to 9 | 29 | 6 |
| 10 | 4 | 1 |
| 11 to 14 | 5 | 5 |
| 15 or more | 22 | 75 |

SOURCE: *Continuous Longitudinal Manpower Survey,* Westat, Inc.

a. Excludes persons who were enrolled in FY 1978 but were found to be not eligible under both the old and new eligibility criteria.

b. Less than 0.5 percent.

c. The CLMS categories of "not in the labor force" and "weeks unemployed—none" include persons, who for purposes of determining eligibility for PSE, are defined in the CETA regulations as unemployed. Prior to the 1978 amendments, this group included discouraged workers—those who did not actively seek employment because they believed jobs were not available, as well as persons receiving SSI or AFDC (whether employed or not), and persons who worked no more than 10 hours a week. Persons with low incomes were eligible for PSE both before and after the 1978 amendments, even if employed, and may be included in the CLMS category "weeks unemployed—none."

This procedure indicates that the eligibility criteria were most important for increasing the share of enrollment for persons in families receiving public assistance and minorities. Lower wages and other factors were more important than the tighter eligibility criteria for increasing the shares of women, youth, and the poorly educated (table 18). The latter effects are supported by the observations of local officials on the effects of lower wages.

*Perceptions of CETA administrators.* When CETA administrators were asked in the October 1980 survey to indicate whether the eligibility or the wage changes had the greater effect on the types of persons enrolled in PSE, about two-thirds said that the eligibility requirements had the greater impact; one-third thought that the wage changes were more significant. When the same question was asked in the June 1979 survey, conducted only two months after the wage provisions became effective, the responses were equally divided.

## Objectives of Local Officials

In addition to the legal requirements, the types of persons enrolled in PSE depended, in part, on how local officials viewed the objectives of the PSE program and the types of persons that should be serviced. It is apparent from the responses of some prime sponsors that there were inherent conflicts between the targeting objectives and other local purposes. Enrolling the seriously disadvantaged, for example, may preclude useful public services or adversely affect the placement of enrollees in unsubsidized jobs.

*Persons to be served.* Most of the CETA directors in the survey concurred with the major thrust of the 1978 PSE amendments—targeting on the seriously disadvantaged. Eight-five percent said the PSE programs should enroll persons with serious labor market disadvantages. About 40 per-

**Table 18**
**Changes in Enrollee Characteristics Attributable**
**to Eligibility and Wage Changes, Fiscal 1978-1980**

| Characteristic | Total change 1978-1980 | Changes due to | | Proportion of change due to tighter eligibility (percent) |
|---|---|---|---|---|
| | | New eligibility criteria | PSE wage and other factors | |
| | | (Percentage point changes) | | |
| Female ................. | + 8 | -1 | + 9 | 0 |
| Youth .................. | + 5 | 0 | + 5 | 0 |
| Less than high school education ... | +10 | +2 | + 8 | 20 |
| Member of a minority group ...... | + 9 | +5 | + 4 | 56 |
| Family receiving public assistance .. | + 9 | +8 | + 1 | 89 |
| Family income at or below 70 percent of lower living standard ................ | +17 | +6 | +11 | 35 |

SOURCE: Special tabulation, *Continuous Longitudinal Manpower Survey*, Westat, Inc.

cent also identified new entrants into the labor market who were having trouble getting their first job (table 19). Some CETA directors (37 percent) selected experienced laid off workers as a target group. In most of these cases, it appeared that the intent was to enroll workers who, though previously employed, could be considered as seriously disadvantaged. However, in 15 percent of the study areas the identification of this group may indicate a view that the most qualified of the eligible population should be enrolled to serve the major local objective of providing useful public services or to enroll candidates most likely to move to regular employment.

**Table 19**
**CETA Directors' Views of Types of Persons**
**Public Service Employment Programs Should Seek to Enroll**
**Sample Prime Sponsor Areas, 1980**

| Type | Percent of reporting areas |
|---|---|
| Workers seriously disadvantaged in the job market ......................... | 85 |
| New entrants to the job market who are having problems finding a job .............. | 41 |
| Experienced workers who have been laid off from a former job ....................... | 37 |

SOURCE: Reports from 27 areas.

NOTE: Detail adds to more than 100 percent because some respondents identified more than one type of worker to be served.

When asked whether the new PSE provisions facilitated the attainment of the tighter targeting objective, most CETA directors answered affirmatively, although a few did experience difficulty in enrolling seriously disadvantaged persons. In one area, the cumbersome procedures and the documents required to demonstrate eligibility discouraged the most seriously disadvantaged persons from persevering with their applications. In another instance, the recruitment system was inadequate to reach many of the disadvantaged.

The low PSE wage was also mentioned as an obstacle in enrolling persons receiving welfare.

For most areas, the perceptions of the CETA directors of who should be served and their ability to enroll the seriously disadvantaged indicate that the more restrictive eligibility requirements of the 1978 amendments were accepted by local officials, albeit reluctantly in some places, and produced the desired targeting results.

*Program objectives.* The program objectives of PSE operators can be classified as "client oriented" and conducive to enrolling the disadvantaged, or "community service oriented" and more open to enrolling qualified workers. Client oriented objectives such as "jobs for the unemployed" and "training for disadvantaged workers" were each identified as among the most important goals of PSE by about 70 percent of the CETA administrators. About 40 percent considered service oriented purposes such as "providing essential public services" to be among the major objectives of PSE (table 20). Some administrators were pursuing both goals.

**Table 20**
**CETA Directors' Views of "Most Important" Public Service**
**Employment Program Objectives**
**Sample Prime Sponsor Areas, 1980**

| Most important objective | Percent of reporting areas |
|---|---|
| Providing a job for the unemployed ........... | 71 |
| Providing training for disadvantaged workers .... | 68 |
| Providing essential public services ............. | 39 |
| Relieving the fiscal strain of local government.... | 11 |
| Other...................................... | 21 |

SOURCE: Reports from 28 areas.

NOTE: Detail adds to more than 100 percent because several respondents identified more than one most important objective.

There was a great deal of skepticism concerning the ability of PSE to accomplish the objectives identified as most important. Only half of the CETA administrators believed that the 1978 provisions of PSE would achieve these purposes (table 21). The low-wage provisions coupled with the requirement that PSE workers be paid prevailing wages for similar work were reported as the major stumbling block in attaining the desired ends. To meet this double requirement, sponsors created special low-skill jobs that, in many instances, were not helpful to the participant in obtaining suitable employment or to the community in providing the kinds of services they deem most useful.

Some areas shifted PSE positions from government agencies to nonprofit organizations that were thought to be more flexible in creating low-wage jobs. The share of PSE enrollees assigned to nonprofits increased from 24 percent in September 1977 to 38 percent at the end of 1980. However, in view of the limited number of regular job openings in these organizations, opportunities for unsubsidized postprogram employment with nonprofits were considered to be poorer than in government agencies.

### Recruitment Methods
### and Participant Characteristics

All sponsors in the study used more than one recruiting method. Persons walking into a CETA intake center were the source of the greatest number of applicants in 39 percent of the areas and the second best source in another 27 percent. Advertising produced the greatest number of applicants in 18 percent of the areas. Community organizations were most often the second major source of applicants (table 22).

**Table 21**
**CETA Directors' Views on Whether 1978 CETA Amendments**
**Enable the Public Service Employment Programs to Serve**
**Their "Most Important" Objectives**
**Sample Prime Sponsor Areas, 1980**

| Most important objective | Attainment of objective | | | |
|---|---|---|---|---|
| | Total | Yes | No | Don't know |
| | (Number of reporting areas) | | | |
| Providing a job for the unemployed ......... | 20 | 10 | 8 | 2 |
| Training for disadvantaged workers .. | 19 | 8 | 8 | 3 |
| Providing essential public services ......... | 11 | 5 | 5 | 1 |
| Relieving the fiscal strain of local government .... | 3 | 1 | 2 | 0 |
| Other................. | 6 | 1 | 5 | 0 |

SOURCE: Reports from 28 areas.

**Table 22**
**Major Recruiting Methods**
**Sample Prime Sponsor Areas, 1980**

| Recruiting method | Importance ranking | | |
|---|---|---|---|
| | 1 | 2 | 3 |
| | (percent of all replies) | | |
| Walk-ins to CETA intake center ............. | 39 | 27 | 15 |
| Advertising ............................. | 18 | 3 | 23 |
| Community organization................... | 14 | 30 | 15 |
| Employment service or unemployment insurance office....................... | 14 | 20 | 19 |
| Employer identification of potential enrollees............................. | 11 | 3 | 12 |
| WIN/AFDC office...................... | 4 | 17 | 8 |
| Other ............................... | 0 | 0 | 8 |

SOURCE: Reports from 28 areas.

The survey found a sharp decline in dependence on state employment service agencies. They were the major source of applicants in 43 percent of the survey areas in 1977,[15] but in only 14 percent of the areas in 1980. The reduced use of the employment service is due principally to the changes in the financial liability provisions of the reauthorization act. Prior to 1978, prime sponsors were exempt from liability for ineligible enrollees if the employment service had determined the eligibility of applicants. The intent of this policy was to increase the use of the employment service and facilitate the large and rapid buildup of PSE in 1977. With this "no liability" incentive, most sponsors entered into agreements that assigned recruitment and eligibility determination functions to the employment service. When the reauthorization act removed the liability exemption, sponsors found the employment service much less attractive although they still considered it an important recruiting source (see chapter 3).

The methods used by prime sponsors to recruit PSE applicants may be characterized as "participant oriented," "job oriented" or "neutral," and the specific recruitment techniques employed may influence the type of participants who were enrolled in PSE programs. Reliance on local welfare offices and community based organizations (CBOs) orients enrollment to the more seriously disadvantaged, and these methods were classified as participant oriented. On the other hand, if persons to be enrolled, are identified and referred to CETA by the potential employer, or found through advertising, or by searching the employment service or unemployment insurance files, the participants are likely to be more highly qualified, and these methods were considered job oriented. "Walk-ins" to a CETA intake center were viewed as neutral in their effect.

---

15. Mirengoff et al., *CETA: Assessment,* p. 79.

There appears to be an association between the recruitment strategies of prime sponsors and changes, between 1978 and 1980, in the characteristics of the PSE enrollees. For example, in areas where the recruitment techniques were largely "participant oriented," the proportion of enrollees with less than a high school education and the share from persons in families receiving welfare payments increased more sharply than in areas where recruitment was "job oriented" (table 23).

Factors which tended to increase the enrollment of more able workers had little impact. Although economic conditions had worsened in a majority of the sample areas, only a few reported that the business downturn had increased the flow of more qualified applicants. The reduction in program size which permitted prime sponsors to fill their openings without dipping as deeply as before into the applicant pool increased the proportion of enrollees with good job skills in only two areas.

### Effect of 1978 Amendments on Recruitment Efforts

Despite declining enrollment levels, more effort was required to recruit PSE enrollees after the 1978 amendments. The eligibility and wage changes increased the effort needed in three-fourths of the study areas. The more restrictive eligibility required the prime sponsor to enroll a clientele more difficult to reach and less familiar with filling out government forms. Lower wages generated PSE jobs that were less attractive to eligible persons who had options in the regular job market. Although there was an overall reduction in the size of their programs, a third of the prime sponsors reported that frequent changes in guidelines for enrollment complicated and added to the recruitment effort (table 24).

**Table 23**
**Change in Characteristics of Public Service Employment Enrollees**
**by Type of Recruiting Activity, Sample Prime Sponsor Areas, Fiscal 1978-1980**

| Most important recruiting activity | Enrollee characteristics | | | | Number of reports |
|---|---|---|---|---|---|
| | Female | Under 22 years of age | Less than high school education | Public assistance recipient | |
| | (Percentage point changes) | | | | |
| All areas .............................. | + 8 | +3 | + 3 | + 4 | 25 |
| Oriented to the disadvantaged[a] ...... | +10 | +2 | +10 | +10 | 5 |
| Oriented to job requirements[b] ....... | + 8 | +3 | 0 | 0 | 12 |
| Walk-ins ............................. | + 7 | +4 | + 2 | + 5 | 8 |

SOURCE: Reports from 25 areas.

a. Includes outreach by community based organizations and solicitation of applicants through WIN or AFDC offices.

b. Includes media advertising, identification of potential PSE employees by hiring agencies, and solicitation of persons in employment service or unemployment insurance files.

### Table 24
### Effect of Selected Factors on Recruitment Effort
### Required for PSE, Sample Prime Sponsor Areas, 1980

| Factor | More activity required | No effect | Less activity required |
|---|---|---|---|
| | (Percent of reporting areas) | | |
| New eligibility criteria.......... | 75 | 25 | 0 |
| More restrictive wage limits ....... | 75 | 21 | 4 |
| Economic conditions. | 25 | 61 | 14 |
| Changing PSE enrollment levels .. | 36 | 32 | 32 |

SOURCE: Reports from 28 areas.

## *Eligibility Determination and Verification*

To make sure that the tighter eligibility rules would be strictly enforced the 1978 CETA reauthorization required the Secretary of Labor to "ensure that the prime sponsor has demonstrated a recognizable and proven method of verifying the eligibility of all participants" (Sec. 104c.3).

The regulations (Sec. 676-76-3) prescribe a procedure for eligibility determination and verification (ED&V). It consists of three steps: (1) completion of an application form signed by the applicant,[16] designed to provide the information necessary to determine eligibility; (2) within 30 days after enrollment, a desk review to determine the consistency and reasonableness of the application; and (3) once a quarter, verification of the accuracy of the information on residence, unemployment history, welfare status, and family income

---

16. The following information is required from applicants: (1) name, (2) social security number, (3) birthdate and age, (4) citizenship, (5) residence, (6) prior CETA participation, (7) family status, (8) economic disadvantage, (9) labor force status, (10) family income, (11) farm residence, (12) economic status, (13) work history, (14) veteran status, and (15) whether applicant's immediate relatives are employed in government or CETA programs.

for a sample of the new enrollees. Verification may consist of documentary evidence or confirmation by a third party. Previous regulations did not stipulate any specific verification procedures.

*Current ED&V practices.* Sponsors took the new procedures seriously and sought to comply with the regulations. Two-thirds conducted initial intake themselves; others relied on either the employment service (24 percent) or subcontractors (19 percent) for this activity. Where intake was not conducted by sponsors, their staffs are assigned to review the applications shortly after receipt.

Although the mandated system did not require documentation at the time of intake, nearly half (48 percent) of the sample sponsors required complete documentation before enrollment. They considered this approach to be more cost effective and more likely to reduce liability risks. Most sample sponsors followed the stipulated procedures for conducting the two steps in the verification process: the 30-day review and the quarterly sample. Both documentary evidence (birth certificates, drivers' licenses, tax returns) and collateral contacts (employers, service agency staff, neighbors) were used for verifying information. In most cases, the 30-day review was conducted by the sponsor's management information unit, and the quarterly sample verification was undertaken by the Independent Monitoring Unit (IMU). Four sponsors reported continuing a practice initiated around the time of the reauthorization act of verifying all enrollees' eligibility rather than a sample to make doubly sure that only eligible applicants were enrolled.

Local area implementation of ED&V provisions was an evolving process. Asked to look back to the period prior to enactment of the 1978 amendments, nearly all sample sponsors (96 percent) reported changes in their ED&V procedures. While 40 percent indicated that they had previously employed procedures similar to those required by the reauthorization act, they were not as thorough as the amendments currently require. Sponsors did not, for example, require extensive documentation for eligibility, a few specifying little more than self declarations. Verification procedures were not common and, when undertaken, frequently focused only on applicants whose eligibility was in question.

Most of the sponsors interviewed in the June 1979 survey[17] reported that they were implementing the eligibility determination provisions of the 1978 amendments. The October 1980 survey revealed that more than half (57 percent) have since changed their procedures. The most common change was a shift in responsibility for the 30-day reviews from the sponsors' intake units to their management information units. Accompanying this change was the increased use of IMUs for the quarterly sample verification, as well as a marked decline in reliance on the employment service for verification assistance.[18]

*Impact of ED&V.* Officials in about 90 percent of the study areas reported that the mandated changes reduced the likelihood of ineligible applicants entering CETA programs. A few respondents (7 percent) felt that their procedures in place before reauthorization were sufficient to prevent improper enrollments.

A majority of the field research associates (54 percent) felt that the administrative cost of the current ED&V provisions

17. William Mirengoff, Lester Rindler, Harry Greenspan, Scott Seablom, and Lois Black, *The New CETA: Effect on Public Service Employment Programs* (Washington: National Academy of Sciences, 1980), pp. 125-27.

18. For a more comprehensive treatment of ED&V see *A Study of CETA Eligibility Determination and Verification Systems* (Washington: Office of Program Evaluation, Employment and Training Administration, U.S. Department of Labor, March 1981).

were excessive and outweighed their benefits. One associate observed:

> It is clear that while the need for better eligibility controls once existed—and that the development of those controls has been a necessity—the cost of maintaining them indefinitely may be greater than the benefits derived over time . . . the time-and-travel costs of the 14 PS staff members now assigned to conduct the quarterly eligibility verification sample [for a balance of state prime sponsor] exceeds by far the amount of federal dollars saved through the detection and elimination of ineligible participants. . . . By adding such responsibilities without increasing the allowable administrative costs these sponsors can legally incur, federal officials are practically guaranteeing that limited staff resources will continue to be diverted from matters of substance to matters of form and technical compliance.

## Serving Special Groups

In addition to setting unemployment and income criteria for the enrollment of CETA participants and holding sponsors financially liable for ineligibles, Congress identified a number of specific groups that were to be given special emphasis, special consideration, or equitable treatment. The procedures for stimulating enrollment from these groups were to be described in the prime sponsors' comprehensive plans, but there was no penalty for setting low goals or failing to meet targets except for possible criticism from Department of Labor reviewers.

Congress used the following language to identify at least 15 target groups:[19]

19. Pub. L. 95-524, 95th Congress, October 27, 1978, Secs. 103(b) (2), 121(b) (1) (A), and 122(b).

- PSE under this act is intended for eligible persons who are the most severely disadvantaged in terms of their length of unemployment and their prospects for finding employment.

- Special consideration in filling public service jobs shall be given to eligible disabled and Vietnam-era veterans, eligible persons who are public assistance recipients, and persons who are eligible for public assistance but not receiving such assistance.

- Special emphasis in filling public service jobs shall be given to persons who face particular disadvantages in specific and general labor markets or occupations, taking into account the household support obligations of persons applying for such jobs including offenders, persons of limited English language proficiency, handicapped individuals, women, single parents, displaced homemakers, youth, older workers, individuals who lack educational credentials, public assistance recipients, and other persons who the Secretary determines require special assistance.

- Employment and training opportunities for participants shall be made available by prime sponsors on an equitable basis in accordance with the purposes of this act among significant segments (age, sex, race, and national origin) of the eligible population giving consideration to the relative numbers of eligible persons in each segment.

It would be difficult to find an unemployed, low-income person who does not fit into one of these categories. But if all were to receive special attention, none would be really targeted.

## Selecting Enrollees from
## Eligible Applicants

Prime sponsors responded to the requirement to target PSE enrollment on special subgroups in various ways. Nine of the 28 study areas had no formal system and made little effort to give preference to the groups identified in the legislation. In six of these areas, local officials took the position that targeting would take care of itself if enrollment came from the eligible population. In two of the areas, applicants were sparse and there was no opportunity to choose some over others. One sponsor adopted a "first in; first out" policy as the fair way to run the program.

Among the 19 areas that made special efforts to enroll the target groups, 10 used rating systems to identify the individuals to be given priority. The more complex systems assigned values to as many as 14 applicant categories. In the less complex rating schemes, there were as few as four categories and each was given equal weight. The categories most often included in the rating systems were veterans, public assistance recipients, women (including displaced homemakers), the handicapped, ex-offenders, minority groups, and the economically disadvantaged.

One system, for example, rated eligible applicants on 10 characteristics weighted from 1 to 10:

| Characteristic | Priority rating points |
|---|---|
| Veteran | 10 |
| Head of household | 9 |
| Economically disadvantaged | 8 |
| Youth | 7 |
| Minority | 6 |
| Older worker | 5 |
| Female | 4 |
| Handicapped | 3 |
| Drug abuser | 2 |
| Ex-offender/offender | 1 |

Even where priority rating systems were designed, they were frequently ignored. In most areas, referrals were handled by a counselor on the basis of operational efficiency—applicants who were at hand and able to perform the job duties were the first to be referred.

## Program Assignment Practices

Program assignments were based on several considerations. Following the determination of eligibility, an assessment was made of the applicants' interests, skills and training needs, and these most frequently determined the assignment—provided openings were available in the selected activity. In about one-third of the survey areas the applicants' training needs dictated the program assignment. The availability of openings was most important in more than a fourth of the areas (table 25). If applicants were eligible for PSE as well as for Title IIB training programs, most prime sponsors referred the better qualified to PSE and routed the less well qualified to training programs.

### Table 25
### Factors which Influenced the Assignment of Applicants
### to Specific CETA Programs
### Sample Prime Sponsor Areas, 1980

| | Importance ranking | | |
|---|---|---|---|
| Factor | 1 | 2 | 3 |
| | (Percent of reporting areas) | | |
| All Factors............................... | 100 | 100 | 100 |
| Applicants' training needs.................. | 32 | 16 | 23 |
| Availability of openings.................... | 27 | 23 | 29 |
| Applicants' qualifications ................. | 16 | 39 | 20 |
| Preference of the applicant ............... | 18 | 11 | 14 |
| Income needs of the applicant.............. | 4 | 4 | 4 |
| Applicant member of a target group.......... | 4 | 7 | 7 |
| Other ................................... | 0 | 0 | 4 |

SOURCE: Reports from 28 areas.
NOTE: Detail may not add to 100 percent because of rounding.

In a few areas, program options were constrained because intake was done by service deliverers who operated a single program. In these instances, applicants were often limited to the program offered by the agency. Only if applicants could not be enrolled in the agency's program were they encouraged to explore other CETA opportunities. One prime sponsor referred all applicants to job search training immediately after determining eligibility. If not placed in an unsubsidized job as a result of the job search, applicants went on to assessment and assignment to other programs.

Research associates in a majority of the study areas (57 percent) believed that applicants were generally referred to CETA programs most suitable for them, but there was substantial skepticism in the remaining areas. They cited the failure to match client needs with appropriate CETA programs—often due to insufficient openings. The applicants were sent to the slots available. Some sponsors did keep waiting lists. However, when openings occurred, the applicants on the list were often overlooked and the referral was likely to go to a new applicant.

Two-thirds of the study areas reported that their program assignment practices were not affected by the 1978 amendments. Most of the areas in which program assignment practices were modified reported that the Employability Development Plan (EDP) requirement resulted in a more thorough assessment and a better match of program services with participant needs.

## Selection Practices of Training Agencies and PSE Employers

In about 90 percent of the study areas, agencies which contracted with local prime sponsors to provide training had enrollment requirements that screened out some CETA eligibles. Generally, the qualifications required for specific types of training were discussed with the training agency and sometimes adjusted during contract negotiations. Counselors and intake staff considered the requirements of the training agency in making their referrals. In other instances, the contract permitted the training agency to test referrals and accept or reject them on the basis of a required minimum score.

Some kind of educational attainment was the most commonly cited requirement. For some clerical courses, sixth grade reading and math levels were required. Referrals to courses in community colleges or technical schools required high school equivalency. For some occupational training courses, such as programmer, special tests were administered.

Sponsors were generally inclined to accept the screening practices of training agencies. Only in a few areas did rejections of applicants result in disagreement between the prime sponsor and the training agency. The sponsors' attitudes were summarized by one CETA director who said, "This type of creaming is only realistic." In all areas, applicants who had been rejected by a training agency were considered for other CETA opportunities if they returned to the CETA office. One area reported that such persons often did not return.

When referring applicants to PSE jobs, prime sponsor and employment service counselors generally tried to refer persons whose abilities matched the skill requirements of the job. PSE jobs established after the 1978 amendments generally required fewer skills than those set up earlier. Nevertheless, in two-thirds of the study areas, PSE employing agencies had job requirements that screened out some of the applicants referred by the prime sponsor. Rejections occurred, for example, because a specific skill such as typing was inadequate or because the hiring agency insisted upon the job standards used for their regular positions. Persons with criminal records were deemed to be inappropriate for some kinds of employment.

For PSE employers who appeared to have unreasonably high job standards, CETA staff attempted to negotiate reduced requirements. In at least one-fourth of the study areas, the contracts with the PSE hiring agencies specified that persons from the target groups were to be hired. A few reviewed the performance of agencies in hiring the seriously disadvantaged, and decisions on contract renewal were based in part on the findings.

Although rejections occurred in two-thirds of the areas, prime sponsors did not view this as a major problem. In the main, they tried to refer persons who posessed at least the minimum requirements for the PSE jobs, and PSE employers understood that the program was aimed at disadvantaged persons. In almost all cases, applicants who were turned down by one employer were referred to other PSE jobs or to a CETA training program. If an enrollee was turned down for two or three jobs, the EDP might be reviewed and the need for training prior to a PSE job considered. In some areas efforts were made to develop jobs to match the skills of the applicant.

### Effectiveness of Recruitment and Selection Practices

Three-fourths of the research associates who conducted the on-site surveys considered the recruitment and selection procedures to be effective in enrolling persons from the target groups. However, those most in need were not always selected. Recruitment was designed to bring in applicants from the target groups, but the persons who made the selections were more concerned with how well the applicants' qualifications met the job or training requirements. In areas where there were more eligible applicants than openings, the better applicants were often selected. This was especially true for PSE jobs if the employer had the opportunity to choose from two or more referrals.[20]

In a fourth of the areas, the enrollment of persons from the special target groups, and particularly the most needy, was not a major concern of the prime sponsor. In three areas, enrollment was described as haphazard, and no special effort was made to recruit the most seriously disadvantaged. In two other areas, the prime sponsors sought to enroll the most capable of those who were eligible. One sponsor looked for enrollees most likely to succeed in their training or PSE assignments so that they could, with some assurance, be placed in unsubsidized employment. A fiscally distressed city sought capable PSE workers to provide essential municipal services.

## Public Assistance Recipients and Unemployment Insurance Claimants

Fifteen of the 28 study areas made special efforts to recruit PSE enrollees from families receiving public assistance. Most frequently, this involved arrangements with the local AFDC Work Incentive (WIN) office or county welfare office. In some instances, the prime sponsor stationed an intake officer at the local welfare office; in others the welfare agency referred its clients to a CETA intake office. In Chester County, Pennsylvania, the prime sponsor and the county Board of Public Welfare entered into an agreement under which the CETA office provided the welfare agency with information on job and training opportunities. The welfare agency screened its clients, prepared an initial EDP and made referrals to the CETA office for specific jobs or training openings. Prime sponsor staff reviewed the

20. For a discussion of the types of workers suitable and unsuitable for PSE jobs see Richard P. Nathan, Robert F. Cook, V. Lane Rawlins and Associates, *Public Service Employment: A Field Evaluation* (Washington: The Brookings Institution, 1981), pp. 36-47.

documentation, interviewed the client, and made the final decisions. This arrangement proved very effective—about half of the prime sponsors' PSE enrollees in 1980 came from the county welfare rolls.

Prime sponsors who made no special effort to recruit public assistance recipients reported that they had an adequate supply of such applicants from voluntary walk-ins, or from the welfare agencies that took the initiative in referring clients. One prime sponsor, believing that too many AFDC recipients had been enrolled, was making efforts to enroll other underrepresented groups. In two areas, special demonstration projects funded by the Department of Labor to test the employability of welfare recipients were absorbing the bulk of the AFDC recipients who were available for employment. Consequently, public assistance recipients were a relatively small share of PSE enrollees in these areas.

*Problems in recruiting welfare recipients.* The study areas were almost equally divided between those that found low PSE wages to be a deterrent to the enrollment of welfare recipients and those that did not. These differing experiences are due in part to the wide range in welfare payments among the states. The economic incentive to enroll in PSE jobs was greater in states with low welfare payments. On the other hand, the incentive for state and local officials to reduce public assistance rolls by moving welfare recipients into PSE was stronger in areas with higher welfare payments.[21]

Prime sponsors in about 40 percent of the study areas encountered no special problems in working with welfare agencies, and many enjoyed close working relationships. In three areas, however, CETA officials complained that welfare agencies made no effort to encourage their clients to accept PSE jobs. These welfare officials were skeptical of the

---

21. In 1979 the monthly average AFDC payment per family ranged from $84 in Mississippi and $108 in Texas to $370 for New York and $389 for Hawaii.

benefits of PSE or considered other programs, such as vocational rehabilitation, to be preferable. Transportation difficulties, the absence of child care facilities, and the lack of job skills also constrained the enrollment of welfare clients (table 26).

**Table 26**
**Problems in Recruiting for PSE from Families Receiving AFDC**
**or Other Public Assistance**
**Sample Prime Sponsor Areas, 1980**

| Problem | Percent of reporting areas |
|---|---|
| Low PSE wage ............... | 46 |
| Poor cooperation by welfare agency............. | 11 |
| Other ...................... | 18 |
| No problems ................ | 39 |

SOURCE: Reports from 28 areas.
NOTE: Detail adds to more than 100 percent because some areas reported more than one type of problem.

*Penetration of welfare and unemployment insurance populations.* Only a small portion of persons who received transfer payments, such as cash welfare or unemployment insurance, were enrolled in PSE programs. In fiscal 1979, about 50,000 persons in families receiving Aid for Dependent Children and 33,000 persons who had been unemployment insurance (UI) claimants enrolled in PSE. This was about 2.5 percent of the number of AFDC eligibles and 3.4 percent of the number who received unemployment insurance (table 27).[22]

22. The AFDC eligibles refer to those registered with the Work Incentive Program and thus classified as able-bodied and without children under six years of age.

### Table 27
### Percent of Eligible AFDC and Unemployment Insurance Recipients Enrolled in PSE, Fiscal 1978 and 1979
(number in thousands)

| Type of beneficiary | New PSE enrollees | Eligible population | Percent of eligibles |
|---|---|---|---|
| Recipients of aid for families with dependent children: | | | |
| 1978 . . . . . . . . . . . . . . . . . | 51 | 2,178[a] | 2.3 |
| 1979 . . . . . . . . . . . . . . . . . | 53 | 2,142[a] | 2.5 |
| Unemployment insurance beneficiaries: | | | |
| 1978 . . . . . . . . . . . . . . . . . | 65 | 4,000[bc] | 1.6 |
| 1979 . . . . . . . . . . . . . . . . . | 33 | 977[bc] | 3.4 |

a. AFDC/WIN registrants eligible for PSE.

b. Calendar year.

c. The eligible population of UI beneficiaries was much larger in 1978 than in 1979 because persons unemployed for 30 days or more were eligible for PSE in 1978 regardless of family income but had to meet low-income, long term unemployment critieria in 1979.

*Benefits to welfare and UI recipients from PSE jobs.* As noted earlier, many welfare recipients were deterred from taking a PSE job because the economic advantages were small or nonexistent. For persons receiving welfare or UI, the earnings from PSE were offset by a reduction or elimination of the welfare or UI payments.[23] The greater the UI or welfare payment, the smaller the financial benefit from a PSE job. Persons who had received UI payments of less than $60 per week averaged $143 in their PSE jobs—a gain of more than $83. Those whose UI payments had ranged from $100 to $119 realized, on the average, only $70 more per week as a result of PSE enrollment. The additional nominal

23. Prior to the Budget Reconciliation Act of 1981, persons from families receiving AFDC/WIN did not suffer a dollar for dollar offset if employment was obtained. The first $30, one-third of the remaining earnings, and certain work related expenses were disregarded in recomputing the allowable AFDC payment. The 1981 budget action limited the disregards to the first four months of employment.

income from the PSE wage was smaller for welfare recipients than for UI claimants at each level of transfer payment, especially for those receiving relatively high levels of welfare (tables 28 and 29). Moreover, the difference between the welfare or UI payment and the PSE wage was not all net gain because of income taxes, transportation, and other costs of employment. For many persons receiving welfare, there were significant losses of nonmonetary benefits such as food stamps and free or low-cost medical care.

*Effects of the 1978 amendments.* Welfare recipients were mentioned frequently by prime sponsors as the group whose participation in PSE was affected by the 1978 amendments. The amendments had mixed effects, but on balance, favored enrollment from this group. The increase in the proportion of welfare recipients occurred despite reports from almost half the areas that the PSE wage provided little or no economic advantage to persons receiving welfare. The major reasons for their greater participation were the change in eligibility criteria, the ease of verifying welfare client eligibility (hence less danger of prime sponsor liability for in-eligible enrollments), and the effect of the lower PSE wages on applications from nonwelfare eligibles.

Welfare clients were eligible for PSE jobs both before and after the 1978 amendments. However, subsequent to the amendments, there was less competition from the nonwelfare population. Persons from families receiving AFDC who were registered with the Work Incentive (WIN) Program made up the bulk of all public assistance recipients who were available for work. As a result of the changes in eligibility, the AFDC/WIN share of the population eligible for PSE increased from 12 percent of Title II and the non-project portion of Title VI prior to the 1978 amendments to 38 percent of Title VI and 55 percent of Title IID afterwards. Before the eligibility change, there were seven non-AFDC

## Table 28
### Average Weekly PSE Wage by Size of Unemployment Insurance and Welfare Payments Prior to Enrollment, Fiscal 1978

| Weekly unemployment insurance or welfare payment[a] | Average weekly PSE wage of recipients of | |
|---|---|---|
| | Cash welfare | Unemployment insurance |
| Less than $60 . . . . . . . . . . . . . . . . | $132 | $143 |
| $60 to $79 . . . . . . . . . . . . . . . . . | 142 | 150 |
| $80 to $99 . . . . . . . . . . . . . . . . . | 143[b] | 161 |
| $100 to $119 . . . . . . . . . . . . . . . | 143[b] | 180 |

SOURCE: *Continuous Longitudinal Manpower Survey,* Westat, Inc.

a. Monthly welfare payment was adjusted to a weekly basis for comparison with UI payments.

b. Estimate based on a weighted count smaller than 7,500 and therefore not statistically reliable (estimated relative standard error greater than 12-15 percent).

## Table 29
### Average Difference Between UI or Welfare Payment and Weekly PSE Wage, by Size of UI or Welfare Payment Fiscal 1978

| Weekly unemployment insurance or welfare payment[a] | Average difference: | |
|---|---|---|
| | Cash welfare | Unemployment insurance |
| Less than $60 . . . . . . . . . . . . . . . . | At least $73 | At least $84 |
| $60 to $79 . . . . . . . . . . . . . . . . . | 72 | 80 |
| $80 to $99 . . . . . . . . . . . . . . . . . | 55[b] | 71 |
| $100 to $120 . . . . . . . . . . . . . . . | 33[b] | 70 |

SOURCE: *Continuous Longitudinal Manpower Survey,* Westat, Inc.

a. Monthly welfare payment was adjusted to a weekly basis for comparison with UI payments.

b. Estimate based on a weighted count smaller than 7,500 and therefore not statistically reliable (estimated relative standard error greater than 12-15 percent).

eligibles for every AFDC eligible. After reauthorization, the ratio was less than 2 to 1 for Title VI and about equal for Title IID.[24] Further, the nonpublic welfare applicants were, by virtue of the new income and unemployment criteria, more disadvantaged than their earlier counterparts. Thus, in terms of numbers and characteristics, the public assistance recipients had less competition for PSE jobs.

The stringent requirements of the reauthorization act for determining and verifying eligibility and the greater likelihood of prime sponsor financial liability for ineligible enrollees also worked to promote the enrollment of public assistance recipients. Unlike other applicants whose employment and income status was difficult to verify, the status of public assistance recipients could easily be documented through the records of welfare offices.

The lower PSE wage provisions had a dual impact on the enrollment of persons receiving public assistance. It discouraged competition from persons better able to compete in the regular job market. But in about half the sample areas it also turned away many public assistance recipients who saw no economic advantage in taking a PSE job. Forty-six percent of the prime sponsors interviewed reported that many persons from families receiving AFDC or other public assistance were unwilling to accept PSE jobs because of the wage level. For these families, the PSE wages after taxes were reported to be not much higher than—sometimes even below—the value of cash welfare allowances plus related benefits such as medical services and food stamps.

There is reason to believe that these statements are not merely excuses for poor performance. Sponsors who reported that welfare recipients were reluctant to apply for PSE after the 1978 amendments had above average shares of

---

24. See Appendix.

public assistance recipients before reauthorization and maintained the proportions after 1978. However, sponsors who said that persons on public assistance were generally receptive to PSE reported a sharp increase in the share for this group after reauthorization—from 17 to 24 percent of total enrollment (table 30).

**Table 30**
**Enrollment of Public Assistance Recipients**
**in Public Service Employment**
**by Wage Effect, Sample Prime Sponsor Areas**
**Fiscal 1978 and 1980**

| | Welfare receipints as percent of total enrollment | | Number of reporting areas |
|---|---|---|---|
| Wage effect on enrollments | 1978 | 1980 | |
| Areas in which wage discouraged enrollment ...... | 24 | 25 | 13 |
| Areas in which wage did not discourage enrollment ....... | 17 | 24 | 14 |

SOURCE: Reports from 27 areas.

## Veterans

Despite special efforts to recruit veterans, the share of PSE enrollment for this group declined each year in the 1976-1980 period. The decline was sharpest after the 1978 amendments (table 31). Eleven of the 28 study areas used such special recruitment techniques as arrangements for referrals from veterans' organizations, special identification of veterans in the list of applicants, and holding openings for an initial period to give veterans priority in applying for job opportunities. A number of the study areas attributed recruitment difficulties to the low wage and the fact that few eligible veterans were available.

### Table 31
### Veterans' Share of New PSE Enrollments
### Fiscal 1976-1980

| Type of veteran | 1976 | 1977 | 1978 | 1979 | 1980 |
|---|---|---|---|---|---|
| | (Percent of total enrollment) | | | | |
| All veterans ............... | 29 | 28 | 24 | 20 | 15 |
| Special disabled ............ | 6 | 5 | 4 | 3 | 1 |
| Vietnam-era ............... | 12 | 12 | 9 | 7 | 6 |
| Other .................... | 11 | 12 | 11 | 9 | 9 |

SOURCE: Special tabulations of the *Continuous Longitudinal Manpower Survey,* Westat, Inc.

NOTE: Detail may not add to total because of rounding.

## Women

Women are identified in the CETA statute as a significant segment and displaced homemakers as a special target group. Seven areas reported special recruitment efforts on their behalf. These generally took the form of contacts with agencies which had a special interest in working with displaced homemakers or welfare recipients.

The proportion of women in PSE rose from 38 percent in 1978 to 46 percent in 1980. Several explanations for this increase were offered: women's willingness to accept the lower wage jobs; increased interest in the employment problems of displaced homemakers; interest in overcoming the sex stereotyping of jobs; and the change in the requirements for serving "significant segments" of the population. The initial DOL regulations required sponsors to designate "significant segments"—groups which experienced special difficulty in the labor market—and to provide service to these groups in relation to their proportions among the unemployed. The 1978 amendments, however, went further. They specified age, race, sex, and national origin as the significant segments. Moreover, the legislation required the DOL to monitor the implementation of those provisions, and it required prime sponsors to justify instances where service to the significant segments fell short of their incidence in the eligible population. A number of areas responded to these mandates by giving women priority in enrollment. The share of women in PSE programs, however, had been on the rise even before the 1978 amendments due, in part, to special efforts by some prime sponsors to reduce sex stereotyping of jobs. A few sponsors actively encouraged the employment of women in such jobs as truck driver, carpenter, and groundskeeper. Women also benefitted from reduced emphasis on and ability to enroll veterans.

### Other Target Groups

Other groups which were specially targeted in a number of the study areas were handicapped persons, ex-offenders, and Spanish speaking persons. Although persons with less than a high school education were not identified as a target group in the legislation, the emphasis on enrolling the low-income, long term unemployed had the effect of reaching them.

# Countercyclical/Counterstructural Purposes and Results

Congress intended to establish separate PSE programs for the structurally unemployed (Title II/IID) and for the cyclically unemployed (Title VI). However, neither the initial nor the subsequent eligibility criteria were sufficiently different to produce clearly distinguishable structural and countercyclical programs. PSE admission rules did not funnel only the structurally unemployed to Title II/IID, nor did they restrict enrollment in Title VI to the cyclically unemployed.

The 1976 and 1978 amendments tended to blur rather than sharpen the differences between the two programs. By 1978, the countercyclical Title VI program had enrolled larger proportions of the structurally unemployed than the counterstructural Title IID PSE program. Much larger shares of new Title VI enrollees had been unemployed 15 weeks or more and had incomes at or below 70 percent of the BLS lower living standard. This reflected the tighter income and unemployment criteria applicable to the expanded segment of Title VI after the 1976 amendments. Moreover, enrollees in Title VI were more likely than those in Title II to have other characteristics of the structurally disadvantaged—limited education, minority membership, and welfare status.

After the 1978 amendments, the proportion of disadvantaged persons in both Title IID and Title VI increased sharply. The shift was larger for Title IID due to the more extensive changes in eligibility criteria and somewhat tighter wage limits in that program. By 1980 there was little difference between Title IID and VI in the participation rates by race/ethnic group, age, low educational attainment, and unemployment history. The differences that did occur were consistent with the more restrictive eligibility and wage limits for Title IID. Title IID enrolled higher percentages of persons in low-income families and those unemployed for 15 weeks, and lower proportions of enrollees with post-high school education (table 32 and figure 7).

Although the 1978 CETA reauthorization continued separate PSE programs, the eligibility criteria and the wage limits restricted both programs primarily to persons who were at a serious disadvantage in the labor market.

## Table 32
## Characteristics of New Enrollees in CETA Title II/IID
## and in Title VI Public Service Employment
## Fiscal 1976, 1978, and 1980

| | Percent of all new enrollees | | | | | |
|---|---|---|---|---|---|---|
| | 1976 | | 1978 | | 1980 | |
| Characteristic | Title II | Title VI | Title II | Title VI | Title IID | Title VI |
| Female ................. | 33 | 33 | 41 | 37 | 47 | 44 |
| Age: 16 to 21 ............ | 19 | 24 | 22 | 23 | 28 | 28 |
| Education: | | | | | | |
| Less than high school .... | 32 | 23 | 19 | 27 | 36 | 34 |
| Post-high school ........ | NA | NA | NA | NA | 21 | 26 |
| Member of a | | | | | | |
| minority group......... | 31 | 29 | 32 | 40 | 48 | 49 |
| Family receiving public | | | | | | |
| assistance[a] ............ | 15 | 15 | 19 | 22 | 33 | 29 |
| Family income at or below | | | | | | |
| 70 percent of lower | | | | | | |
| living standard[b]........ | 41 | 46 | 65 | 77 | 96 | 86 |
| Unemployed 15 weeks | | | | | | |
| or more................ | 25 | 33 | 35 | 47 | 47[c] | 43[c] |

SOURCE: Special tabulations, *Continuous Longitudinal Manpower Survey,* Westat, Inc. Data for 1980 are from a sample of prime sponsor records, in place of interviews of a sample of enrollees and must be considered preliminary.

a. Includes cash and noncash public assistance.

b. For 1976, this included persons in families receiving cash welfare or having income below the OMB poverty level.

c. Last half of fiscal year 1979; data for 1980 not available.

# Figure 7
## Percent of New Enrollees with Selected Characteristics
## CETA Title II/IID and Title VI, Fiscal 1976, 1978 and 1980

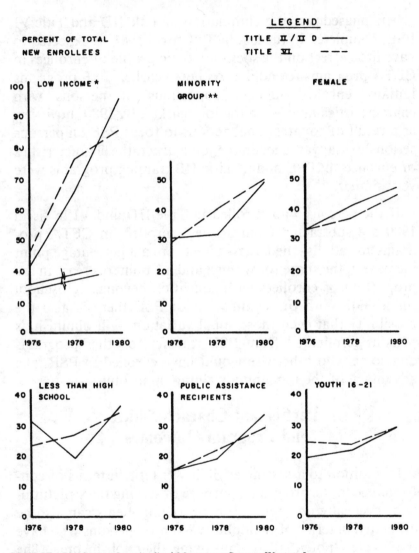

SOURCE: *Continuous Longitudinal Manpower Survey,* Westat, Inc.

*For 1976 this included persons in families receiving cash welfare or having income below the OMB poverty level.

**Hispanics, blacks and other nonwhite.

# Effect of the Elimination of PSE
# on the Characteristics of CETA Enrollees

The phasedown and elimination of Title IID and Title VI PSE, completed in the last half of fiscal 1981, is expected to have little effect on the socioeconomic profile of enrollees in CETA programs for adults. As noted earlier, PSE programs initially enrolled higher proportions of persons with characteristics favored in the job market. By 1980, however, as a result of congressional actions to focus PSE on persons seriously disadvantaged in the job market, the characteristics of enrollees in PSE and in Title IIB training programs were very similar.[25]

If the persons who enrolled in Title IID and VI in fiscal 1980 are subtracted from all new enrollees in CETA programs for adults, the largest effects are a 3 percentage point increase in the share for women and a 3 point decrease in the proportion of enrollees with education beyond high school (table 33). With the elimination of PSE there is also the possibility that even those small variations will diminish as persons terminated from PSE transfer to other programs and some who otherwise would have enrolled in PSE take advantage of the remaining training opportunities.

# Participant Characteristics
# and Program Outcomes

In addition to assessing eligibility criteria in terms of conformance to the program's purpose of serving the structurally or cyclically unemployed, entry requirements can also be evaluated in terms of their ability to enroll persons who have the greatest potential for improving their job income. The available evidence supports the conclusion that enrollment

---

25. See page 116.

## Table 33
## Characteristics of New Enrollees in CETA Programs for Adults
## With and Without PSE, Fiscal 1980[a]

| Characteristic | All adult programs | Adult programs less Titles IID and VI |
|---|---|---|
| | (Percent of total) | |
| Sex | | |
| Male | 51 | 48 |
| Female | 49 | 52 |
| Member of a minority group | 47 | 47 |
| Age | | |
| Under 22 | 28 | 27 |
| 22 to 44 | 63 | 64 |
| 45 and over | 10 | 8 |
| Education | | |
| School dropout | 34 | 35 |
| Student, not a high school graduate | 2 | 2 |
| High school graduate | 45 | 46 |
| Post-high school education | 19 | 16 |
| Income not higher than the poverty level or 70 percent of the lower living standard | 94 | 96 |
| Family receiving public assistance | 30 | 29 |

SOURCE: *Continuous Longitudinal Manpower Survey,* Westat, Inc. Data are from a sample of prime sponsor records, in place of interviews of a sample of enrollees, and must be considered preliminary.

a. Included in CETA programs for adults are Title IIB, C, and D; Title VI; and Title VII. Included in PSE are Titles IID and VI.

of seriously disadvantaged persons provides the biggest payoff. Persons who had the lowest earnings in the year before enrolling in CETA made larger gains than enrollees with higher pre-CETA earnings.[26] The congressional decision to serve the seriously disadvantaged among the structurally unemployed is supported in terms of program pupose and efficiency.

---

26. See chapter 8.

# Summary

The effect of the 1978 amendments was to limit enrollments in PSE programs almost entirely to persons with low incomes and to increase sharply the share of PSE jobs going to the severely disadvantaged. By 1980, low income persons were 92 percent of new enrollees, 17 points above the 1978 level. In addition, larger proportions of welfare recipients, women, youth, members of minority groups, and persons with less than a high school education had entered the program.

The reauthorization act changes also brought the proportion of disadvantaged persons in PSE programs more closely in line with the proportion of such persons among the long term unemployed and of persons enrolled in CETA training programs.

A corollary of the changes in the socioeconomic profile of PSE participants after 1978 has been the enrollment of persons with fewer job skills than earlier participants.

### Eligibility and Wage Restrictions

The two driving forces behind the changed profile of PSE enrollees were the eligibilty and wage changes in the 1978 amendments. The eligibility restrictions had the greater influence for increasing the share of enrollment for minorities and persons with low incomes. The wage limitations were primarily responsible for the larger proportions of women, youth, and the poorly educated.

The tighter eligibility rules reduced the population eligible for PSE from 18.3 to 5.7 million and increased the proportion of the available population who were poorly educated, members of minority groups, female, or on welfare. Only persons with low incomes could now enroll. The lowered wages discouraged applications from persons who were better prepared to function in the regular job market. The effect of this was to open more PSE opportunities for the disadvantaged.

The success of the eligibility and wage restrictions in reserving PSE for the seriously disadvantaged was not achieved without cost to other objectives of the program. The emphasis on enrolling the hard-to-place was at cross purpose with the placement objective of CETA. Further, the low level jobs created to meet the new wage restrictions were less useful to the participant and the community.

The percent of new enrollees who were from welfare families increased even though, in about half the survey areas, PSE wages provided little if any economic benefit. Nevertheless, the PSE program had little impact on programs providing transfer payments. Only 2 percent of the available AFDC population and 4 percent of eligible persons receiving UI were enrolled in 1979.

The legislative provisions that identified 15 or more groups for "equitable treatment," "special emphasis" or "special consideration" were largely ignored in about one-third of the study areas. In the remaining areas, efforts to implement the provisions often did not work well. Requiring special emphasis for so many groups was self-defeating.

Congressional insistence on serving the seriously disadvantaged is supported by information indicating that enrollees with lowest preprogram earnings benefit most from CETA programs.

Local officials accepted the objective of serving the seriously disadvantaged. Nevertheless, minimum qualification requirements for some jobs and training opportunities were set and employers selected the best qualified person if more than one was referred. These actions were perceived as acceptable screening.

The detailed requirements in the regulations for eligibility determination, review, and verification were seen as reducing the likelihood of ineligible enrollees, but, in a majority of the study areas, the costs were said to be greater than the benefits.

Congress sought to address the problems of two categories of jobless persons—the structurally and cyclically unemployed—and establish separate titles for each group (Title II/IID and Title VI). However, neither the original legislation nor the subsequent amendments provided the differential enrollment criteria that made this distinction effective. In 1980, both programs were serving structurally unemployed populations with largely similar socioeconomic characteristics.

### Eligibility Criteria, Eligibility Determination and CETA Decentralization

The need for criteria that limit participation in CETA programs is inherent in a system that seeks to provide employment and training to persons who have been least successful in the regular job market. However, excessive specificity restricts state and local freedom to decide who among their population require services. More broadly, it raises the question of the degree to which the decentralized design of CETA is compromised to meet substantive national objectives. The evidence of the survey—that the tigher eligibility criteria of the 1978 amendments were a major factor in the enrollment of higher proportions of seriously disadvantaged persons—indicates that the criteria were appropriate in relation to the objectives. However, there is a serious question as to the net benefit of the detailed eligibility determination and verification procedures in the 1978 amendments and the implementing regulations. The procedures presently required for all CETA programs could be simplified to increase flexibility and local control without relieving prime sponsors of liability for the enrollment of ineligible persons.

# 5 Needs Assessment and Training

When the reauthorization act was under consideration in 1978, the U.S. unemployment rate had declined to 6 percent from a high of 8.5 percent in 1975. Nevertheless, among groups with special difficulties in the labor market, unemployment was still unacceptably high. Under these circumstances, there was strong support from the Administration, public and private groups, and Congress to focus the CETA programs more directly on those in the labor force who were most disadvantaged.

Recognizing that the effect of the tightened eligibility and wage provisions of the reauthorization act would be to enroll persons less job-ready than the earlier participants, Congress mandated new program tools to improve their employability. Two areas were emphasized: better assessment of enrollees, and the linking of public service employment (PSE) with training.[1]

To enhance the employability of CETA participants, the reauthorization act required an individual employability development plan (EDP) for each person enrolled in a Title

---

1. See statement of Senator Gaylord Nelson in introducing the Senate Committee Bill, *Congressional Record,* August 22, 1978, p. S13953.

II program.[2] The plan is to be used in selecting the most appropriate employment or training program, taking into consideration the individual's skills, interests, and employment objectives as well as job prospects. The language of the act implies, but does not stipulate, that employability development plans are to be prepared also for Title VI participants who need assistance. To improve further the employability of PSE enrollees, Congress set aside a percentage of each sponsor's annual PSE allotment to be used for training.

The concept of linking training with PSE is not new. The original CETA visualized combining PSE with other services and giving special consideration to jobs that provide complementary training. However, it was not mandatory, and most sponsors preferred to avoid the administrative and program complexities involved in forging such links. Nationally, only fractional amounts of public service employment expenditures were used for training prior to 1979.

There were several assumptions implicit in the reauthorization act's design for participant assessment and the meshing of training and public service employment:

- Individual assessment and training methods which had been developed for readily employable persons could be quickly adapted to their hard-to-employ counterparts; clients could move smoothly from recruitment to assessment, training, and placement.
- Assessment and training activities could be combined with an ongoing subsidized employment experience.
- Despite the wide diversity, a uniform set of requirements and procedures could be applied to all areas.

---

2. Title II includes both comprehensive employment and training programs (Title IIB), upgrading and retraining (Title IIC), and PSE for the economically disadvantaged (Title IID). Prior to the reauthorization act, comprehensive employment and training programs were authorized under Title I of CETA; Title II authorized PSE for areas of substantial unemployment (see chart 1).

• Finally, the new legislative and regulatory requirements could be implemented with little disruption in the administration of CETA programs. Even if some disruptions were to occur, they would be more than balanced by the benefits—increased placement of hard-to-employ participants.

In short, a successful design combining assessment, training, and employment for disadvantaged participants could be constructed. The extent to which these assumptions have been borne out are examined in this chapter. It describes the arrangements that sponsors made to meet these requirements, the problems they faced, and the impact of the new requirement on clients and on program operations. Two central questions are addressed. First, does the preparation of EDPs and the coupling of training and PSE facilitate the transition of participants to unsubsidized employment or merely add another task for overburdened CETA managers? Second, have the new requirements increased the federal presence in local program operations and reduced local autonomy?

## Employability Development Plans

The assessment of clients' needs has always been an essential ingredient in vocational counseling. Widely employed in the pre-CETA manpower programs, it continued to be practiced in the Title I (later Title IIB) programs of CETA. While the original act did not specifically require employability development plans, it mentioned, as an optional activity, the "assessment of the individual's needs, interests, and potential in the labor market and referral to appropriate employment, training, or other opportunities." There was no similar requirement for PSE enrollees, but the original act did require plans for public service employment to include a description of "programs to prepare the participants for their job responsibilities."

The significance of the reauthorization act is that it (a) makes the language of the original act explicit, (b) mandates a formal procedure for linking assessments of participants with definite plans for finding unsubsidized employment for them, and (c) extends the assessment practice to PSE enrollees in Title IID (structural unemployment) programs and to some Title VI enrollees.

It is the accompanying DOL regulations (Sec. 677.2), however, that specify the five items to be included in each EDP:

1. Assessment of the participant's employability readiness;
2. Barriers to employment faced by the participant;
3. Specific employment and training needs;
4. Specific services and activities to meet those needs; and
5. Individual plans for transition from program activities to placement in unsubsidized employment.

In effect, CETA training and employment are to be blended with specific plans for improving the client's chances to overcome personal and institutional barriers to employment.

### Current Practices

The EDP requirement is being implemented. All prime sponsors in the survey report preparing EDPs for Title IIB/C and IID clients. Moreover, although not specifically required to do so, 90 percent also prepare plans for Title VI enrollees and over 60 percent prepare an equivalent of the EDP for Title IV youth programs. There are, however, some prime sponsors who are not persuaded that EDPs are necessary for all enrollees and, in such cases, their compliance is merely pro forma. On balance, the introduction of the EDP provision has given more prominence to the assessment process.[3]

Since reauthorization more sponsors have assumed the direct responsibility for conducting assessment (table 34). The use of educational institutions to perform assessment has also increased, while the role of the employment service has declined. The wide geographic coverage of the balance-of-state prime sponsors makes it impractical for the state office to conduct the assessment activities. In Maine and Texas, the EDPs are prepared at the county level, in the former by community based organizations, and in the latter by councils of government. Arizona uses the local employment service offices to do the job while in North Carolina each program deliverer is responsible for its own clients.

In view of the EDP's importance in the assessment process, the qualifications of the staff assigned to this task are of particular interest. Findings on one measure of staff qualifications—educational attainment—are shown in table 35.

Prime sponsor or principal subcontractor staffs assigned to prepare EDPs generally appear to be qualified for the task. More than half hold bachelor's or master's degrees in counseling or in a counseling related field; over one-fifth have college degrees in a specialty other than counseling; and one-fourth have completed only high school. The staff with training in counseling are more frequently employed by prime sponsors where there is relatively low ratio of clients to counselors. Persons preparing EDPs who are college educated but not trained in counseling, on the other hand, often work in settings characterized by high client loads.

---

3. As used here "assessment" refers to the process of determining an applicant's skills, interests, and need for training or services. "Employability development plan" is a plan of action which includes the results of assessment and prescribes specific training, services, or employment activities.

Most often, counselors prepare client EDPs prior to assignment to training or to a PSE opening, but there are variations. More than 25 percent of prime sponsors develop some EDPs after job assignments, and almost 10 percent report a similar practice with some IIB assignments.

Previous research suggested that counseling is more effective when the association of the counselor and the client is continuous and scheduled at regular intervals.[4] Our data indicate that counseling for PSE clients was continuous, but not regularly scheduled. Most prime sponsors (63 percent) reported that individual Title IID and VI enrollees were assigned on a continuing basis to one counselor who prepared the EDP and handled all other counseling assignments. However, the contact was likely to be irregular or infrequent. The irregular contact pattern prevailed even among prime sponsors having low client to counselor ratios. Over two-thirds of the sponsors (68 percent) reserved their more intensive counseling for their IIB clients. Like their PSE counterparts, IIB enrollees were assigned to one counselor, but the frequency of contact and length of each session were likely to be greater. Several sponsors justified this differential treatment on the grounds that such counseling was more essential for enrollees in training than in employment programs.

## Components of the Assessment Process

The requisites of a comprehensive participant assessment include aptitude and skill testing, ascertaining functional educational levels, and identifying the need for such supportive services as transportation, health care, child care, and

---

4. See E.S. Bordin, B. Nachman and S.J. Segal, "An Articulated Framework for Vocational Development," *Journal of Counseling Psychology,* 10 (1963), pp. 107-16; C.G. Hendricks, J.G. Ferguson and C.E. Thoreson, "Toward Counseling Competence: The Stanford Programs," *Personnel and Guidance Journal,* 10 (1973), pp. 418-24; and J.J. Horan, *Counseling for Effective Decision Making: A Cognitive-Behavioral Perspective* (North Scituate, MA: Duxburg Press, 1979).

Table 34
Organizations Responsible for Participant Assessment
Prior To and After Reauthorization Act
Sample Prime Sponsor Areas

| | Number of sponsors[a] | | | | | |
| | Title I (IIB) | | Title II (IID) | | Title VI | |
| Organization | Before | After | Before | After | Before | After |
|---|---|---|---|---|---|---|
| Prime sponsor/program agent | 19 | 21 | 14 | 20 | 15 | 19 |
| Employment service | 7 | 5 | 8 | 6 | 7 | 7 |
| PSE employer | 0 | 0 | 2 | 2 | 2 | 2 |
| Educational institution | 5 | 7 | 1 | 5 | 1 | 4 |
| Other organization | 8 | 7 | 4 | 4 | 3 | 5 |
| No assessments | 1 | 0 | 4 | 0 | 5 | 0 |

a. Adds to more than 28 because some used more than one type of organization for assessment.

Table 35

**Educational Attainment of Staff Preparing EDPs by Ratio of Clients to Counselor Sample Prime Sponsor Areas**

| Ratio of clients to counselor | High school education | Staff with | | | | | Total number of staff |
|---|---|---|---|---|---|---|---|
| | | Counseling degree | | Other degree | | | |
| | | B.A. | M.A. | B.A. | M.A. | | |
| | | (Percent) | | | | | |
| Total.............................. | 25.6 | 37.2 | 15.6 | 19.6 | 2.0 | | 250 |
| High ratio (141:1 and above)......... | 26.4 | 34.9 | 14.0 | 22.5 | 2.3 | | 129 |
| Low ratio (140:1 and below) ......... | 24.7 | 39.7 | 17.4 | 16.5 | 1.7 | | 121 |

SOURCE: Reports from 21 areas.

legal services. As table 36 indicates, each of these components was prepared for Title IIB enrollees by most of the prime sponsor sample prior to 1978. However, after reauthorization, dramatic gains were made in the array of assessment components for enrollees in Title VI and particularly in Title IID. For example, Title IID enrollees in less than half the survey areas were tested for skills and aptitudes prior to reauthorization. After the amendments over 75 percent of prime sponsors made these assessments.

Nearly all sponsors (25 out of 28) updated EDPs for PSE and Title IIB enrollees, but the frequency and approach varied. Eight sponsors updated enrollee EDPs monthly or weekly; an equal number updated from two to six times a year; seven varied the frequency depending on client needs; and two updated prior to termination. In a majority of cases (15 sponsors), both participants and supervisors or instructors were contacted and information collected was limited to items contained in the enrollee's original EDP.

## Utility of the EDPs

While most prime sponsors agreed that the EDP provision had improved the assessment process, considerably fewer found that it helped program planning and operations.

More than 60 percent said that the employability development plans improved the assessment function, a more positive reaction than was found in an earlier study. (At that time, July 1979, about one-half considered EDPs worthwhile.[5]) The sponsors were not so positive, however, that the EDP requirement had resulted in plans better tailored to participant needs. The affirmative view representing half the

---

5. Mirengoff et al., *The New CETA*, p. 117.

Table 36
Components of Participant Assessments Before and After Reauthorization Act
by Title, Sample Prime Sponsor Areas

| | Number of sponsors | | | | | |
| --- | --- | --- | --- | --- | --- | --- |
| | Title IIB | | Title IID | | Title VI | |
| Assessment component | Before | After | Before | After | Before | After |
| Aptitude test | 23 | 28 | 13 | 23 | 12 | 21 |
| Skills test | 23 | 26 | 14 | 22 | 15 | 22 |
| Basic education level | 24 | 26 | 12 | 23 | 14 | 21 |
| Need for: Transportation | 25 | 28 | 18 | 23 | 21 | 24 |
| Physical health care | 21 | 24 | 14 | 21 | 15 | 20 |
| Mental health care | 21 | 23 | 12 | 19 | 14 | 19 |
| Child care | 24 | 27 | 15 | 21 | 18 | 20 |
| Legal aid | 17 | 21 | 13 | 20 | 14 | 19 |
| Other | 8 | 9 | 7 | 8 | 6 | 7 |
| Employability development plan[a] | 22 | 28 | 16 | 28 | 17 | 26 |

SOURCE: Reports from 28 areas.

a. "Before reauthorization act" columns refer to the number of sponsors using the equivalent of an EDP at the time.

respondents was expressed by one of the field observers who found that:

> The . . . contribution of the EDP seems to be greater attention paid to the assessment process, with intake counselor and the participant agreeing on an . . . appropriate plan. The EDP enhances the counselor's sensitivity to the participant's needs and goals.

The contrary view was taken by a respondent who observed that:

> There still remains considerable pressure to assign applicants to whatever program is open, and for each intake center to give preference to vacancies in programs operated by its own parent organization. There are [also] no arrangements for a succession of services involving an inter-agency flow of clients.

Affirming the positive contribution of EDPs, administrators pointed out that they identify client objectives more effectively and enable staff to work more directly on achieving these objectives. They were considerably less sanguine, however, on the use of EDPs as tools for planning and developing training programs. Fewer than one-third used the plans for these purposes. In most instances, the EDP was viewed as a tool to be used in the context of existing programs and community resources. While the EDPs could provide the information necessary to determine the aggregate program needs of participants, such use was infrequent. A field observer reported:

> EDPs are not used to determine aggregate client needs so that programs to meet these needs can be developed. No such rationality exists in this system. The selection of programs is based largely on

political considerations, and clients are referred to them on the basis of openings, and to a lesser extent, client skill levels.

Those who did not see the EDPs as improving the assessment process complained about the added paperwork, demands for additional staff, and the slowing of intake. They viewed the EDP as an unnecessary burden routinely performed to meet federal requirements. As one field observer noted:

> They have improved assessment somewhat, but their impact on planning and operation has been nil . . . the EDP starts out OK, but it is skewed to take advantage of whatever openings the prime sponsor has at the time . . .

### Supportive Services

Properly executed, the assessment process identifies, not only training and employment needs and objectives, but also the supportive services necessary to overcome personal and environmental impediments to employability. The U.S. Department of Labor has identified two "principles" to guide prime sponsors in the development and use of supportive services:[6]

- Participant need for supportive service tends to be individualistic and requires attention on a case-by-case basis in order to be effective.
- Many other agencies and organizations in a prime sponsor's area are heavily involved in supportive services. . . . Prime sponsors should develop a supportive service design which makes full use of the area's resources.

---

6. Manpower Administration, U.S. Department of Labor, *Program Activities and Services Guide for Prime Sponsors Under CETA,* April 1974, p. II-9.

The survey suggests that although resources were present, their use was limited. A wide range of supportive services including transportation, health care, child care, and legal aid, are present in more than three-quarters of the sponsor areas. Despite their presence in the community, most informants reported that the PSE participants were often not served because appropriate services were not accessible, were too costly, or adequate arrangements for referrals were not made.

Child care and transportation were the services most often needed and used by participants. They were, however, more frequently selected as "most needed" than as "most used" (table 37). Transportation was cited as the foremost need in rural areas, child care and basic education as the most needed and used in the larger urban areas. Although the EDPs were useful in individual counseling situations to identify the need for and availability of supportive services, they generally played no role in the planning or development of supportive service programs in the community.

**Table 37**
**Local Officials' Perceptions of Supportive Services**
**Most Needed and Used by CETA Title IIB/C, Title IID**
**and Title VI Clients, Sample Prime Sponsor Areas**

| Service | Selected as most needed | Selected as most used |
|---|---|---|
| | (Percent of areas selecting service) | |
| Child care.................... | 33 | 25 |
| Transportation ............... | 32 | 26 |
| Physical health .............. | 2 | 9 |
| Legal aid ................... | 2 | 5 |
| Mental health ............... | 0 | 2 |
| Other ...................... | 3 | 3 |

SOURCE: Reports from 22 areas.

### *Administrative and Program Issues*

A previous study, conducted only two months after the effective date of the reauthorization act,[7] found sponsors uncertain about their ability to implement the new EDP requirements. They were particularly worried about the preparation of forms, frequency of followup, and the assignment of additional responsibilities to already overburdened staffs.

The current survey, conducted 16 months later, found that once they got over the initial shock, most sponsors made accommodations to meet the new requirements. One-fourth had conducted similar assessments prior to reauthorization and had no difficulty in implementing EDP requirements. Among the majority who experienced difficulties, the problems centered around increased workload, added paperwork, and the additional time needed for intake. Sponsors also cited inadequately trained staff and difficulties in developing a suitable EDP form. In most cases sponsors solved these problems by reassigning existing staff, modifying assessment procedures, and, in a few cases, by hiring additional personnel.

The introduction of the EDP process, requiring counseling interviews and followup, increased unit workloads for CETA staff in more than 70 percent of the sample areas. However, possibly because of an offsetting decline in the level of PSE enrollments, there was no corresponding increase in the size of staff.

For prime sponsors who had been assessing participants prior to reauthorization, as well as for those who treated the EDP requirement superficially, the added costs were generally marginal. But for others, particularly those who attempt-

---

7. Mirengoff, et al., *The New CETA*, pp. 117-18.

ed to use the EDP to improve assessment, the costs were much greater. One research associate observed:

> The benefits both to improved assessment, more efficient use of counselor time, and the contributions to identifying gaps in services and activities must outweigh the cost of developing the EDP by several magnitudes. The only issue concerning balance of benefits and costs may lie in the requirements to update the EDP. The cost to the client of coming into the office and the staff costs associated with calling on the client seem almost as high as the costs of initial development of the EDP.

Respondents suggested several ways in which the assessment process could be further improved. Most frequently heard was greater federal direction and guidance. Many respondents expressed a need for specific procedures for preparing EDPs: guidance in selecting skills and attitude tests, advice as to timing and frequency of followup assessments, and staff training in adapting to disadvantaged clients the approaches developed for mainstream workers. The counterpoint was also heard; several respondents viewed the EDP requirements as centralization gone awry. One southwestern sponsor argued that the assessment process should be left to local discretion: "With federally required EDPs, everyone is back merely to meeting federal requirements rather than focusing on serving the clients."

## Training in Public Service Employment Programs

By adding a training component to PSE programs, Congress sought to enhance the employability of the seriously disadvantaged unemployed who were now the focus of PSE, especially in Title IID programs. Under the original CETA legislation, prime sponsors could use part of their PSE funds for training. They could assign some of their PSE enrollees to classroom, on-the-job, or work experience activities normally provided for Title I (later IIB) clients. Or they could provide PSE participants with supplemental training in conjunction with their employment. Actually, few prime sponsors chose either course; only a fraction of Title IID or Title VI enrollees were given any formal training.[8]

To ensure that the new training requirements would be met, Congress stipulated the proportions of PSE allocations to be spent on PSE training. Starting with 10 percent of Title IID allotments in fiscal 1979, the percentage was to increase to 15 percent in fiscal 1980, 20 percent in 1981, and 22 percent by 1982. In Title VI, 10 percent of the fiscal 1979 allotments and 5 percent for each succeeding year were to be reserved for training, employability counseling, and services.

To enforce the training requirements, regional offices of the Department of Labor must review expenditures of prime sponsors periodically. If not up to the required funding level, the prime sponsor must prepare a "corrective action" plan. During fiscal 1980, expenditures to train PSE enrollees were $137 million for Title IID and $86 million for Title VI—amounting to 9 and 6 percent respectively of total expenditures for PSE enrollees.[9]

However, some observers felt that the regional offices should concentrate less on numbers and more on the quality of training. The emphasis, they believe, should be on how

---

8. In fiscal 1978, slightly over 1 percent of PSE expenditures was used for training, training allowances, and services to clients. This includes training a small proportion of Title IID and Title VI enrollees assigned exclusively to classroom and on-the-job training, as well as those PSE workers who received some part-time training or supportive services.

9. In calculating the proportion of expenditures chargeable to the 15 percent set-aside for Title IID and 5 percent for Title VI, percentages are applied only to the portion of funds spent for participants in public service jobs. Because of reporting limitations in fiscal 1980, the $137 million and $86 million include expenditures for training but not for wages and allowances of trainees. If wages and allowances were included, the percentages would be higher.

well training is integrated with the PSE experience, and how closely it relates to occupational demand. Federal pressure to meet a fixed expenditure quota without regard for these considerations may encourage training of dubious value or may result in paying for training that could be available from public institutions at lower costs.

The post-reauthorization patterns of PSE training, their comparisons with earlier practices, and the experiences of sponsors in linking training with employment prospects are examined in this section.

## Patterns of PSE Training

PSE training patterns can be examined in two ways: first, by the form of training sponsors offered and, second, by the proportion of trainees in each type. All sponsors in the study sample offered some form of training. The basic patterns used almost universally to meet the training requirements were skill training (96 percent of areas) and job search training (92 percent of areas). Work orientation and adult basic education (both offered at 77 percent of the sites) were also commonly provided, and in many instances job search orientation with skill training was offered. Skill training and adult basic education were offered in schools and skill centers. Most courses (56 percent) were given on release time and for less than 20 hours per week.

For the United States as a whole, 33 percent of Title IID and 28 percent of Title VI PSE enrollees received training in fiscal 1980. During that same period 34 percent of Title IID and 22 percent of Title VI enrollees in the study sample receiving training. Occupational skill training was the principal type received by both Title IID and VI enrollees, followed by job search and orientation to work environment (table 38). As the differences in participant characteristics might suggest, a slightly higher proportion of Title IID enrollees took occupational skill and basic education as the principal courses, while Title VI enrollees more frequently were given job search and work orientation training.[10]

**Table 38**
**Principal Types of Training of Public Service Employment Participants**
**Sample Prime Sponsor Areas, Fiscal 1980**

| Type of training | Percent distribution of participants trained[a] | |
| --- | --- | --- |
|  | Title IID | Title VI |
| Total .............................. | 100 | 100 |
| Occupational skill ...................... | 49 | 46 |
| Job search and orientation to work environment .................. | 38 | 43 |
| Basic education ....................... | 10 | 7 |
| Other ................................. | 3 | 4 |

SOURCE: Reports from 20 areas. Data are averages of percentages for each area.

a. Based on unduplicated count of participants who received training by major type of training.

Sponsors implemented training requirements in a variety of ways. Some stipulated a set of required courses and the sequence in which they must be taken. Others gave participants more discretion, differentiating between required core courses and supplemental offerings. A southern consortium, for example, prescribes a 28-hour mandatory course in "job survival training." PSE participants who failed to complete the required sessions after two enrollments were terminated from their PSE positions. Successful participants could enroll voluntarily in an adult basic education course offered through the county board of education. All enrollees in the tenth month of PSE employment were encouraged to take a 30-hour job search training course.

---

10. These figures are somewhat higher than those reported in an earlier study (April 1979), but differences in study methodologies do not permit a direct comparison of the two periods. See Robert C. Cook et al., *Public Service Employment in 1980* (Princeton, NJ: Princeton Regional Research Center, 1981. In process).

An eastern prime sponsor offered an array of 32 skill training and basic education courses at a local community college. Title IID and VI enrollees and their counselors selected courses appropriate to current work assignments or EDP findings. These courses were followed by job search training during the last three months.

Not all prime sponsors provided training tied to participant progress in the PSE program. In one midwestern county, for example, the most compelling consideration was to meet federal expenditure requirements. On the theory that "it couldn't hurt," all Title IID and VI enrollees were required to take such courses as cardiopulmonary resuscitation, mathematics, and money management. A prime sponsor in the rural south focused almost exclusively on job search training. Despite the limited course offerings, there were difficult traveling and scheduling problems. As a result, there was little individual programming of training and uneven course attendance.

Sponsors proffered a number of reasons, not necessarily exclusive, for their choice of training programs. Most frequently cited (50 percent of reporting areas) was the desire to provide the type of training indicated by the assessment of participants' needs. Improving the marketability of enrollees was mentioned by 19 percent, and an equal number made their decisions on the basis of client interest. Expediency was also a consideration. Twelve percent of the sponsors preferred to provide uniform types of training across CETA titles.

In response to questions about training plans for fiscal 1981, most sponsors said they did not propose significant changes. Some changes were planned in order to meet federal expenditure requirements, and others involved expanding existing offerings. These efforts resulted in some wasteful expenditures. A research associate from a balance-of-state sponsor noted that:

PSE training requirements had to be implemented too quickly, and the BOS sponsors received no guidance in how to proceed with the task in a service area involving 90 counties. The IID training provisions have encouraged wasteful spending for the sake of nothing more than complying with an arbitrary percentage figure. By placing a premium on meeting expenditure figures, CETA has discouraged the use of low cost community college training and encouraged reliance on high priced consultant services and short-term job search training.

Prior to reauthorization, the linking of training to PSE programs was optional rather than required and was offered to PSE enrollees at over one-third of our sample sites.[11] Since 1978 the program offerings have been expanded rather than altered. Job search and work environment orientation were the courses most commonly added.

Sponsors who, prior to reauthorization, had the infrastructure to use and the experience from which to judge the new training and expenditure requirements were the most critical of the new requirements (table 39). They also were more likely to provide separate programs or facilities for their Title IIB/C and PSE enrollees. Sixty percent of those sponsors who provided PSE training prior to reauthorization had separate programs or facilities for Title IIB/C and PSE enrollees. In contrast, less than 18 percent of the sponsors who did not provide this training prior to reauthorization had separate programs or facilities for their IIB/C and PSE enrollees. Sponsors to whom PSE training was new more readily accepted the post-reauthorization requirements and

---

11. Despite the availability of training at these sites the actual expenditures for training prior to 1978 were minimal, and only a minority of PSE enrollees received training (see p. 180).

viewed the establishment of separate facilities as either un-manageable or unnecessary.

**Table 39**
**Prime Sponsor Perceptions of Expenditure Requirements**
**by Existence or Absence of PSE Training**
**Prior to Reauthorization Act, Sample Prime Sponsor Areas**

| PSE training prior to reauthorization | Perception of expenditure requirements | | | |
|---|---|---|---|---|
| | Title IID | | Title VI | |
| | Appropriate | Not appropriate | Appropriate | Not appropriate |
| | (Number of areas) | | | |
| Training offered ............... | 3 | 7 | 4 | 6 |
| Training not offered ........... | 7 | 10 | 12 | 5 |

SOURCE: Reports from 27 areas.

## Linking Training to Employment

The rationale for infusing public service employment pro-grams with formal training was to improve participants' chances for obtaining unsubsidized employment. In addition to providing temporary, federally supported jobs for the unemployed, PSE programs were now charged with a broader responsibility—to provide occupational and job search skills that would facilitate their joining the mainstream of the labor force.

A majority (57 percent) of the respondents indicated that, on balance, the training provided to PSE enrollees improved their ability to obtain unsubsidized employment. One prime sponsor pointed out that "since the types of PSE jobs presently available are almost entirely dead-end, acquiring skills through training is the participant's primary hope for obtaining an unsubsidized job."

Although other provisions of the reauthorization act, i.e., the limits on duration of enrollment and the introduction of EDPs, were, in part, designed to encourage transition, respondents most often identified the linking of training with PSE programs as the provision having a direct effect on improving transition rates. (See chapter 8.) The subsample of sponsors who stated that training improved transition prospects were also providing the most training.

A comparison of the placement rates of these groups before and after reauthorization suggests an association between training activity and placements for Title IID enrollees. Sponsors training an above average proportion of Title IID enrollees placed 43 percent of their participants in fiscal year 1980, compared with placement rates of 33 percent for those training a below average proportion of enrollees. In 1978 both groups had placement rates of 43 percent. This finding suggests that high levels of training may act to counterbalance the reduction in placements that would accompany both the tighter eligibility requirements and the downward shift in the types of jobs since reauthorization. Comparable rates for Title VI enrollees were 33 percent for both sponsor groupings in 1980 and 34 percent in 1978.

In justifying their support of the training provision's impact on placements, several sponsors said that PSE training added significantly to an enrollee's credibility in applying for unsubsidized employment. A certificate from an educational or training institution often assisted in placement, since it suggested both that the applicant was interested in career development and had obtained training.

There were, however, a minority of respondents (21 percent) who were skeptical of the impact of training on improving placement prospects. They expressed several reservations about current practices: splitting PSE enrollees' time between work and training could weaken both; in contrast to the training offered under Title IIB, PSE training (particularly the job search and work orientation) was often superficial; and factors other than training, such as motivation and labor market conditions, might be as important as training in obtaining employment. However, even these critics supported the concept of combining training with PSE as a strategy for improving employment prospects.

## Implementation Difficulties

Attempts to mesh training with public service jobs in a meaningful way presented new challenges to CETA sponsors in their dealings with participants, employing agencies, and training institutions. The survey suggests that the logistical problems of accomplishing these linkages in ways that meet both the vocational objectives of the enrollees and the job prospects in the labor market could be formidable, particularly in depressed rural areas with few employment and training outlets.

Not surprisingly, a number of sponsors encountered resistance from participants because of interruption of work or loss of income where training allowances are paid instead of wages. Two-thirds of the sponsors interviewed reported resistance from employing agencies inconvenienced by disrupted work schedules. Further, a number of prime sponsors found that training agencies were not adaptable enough to provide training on short notice. The training institutions, in turn, complained about the poor attitude and absenteeism of those PSE enrollees who were reluctant to participate in training programs. To avoid many of these problems some sponsors, as the preceding section indicated, resorted to the expedient of offering a general course in work orientation or job search methods at the beginning or end of the employment cycle.

In addition to resistance from employers, participants, and training institutions, sponsors reported difficulties in achieving the coordination necessary to implement an effective work training program. The absence of coordinated efforts often reflects differing perceptions on program objectives. One field associate observed:

It is not the 'coupling' (of work and training) that does the damage, but it is the imbalance, the undue emphasis on PSE as an employment subsidy for local governments, that does the harm. If participants and employers were given the clear understanding that training was the overarching purpose of their getting together, then PSE work experience could be a valuable component of the overall training.

Despite such operational difficulties, nearly all prime sponsors interviewed believed that the training offered contributed to the ability of many participants to obtain jobs and, on balance, was worth the costs incurred. Most saw a payoff to employers in terms of better performance on the job and an opportunity to identify workers with potential for transition to regular employment. Some also felt that the increased employability of the hard-core unemployed would benefit the community by increasing its pool of trained workers.

## Summary

The reauthorization act sought to design an employment and training system more sharply centered on persons on the lowest rungs of the socioeconomic ladder. To accommodate the special needs of disadvantaged participants, the legislation prescribed employability development plans for Title II and some Title VI enrollees and required that training programs be added to PSE jobs. These amendments are being implemented and have given more weight to the assessment process and more recognition to the need for enriching the PSE experience. A majority of respondents felt that introduction of EDPs has improved the assessment process and that new training requirements have increased participants' chances of obtaining unsubsidized employment.

Figures on placements suggest that sponsors who emphasize training may have higher than average placement rates for their Title IID enrollees.

The implementation of the new requirements has been achieved at some cost. The insistence on minimum rates of PSE training expenditures for all sponsors encourages waste, adversely affects the quality of training, and constrains local flexibility. Other findings:

- Although EDPs were intended primarily for Title IID clients, most prime sponsors have extended the practice to Title VI participants as well.
- The emphasis on assessment reflected in the EDP provisions has resulted in organizational shifts. Some sponsors have taken over this responsibility from the employment service or other delegated agencies.
- Most staff preparing EDPs have had specialized training in counseling. The most qualified counselors are found at sites having the lowest client/counselor ratios.
- Most administrators view the EDPs as having improved the assessment process, but there is less agreement on whether plans are now better tailored to clients' needs. There is also some question as to whether EDPs are used as tools for planning and developing training programs. Some sponsors treat EDPs as a pro forma compliance exercise.
- More than 30 percent of PSE enrollees, in 1980, were receiving some form of training. Occupational skills, job search, and orientation to the labor market were the principal types of training.
- While most respondents believed training of PSE participants enhanced their ability to obtain unsubsidized employment, some were skeptical. They pointed out that the splitting of enrollees' time weakened both the training and job components, and they stressed the im-

portance of nontraining factors in obtaining unsubsidized employment.

- Sponsors who had offered training to PSE participants prior to reauthorization were particularly critical of the new training expenditure requirements, tending to view them as artificially high.
- There are difficult operational problems in meshing training and work schedules and in finding the right combinations of learning and work experience. Sponsors are confronted with resistance from employers because of disruption of work schedules and from some employees who resist training. There are also problems in finding training outlets offering the kinds of training needed.

# 6 Wages, Jobs, and Services

Among the most important of the 1978 amendments were the restrictions on the wage levels that could be paid for public service employment jobs. Major objectives of these restraints were to limit enrollment in PSE to persons who had been least successful in obtaining unsubsidized employment and to curtail the substitution of PSE workers for regular employees of government.[1] The lower wage levels (and the tighter eligibility criteria) resulted in the enrollment of larger proportions of the seriously disadvantaged. However, the new wage limits forced the development of low-skill PSE jobs that were considered by local officials to be less useful in providing public services to the community and less likely to provide the kinds of job experience that would help the participants obtain unsubsidized employment.

---

1. The substitution of CETA enrollees for regular employees of government is examined in Richard P. Nathan et al., *Monitoring the Public Service Employment Program: The Second Round.* See also Mirengoff and Rindler, *CETA: Under Local Control,* pp. 173-90; and Michael Borus and Daniel Hamermesh, "Study of the Net Employment Effects of Public Service Employment—Econometric Analyses," pp. 89-150.

# PSE Wage Changes in 1978

Early CETA legislation limited the wages that could be paid PSE enrollees to a national average of $7,800 and set $10,000 as the maximum that could be paid from CETA funds.[2] However, employing agencies were free to supplement the PSE wage without limit. Many of the PSE jobs paid $10,000 to $15,000 and suggested to Congress that the wage limits permitted abuse. Such high paying jobs were suspect as instances of substitution and of the enrollment of persons who could obtain employment without the assistance of CETA. The 1978 amendments sought to resolve these problems by tightening the eligibility requirements and limiting PSE wages.

## Average Wages

The national average wage for PSE jobs that could be paid from CETA funds was reduced from the $7,800 per year to $7,200 for enrollees entering after April 1, 1979. The 1978 amendments, however, permitted the average wage to be adjusted annually to reflect national wage changes for regular jobs. This increased the PSE average from $7,200 in the last half of fiscal 1979 to $7,653 for fiscal 1980 and to $8,271 for fiscal 1981. The average PSE wage for each area varied from the national PSE average depending upon the relationship of local wages for unsubsidized jobs in each area to the national average.

## Maximum Wages

Prior to the reauthorization, the maximum annual PSE wage that could be paid from CETA funds was $10,000. The

---

2. The Emergency Jobs and Unemployment Assistance Act of 1974 (Pub. L. 93-567) Sec. 209(b) set the average wage at $7,800. The $10,000 maximum was in the basic CETA legislation of 1973.

reauthorization retained the $10,000—for areas where wages for regular jobs were above the national average. However, unlike average wages, maximum PSE wages were not adjusted to reflect rising wage levels.

## Supplementation of PSE Wages

The 1978 amendments constrained the previously unlimited freedom of agencies to use their own funds to supplement the PSE wage. No supplementation was permitted for Title IID jobs. For Title VI, supplements could be no more than 10 percent of the CETA maximum wage, except in a few areas where wages for regular jobs were 25 percent or more above the national average. PSE wages in such areas could be supplemented by up to 20 percent of the area's maximum CETA wage.

## Prevailing Wages

The implementation of the new wage provisions was complicated by the continuing requirement that PSE enrollees be paid "the prevailing rates of pay for persons employed in similar occupations by the same employer."

# Effects of Wage Changes

Following the implementation of the new wage provisions, the average annual wage of new enrollees, which had been rising steadily, dropped by 6 percent from $7,821 in the first half of fiscal 1979 to $7,363 for the last half (table 40). The reduced wage was 10 percent above the poverty level for a family of four ($6,700), and 31 percent below the Bureau of Labor Statistics lower living standard income level ($11,546). Lower PSE wages at a time of rising wages for regular jobs and the established policy that PSE workers must be paid the prevailing wage meant that many PSE positions that became open after 1978 could not be refilled. Prime sponsors responded to these constraints by discontinuing the use of some high-wage positions, writing down the duties of others (restructuring), and developing new types of lower wage PSE jobs. They also shifted PSE positions to nonprofit agencies where it was easier to develop low-wage jobs.

**Table 40**
**Average Wage of New Public Service Employment Enrollees**
**Fiscal 1976-1979**

| Wage | 1976 | 1977 | 1978 | 1979 First half | 1979 Second half |
|---|---|---|---|---|---|
| Average hourly wage ....... | $3.28 | $3.54 | $3.68 | $3.76 | $3.54 |
| Average annual wage[a] ....... | $6,822 | $7,363 | $7,654 | $7,821 | $7,363 |

SOURCE: Special tabulations, *Continuous Longitudinal Manpower Survey*, Westat, Inc.
a. Derived by multiplying the average hourly wage by 2,080 hours.

## Average Wage Effects

*Jobs discontinued.* Eighty-six percent of the areas surveyed dropped some of their PSE positions as a result of the new average wage requirements. In 25 percent of the areas, more than half the jobs were discontinued (table 41). By far, the most important reason for dropping PSE jobs was the absence of positions in government agencies with entry wages low enough to meet the wage provisions of the 1978 amendments together with the requirement that PSE pay the prevailing wage. The lack of skills among PSE applicants that limited their usefulness to the employing agencies and the extra work in reorganizing wage structures and supervising lower skill enrollees also influenced the decisions to eliminate some types of PSE positions (table 42).

**Table 41**
**Proportion of Public Service Employment Jobs Discontinued**
**Because of Lower Average Wage Requirements**
**Sample Prime Sponsor Areas**

| Proportion of jobs discontinued | Percent of reporting areas |
|---|---|
| More than half............................... | 25 |
| One-fourth to one-half......................... | 39 |
| Less than one-fourth........................... | 21 |
| None....................................... | 14 |

SOURCE: Reports from 28 areas.

**Table 42**
**Factors Influencing Decisions to Discontinue**
**Public Service Employment Positions**
**Sample Prime Sponsor Areas**

| Factor | Importance ranking | | |
|---|---|---|---|
| | 1 | 2 | 3[a] |
| | (Percent of reporting areas) | | |
| All reports............................ | 100 | 100 | 100 |
| Few low-wage positions available in employing agencies................... | 63 | 21 | 10 |
| Applicants willing to accept low PSE wage lack necessary skills................ | 8 | 25 | 38 |
| PSE employers reluctant to undertake extra work to develop low-wage jobs............ | 8 | 21 | 19 |
| Inadequate number of applicants willing to accept low PSE wage ................ | 8 | 17 | 10 |
| Organized labor objections to low-wage PSE jobs..................... | 8 | 8 | 14 |
| Other ...................................... | 4 | 8 | 10 |

SOURCE: Reports from 24 areas.
NOTE: Detail may not add to 100 percent because of rounding.
a. Only 22 areas provided a third most important factor.

In the previous survey conducted two months after the effective date of the revised wage requirements, almost all CETA directors anticipated that positions requiring professional, technical, and craft skills would be de-emphasized in favor of low level clerical, laboring, and service worker jobs.[3] These expectations did in fact materialize. In the followup survey, conducted after 18 months of experience with the new wage provisions, three-fourths of the areas where wages were reduced reported that the jobs most frequently eliminated were in the professional, technical, and administrative categories. Paraprofessional, craft, police, and firefighter occupations were ranked second or third as the types of jobs most frequently discontinued (table 43). Least likely to be dropped were clerical, operative, and service worker jobs (other than police and firefighter).

**Table 43**
**Types of Public Service Employment Jobs Most Frequently**
**Discontinued Due to the Lower Average Wage Requirement**
**Sample Prime Sponsor Areas**

|                                              | Ranking | | |
|----------------------------------------------|---------|---------|---------|
| Occupational group                           | 1 | 2 | 3 |
|                                              | (Percent of reporting areas) | | |
| Professional, technical, and administrative.... | 75 | 21 | 0 |
| Paraprofessional........................      | 4 | 42 | 0 |
| Clerical...............................       | 4 | 0 | 0 |
| Craft workers .........................      | 0 | 12 | 46 |
| Operatives ...........................       | 0 | 0 | 8 |
| Laborers..............................       | 4 | 4 | 12 |
| Service workers: Police and firefighters....... | 12 | 21 | 25 |
| Other service workers ....... | 0 | 0 | 8 |

SOURCE: Reports from 24 areas.
NOTE: Detail may not add to 100 percent because of rounding.

*Job restructuring.* A second method practiced by prime sponsors to meet the lower wage requirements was to restructure PSE positions by reducing their skill content. Government agencies in all but one of the 24 reporting areas

---

3. Mirengoff et al., *The New CETA*, p. 83.

required to reduce PSE wages used this method, as did non-profit organizations in 20 of these areas. Clerical jobs were most frequently redesigned in both government agencies and nonprofit organizations. Professional and paraprofessional jobs were restructured in some instances and discontinued in others (table 44 and figure 8). Although low-skill occupations were less frequently restructured, some laborer and service worker jobs were modified. Thus to some degree, the effort to meet the new wage levels reduced the skill content of jobs which were already of a low order. In about a third of the survey areas some jobs were merely retitled without a real change in job content. Restructuring in some city agency PSE jobs in Philadelphia consisted of four days of work per week at regular (union) wages and one day of training and counseling at the minimum wage.

### Table 44
### Types of Jobs Most Frequently Restructured to Meet
### Lower Average Wage Requirements
### By Type of Hiring Agency
### Sample Prime Sponsor Areas, April 1979-September 1980

| | Type of hiring agency and ranking | | | | | |
|---|---|---|---|---|---|---|
| | Government agencies | | | Nonprofit organizations | | |
| Occupational group | 1 | 2 | 3 | 1 | 2 | 3 |
| | (Percent of all reports) | | | | | |
| Professional, technical, and administrative...... | 29 | 5 | 0 | 25 | 4 | 5 |
| Paraprofessional......... | 17 | 10 | 15 | 17 | 22 | 14 |
| Clerical................. | 42 | 10 | 5 | 38 | 13 | 9 |
| Craft workers........... | 0 | 5 | 15 | 0 | 4 | 9 |
| Operatives ............. | 0 | 10 | 15 | 0 | 0 | 14 |
| Laborers................ | 4 | 38 | 10 | 0 | 17 | 14 |
| Service workers .......... | 4 | 19 | 35 | 4 | 22 | 18 |
| No restructuring ......... | 4 | 5 | 5 | 17 | 17 | 18 |

SOURCE: Reports from 24 areas.

NOTE: Detail may not add to 100 percent because of rounding.

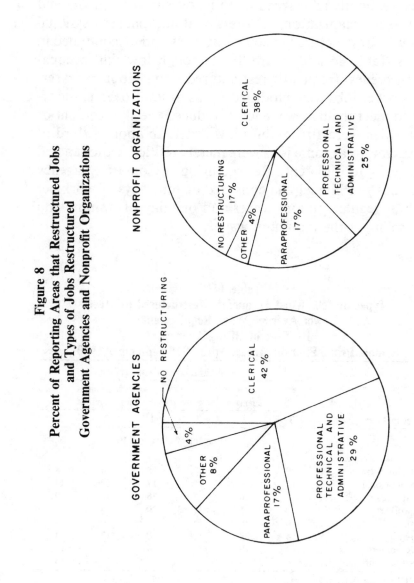

**Figure 8**
**Percent of Reporting Areas that Restructured Jobs
and Types of Jobs Restructured
Government Agencies and Nonprofit Organizations**

*New jobs for PSE.* In addition to discontinuing some higher wage jobs and restructuring others, new types of jobs were created for PSE in 20 of the 24 areas where a reduction in PSE wages was necessary. Job titles such as "laborer aide," "custodial trainee," and "community service aide" were not uncommon and indicate the entry and sub-entry character of the occupation.

At the end of fiscal 1980, after 18 months of operation under the new wage requirements, 42 percent of the CETA directors reported that more than half of their current PSE jobs were either new or restructured.

| Proportion of PSE jobs new or restructured | Percent of reporting areas |
|---|---|
| More than half ............. | 42 |
| One-fourth to one-half ...... | 21 |
| Less than one-fourth ........ | 38 |

SOURCE: Reports from 24 areas.

*Problems in creating lower wage jobs.* About 85 percent of the prime sponsors who restructured or created new jobs to reach a lower average wage ran into difficulties. In some agencies, the personnel structure or policies precluded sub-entry positions. In other instances, elected officials and supervisors felt that the low level of service obtainable from sub-entry positions and the amount of the supervision required by workers in those jobs removed the incentive to participate in PSE programs. In one-third of the areas where PSE wages had to be reduced, some government employing agencies withdrew from the program. There were also reports of resistance to restructuring from nonprofit organizations and unions.

In about half the areas where jobs were restructured or new jobs created, prime sponsors had to exert extra effort to negotiate revised job structures for PSE and to assist hiring agencies that were writing new job descriptions. Smaller organizations and nonprofit agencies in particular needed such help. Because of the difficulty of job restructuring in government agencies, greater shares of the program were shifted to nonprofit organizations. Despite these efforts, additional job restructuring and new job creation were still necessary in half the study areas to reach or remain in conformance with the average wage requirements.

## Wage Supplementation Effects

Supplementation of the CETA wage which had been widely used prior to the amendments was largely abandoned after 1978. By 1980, supplementation was eliminated or used for less than one percent of the PSE jobs in three-fourths of the study areas and was used for no more than 5 percent of the enrollees in most of the other areas. The drop in wage supplementation did not occur immediately after the 1978 amendments because persons receiving supplements prior to October 1978 were "grandfathered" for the period of their enrollment in PSE (table 45). Two areas continued relatively high rates of supplementation in 1980. Both were financially distressed cities that were using PSE workers to assist regular employees in providing essential municipal services.

Supplementation was cut back for several reasons. The major element appeared to be the unwillingness of PSE employers to use their own funds to support the kind of low wage positions that were available following the 1978 amendments. Government agencies found that the restrictions on supplementation and other wage limits prevented them from reaching the wage levels necessary for the kinds of PSE jobs they most wanted to fill such as police, firefighters, administrative assistants, and junior professionals. Before 1979, more than half of the wage supplements exceeded the amount permitted after the 1978 amendments and 72 percent of the supplements had been added to jobs that paid a CETA wage of $10,000.[4]

**Table 45**
**Percent of PSE Enrollees Whose CETA Wage Was Supplemented**
**by the Hiring Agencies, Sample Prime Sponsor Areas**
**1977, 1979, and 1980**

| Percent of all PSE enrollees receiving supplements | Percent of reporting areas | | |
|---|---|---|---|
| | September 1977 | May 1979 | June 1980 |
| Total ................... | 100 | 100 | 100 |
| Zero...................... | 8 | 17 | 48 |
| Less than 1 .............. | 0 | 8 | 30 |
| 1 to 5 ................... | 30 | 22 | 17 |
| 6 to 15 .................. | 35 | 26 | 0 |
| 16 or more............... | 26 | 26 | 4 |
| Average percent of enrollees receiving supplements ..... | 15 | 13 | 2 |

SOURCE: Reports from 23 areas.
NOTE: Details may not add to 100 percent because of rounding.

In some instances, sharply lower supplementation reflected a shift in the prime sponsors' view of the PSE program—from one in which jobs were provided to unemployed persons with the skills necessary to provide useful public services to one in which the purpose of serving the most disadvantaged far outweighed the goal of providing useful community services. A number of prime sponsors with this perception ruled out supplementation as an option available to PSE employers.

Supplementation was also used less often because of the shift of a greater share of PSE jobs to nonprofit organizations. These agencies seldom had the resources to augment the CETA wage.

---

4. Ibid., pp. 90-92.

In two-thirds of the study areas, the limit on wage supplementation resulted in the elimination of some PSE jobs. Those hardest hit were the professional, paraprofessional, police, and firefighter positions.

One-third of the areas reported a difference in the kinds of occupations funded under Title VI and Title IID because supplementation was permitted in the former but not in the latter.

## Maximum Wage Effects

Prime sponsors in about half the study areas found that the maximum PSE wage, because it was not adjusted for the rising level of regular wages, was more of a hindrance to program operations in 1980 than in 1979. Between June 1979 and June 1980 the largest governmental units in 26 of the 28 study areas provided cost of living or other general wage increases to their regular employees averaging 7.5 percent. As a result, more of their regular job classes had entry wages which were above the maximum that could be paid to PSE workers. In 15 of 28 areas, PSE jobs had to be dropped after enrollees left because the entry wage exceeded the CETA maximum. Again, the majority of these positions were in the professional, technical, and administrative group but also included police and fire protection jobs in a few areas.

A few prime sponsors were more troubled by the fixed maximum than by the average wage, especially those that were interested in filling higher wage positions and were willing to offset the effect on average wages by developing lower level positions for other PSE enrollees. The fixed maximum made it very difficult to hire a few especially needed employees in exchange for others whose contribution to an agency's mission was smaller.

## Average Wage Had Greatest Impact

Of the three types of wage limitations in the 1978 amendments, the average wage constraints continued to have the
greatest effect on the jobs and services provided by PSE programs. In many areas the average wage was more important
than the maximum wage because a job at or near the maximum would require two or more offsetting jobs at or near
the minimum to meet the required average wage for the area.
For example, after January 1, 1980, the federal minimum
wage was $3.10 per hour or $6,448 per year. In Phoenix, the
average PSE wage was set at $7,362; the maximum was
$10,000. A PSE job at $10,000 would have to be offset by
three jobs at the federal minimum wage to achieve the required average of $7,362.

In over 80 percent of the study areas, the average wage was
also the most difficult of the wage changes to implement—primarily because of the difficulty of developing
low-wage jobs that would not conflict with established job
classification structures but would still provide useful services and job experience.

The influence of the average wage, although still predominant in 1980, had diminished somewhat compared with 1979
(table 46). The CETA maximum wage which, unlike the
average, is not adjusted annually to reflect wage escalation,
was the most important of the wage factors affecting jobs
and community services in a small but increasing number of
areas, or it shared that position with the average wage. The
general complaint in these areas was that the maximum often
prevented them from hiring small numbers of higher wage
personnel necessary to supervise PSE enrollees or perform
other specialized tasks.

**Table 46**
**Wage Changes with the Greatest Effect on Jobs and Services**
**Sample Prime Sponsor Areas, Fiscal 1979-1980**

| | Percent of reporting areas | |
|---|---|---|
| Wage change | 1979 | 1980 |
| Lower average CETA wage ................... | 89 | 64 |
| Limit on wage supplementation ............... | 7 | 4 |
| CETA maximum wage ...................... | 4 | 11 |
| Lower average and limit on supplementation..... | 0 | 4 |
| Lower average and CETA maximum ........... | 0 | 11 |
| Don't know ............................... | 0 | 7 |

SOURCE: Reports from 28 areas.

NOTE: Detail may not add to 100 percent because of rounding.

## New Wage Base in 1981

In December 1980, Congress raised the base for the national average PSE wage from $7,200 to $8,000. The legislative vehicle for this change was PL 96-583 that extended Title VII, the private sector initiative program of CETA. Since the $8,000 wage base was tied back to 1979 and was subject to annual adjustments for general wage escalation, the effective national average wage for fiscal 1981 was $9,190.

## Effects of Enrollee Qualifications on PSE Jobs

Local officials in a large majority of the study areas (86 percent) believed that applicants for PSE jobs after the 1978 CETA amendments were not as well qualified as those available earlier. The limited job skills of the new enrollees influenced the types of positions used for PSE and diminished the usefulness of the public service provided.

## Factors Affecting the
## Skill Levels of Enrollees

The survey explored the effect of three factors thought to influence the enrollment of lower skill persons in PSE: eligibility restrictions, wage limits, and local labor market conditions. The more restrictive eligibility criteria were a factor in all 24 areas where enrollees with fewer skills were reported and the most important factor in 15 of the areas (table 47). Respondents gave low PSE wages as the leading reasons for the decline in the qualifications of enrollees in nine areas and the second most important factor in another ten. In these areas the low skill level of PSE enrollees was attributed, in part, to self screening—persons with marketable skills who were eligible for PSE found that they could earn more in the regular job market. Also, experienced unemployed workers often preferred unemployment insurance payments to a low-wage PSE job.

**Table 47**
**Factors Responsible for Enrollment of Lower Skill Workers**
**Sample Prime Sponsor Areas, 1980**

| Factor | Importance ranking | | |
|---|---|---|---|
| | 1 | 2 | 3 |
| | (Number of areas) | | |
| Eligibility restrictions | 15 | 8 | 1 |
| Wage limits | 9 | 10 | 1 |
| Tight labor market | 0 | 3 | 1 |

SOURCE: Reports from 24 areas.

Changes in labor market conditions had little effect on the quality of applicants for PSE. Only four of the 28 study areas reported that improved employment opportunities was a second or third factor in a reduced supply of skilled applicants for PSE. In a majority of the areas, employment conditions had worsened, but this too had little effect. Except for a few areas, there was little or no increase in skilled applicants because the unemployed with work histories were seldom eligible for PSE or, if eligible, often preferred to draw unemployment insurance benefits.

In sum, the 1978 amendments had the intended effect of discouraging persons with strong skills from competing for PSE jobs with those less prepared for the world of work.

### Impact on Jobs and Services

*Jobs.* In two-thirds of the study areas, the lower skill level of persons who enrolled after the 1978 amendments influenced the types of jobs that were established. The skills needed for craft, professional, paraprofessional, and higher level clerical jobs were less often available, and PSE employers resorted to a variety of "trainee" positions. However, the new wage restraints had a greater effect on PSE jobs and were responsible for most of the restructuring and downgrading of PSE positions.

Other consequences of the changes in the PSE participants' skill profile included the need for more supervision and a loss in productivity.

*Services.* The more limited job skills of the new enrollees did not have a major impact on the kinds of agencies in which they were employed but did affect the level of services. For example, prior to 1978 some government agencies had used PSE in administrative/professional positions such as planner, coordinator, probation officer, or as police and firefighter. In nonprofit organizations enrollees had worked as project leaders, caseworkers, and skilled clerical workers. After 1978 these skills often were not available, and the same agencies used the public service employment slots for lower level clerical and other support positions. As a consequence, both the quality and the quantity of services suffered.

*Training.* The legislative mandate to use a portion of PSE funds for the training of enrollees had very little direct impact on the types of jobs approved or the types of community services provided. However, many officials pointed out that the volume of public services was reduced by the absence of PSE enrollees from their assigned work while in training. In some instances it was necessary to shift PSE jobs from agencies that could not accommodate the interruption of work and from locations that were inconvenient for the training of enrollees.

## Changes Reported by the Continuous Longitudinal Manpower Survey

The response of prime sponsors in the study of the effects of the wage and eligibility changes on occupations is consistent with data from the Continuous Longitudinal Manpower Survey (CLMS). These data indicate that in the six months after April 1978 (the effective date of the lower average wage requirements), the proportion of all new PSE enrollees hired for professional, technical, and administrative jobs dropped from 20 percent to 14 percent. The share for craft workers also declined. These reductions were offset by increases in the proportion of clerical, laboring, and service worker jobs (table 48 and figure 9).

### Table 48
### Percent of New Public Service Employment Enrollees by Occupational Group, Fiscal 1977-1979

| Occupational group | 1977 | 1978 | Second half 1979 |
|---|---|---|---|
| Total new enrollees (est.) . . . . . . . . . . . . | 359,000 | 545,000 | 203,000 |
| | | (Percent of total) | |
| Professional, technical, and administrative . . . . . . . . . . . . . . | 21 | 20 | 14 |
| Clerical . . . . . . . . . . . . . . . . . . . . . . . . | 23 | 24 | 28 |
| Craft workers . . . . . . . . . . . . . . . . . . . | 10 | 11 | 8 |
| Operatives . . . . . . . . . . . . . . . . . . . . . | 5 | 6 | 6 |
| Laborers . . . . . . . . . . . . . . . . . . . . . . . | 22 | 21 | 24 |
| Service workers . . . . . . . . . . . . . . . . . . | 19 | 18 | 21 |

SOURCE: Special tabulation, *Continuous Longitudinal Manpower Survey,* Westat, Inc.
NOTE: Detail may not add to 100 percent because of rounding.

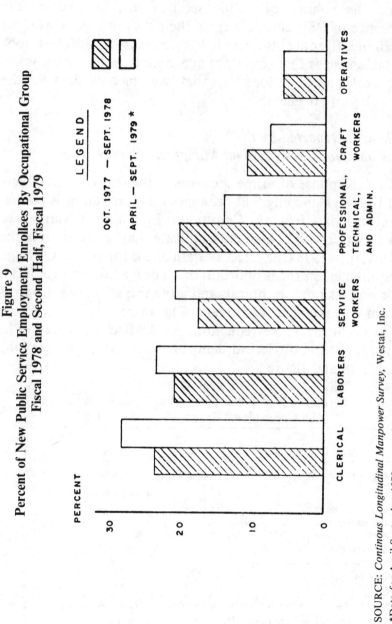

Figure 9
Percent of New Public Service Employment Enrollees By Occupational Group
Fiscal 1978 and Second Half, Fiscal 1979

SOURCE: *Continous Longitudinal Manpower Survey*, Westat, Inc.

*Data for April-September 1979 are used because the wage restrictions of the 1978 amendments were not fully effective until April 1979.

## Occupations of PSE Participants
## and the Long Term Unemployed

Prior to the 1978 amendments, PSE enrolled persons with high level skills in greater proportion than their share of the long term unemployed. Twenty percent of PSE enrollees were in professional, technical, and managerial positions; only 13 percent of the long term unemployed were last employed in these categories. The accommodations made to meet the wage and eligibility provisions of the 1978 amendments brought the PSE share for those occupational groups to about their levels among the long term unemployed and also reduced the share of craft jobs filled by new PSE enrollees relative to the long term unemployed. Conversely, relatively larger proportions of PSE than of the long term unemployed were classified in the lower skill occupations of laborer, service worker, and clerk after 1978 (table 49). These shifts indicate that the program was more often serving its primary target group—persons experiencing the greatest difficulty in obtaining employment.

## The Role of Nonprofit Organizations

Nonprofit organizations (NPOs) have participated in employment and training programs since the early sixties. Their role was acknowledged in the original CETA legislation and given special emphasis in the Conference Report on the 1976 CETA amendments which stated, "The conferees expect prime sponsors to provide a substantial portion of the PSE project funds to nonprofit agencies. . . ." The conferees believed that PSE operated by nonprofit organizations "would insure that real new jobs are created and avoid the substitution of federal funds for services customarily provided by state and local governments."[5] In implementing the

5. U.S. Congress, House, *Emergency Jobs Program Extension Act of 1976, Conference Report,* H.R. Rept. 94-1514, 94th Congress, September 13, 1976, p. 17.

Table 49
Distribution of Occupations of New Public Service Employment Enrollees
and the Long Term Unemployed, Fiscal 1978 and 1979

| | 1978 | | 1979 | |
|---|---|---|---|---|
| Occupational group | Jobs of new PSE enrollees | Last job of the long term unemployed | Jobs of new PSE enrollees[a] | Last job of the long term unemployed |
| | (Percent of total) | | | |
| Total ................................ | 100 | 100 | 100 | 100 |
| Professional, technical, and managerial ............. | 20 | 13 | 14 | 13 |
| Clerical ............. | 24 | 14 | 28 | 14 |
| Sales ............. | 0 | 4 | 0 | 4 |
| Craft workers ............. | 11 | 12 | 8 | 11 |
| Operatives ............. | 6 | 22 | 6 | 22 |
| Laborers ............. | 21 | 9 | 24 | 10 |
| Service workers ............. | 18 | 15 | 21 | 15 |
| No work experience ............. | 0 | 11 | 0 | 11 |

SOURCE: PSE—Special tabulations, *Continuous Longitudinal Manpower Survey*, Westat, Inc. Long term unemployed—*1980 Employment and Training Report of the President*, p. 267.

NOTE: Detail may not add to totals because of rounding.

a. Refers to second half of FY 1979—after the effective date of the new wage and eligibility restrictions.

congressional intent the DOL was more explicit. It interpreted "substantial" to mean at least one-third.[6]

A study made after the 1976 amendments found major differences between PSE programs operated by nonprofit organizations and government agencies with respect to the kinds of persons employed and the services performed. Enrollees in nonprofit organizations were much more likely than those in government agencies to be working in professional and paraprofessional positions; PSE participants employed by government agencies were more likely to be working as laborers. PSE activities sponsored by nonprofits were more often social services and art projects; government agencies were more heavily oriented to public works and maintenance projects and to the development of park and recreation areas.[7]

## Influence of the Reauthorization Act on Nonprofit Organizations (NPOs)

Although the reauthorization act did not specifically modify the role of nonprofit organizations, many of its amendments significantly affected their participation in public service employment programs.

The nonprofit organization share of PSE employment increased sharply in the study areas after the 1978 amendments, from an average of 24 percent of total in 1977 to 38 percent in June 1980. In June 1980, an estimated 140,000 PSE participants were employed by private nonprofit organizations and 230,000, by government agencies. PSE participants were more than 3 percent of total employment in nonprofit organizations and less than 2 percent of all state

---

6. Field Memorandum 316-77, June 17, 1977.
7. Mirengoff et al., *CETA: Assessment,* pp. 147-48.

and local government employees.[8] Although PSE enrollees were only a small proportion of total employment in nonprofit organizations, they were sometimes a large share of the total in the agencies in which they worked.

The major factors in the increased share of PSE going to nonprofit organizations were the limits on PSE wages and the tighter eligibility requirements mandated by the 1978 CETA amendments (table 50). Government agencies found it difficult, or not in their interest, to establish PSE jobs at the low wages that were required. Nonprofit organizations, however, were eager to expand their activities and to serve the disadvantaged and were less deterred by the wage limits. In about one-third of the study areas local officials reported that the nonprofits were more willing than government agencies to employ the seriously disadvantaged.

The pattern, however, was not uniform. In about one-third of the study areas, the nonprofit organization share of PSE declined. The reason given most frequently was the decision by local officials, in the face of a reduced PSE program, to retain PSE positions in government agencies so that important public services could be continued. In these areas, the cutback in PSE was accomplished at the expense of the PSE operations of nonprofit organizations.

The effect of the requirement that PSE enrollees receive training was mixed. None of the respondents cited it as a most important factor in increasing or decreasing the role of NPOs. However, 26 percent mentioned it as a subsidiary factor in increasing the NPO share of PSE, and 15 percent said

---

8. Nonprofit organizations with 4,200,000 employees were assumed to be eligible for PSE. Included were nonprofit health, educational, and social service agencies, museums, etc. See U.S. Department of Commerce, Bureau of the Census, *1977 Census of Service Industries,* 5C77-A-53 (Part 2), pp. 52-53 for information on employment in private nonprofit organizations. In June 1980, employment in state and local governments was 13,400,000. See U.S. Department of Labor, Bureau of Labor Statistics, *Employment and Earnings,* September 1980, p. 58.

it had the opposite effect. In areas where the share for non-profit organizations was reduced, the respondents indicated that the relatively small number of PSE participants and the scattered location of the nonprofit organizations made it difficult to set up training classes. Where the training requirement tended to increase the PSE positions given to nonprofit organizations, it was because they were more willing than government agencies to deal with the complications involved in linking training and PSE jobs.

**Table 50**
**Reasons for Increase or Decrease in the**
**Nonprofit Organization Share of PSE Enrollments**
**Sample Prime Sponsor Areas**

| Reason | Increases: importance ranking | | | Decreases: importance ranking | | |
|---|---|---|---|---|---|---|
| | 1 | 2 | 3 | 1 | 2 | 3 |
| | (Percent of all replies) | | | | | |
| Wage limits in 1978 amendments ...... | 70 | 7 | 0 | 0 | 4 | 0 |
| Eligibility requirements ... | 0 | 26 | 7 | 7 | 0 | 4 |
| Requirement to serve target groups .......... | 4 | 11 | 11 | 0 | 0 | 0 |
| Training requirements .... | 0 | 11 | 15 | 0 | 11 | 4 |
| Change in size of PSE program .......... | 0 | 0 | 4 | 26 | 7 | 0 |
| Sponsor liability for ineligible enrollees ...... | 0 | 0 | 0 | 7 | 4 | 0 |
| Increased monitoring requirements .......... | 0 | 0 | 0 | 7 | 7 | 7 |
| Other................... | 11 | 0 | 4 | 4 | 0 | 7 |

SOURCE: Reports from 26 areas.

Other changes introduced by the 1978 CETA amendments, such as the prime sponsors' increased financial liability for the enrollment of ineligibles and the increased monitoring requirements also influenced, to some degree, the sponsors' decisions on where to allocate their PSE slots. In no instance did these requirements work to increase the

NPOs' share, and in several instances, these factors tended to reduce the number of PSE enrollees placed in nonprofit organizations. Some sponsors, in the face of the new liability provisions, were reluctant to entrust the PSE program to organizations with limited managerial strength. Others felt that it would be more difficult to monitor the activities of nonprofit organizations.

## Effects of Increased Role of Nonprofit Organizations

To assess the effects of the increased participation of non-profit organizations in PSE programs, local officials were asked how the use of these organizations affected the kinds of persons enrolled, the usefulness of the services provided, and the subsequent placement of enrollees in regular jobs.

The major impact expected was a lower rate of transition to unsubsidized employment. Several reasons were cited. In about three-fifths of the areas, most local officials believed that the skills involved in the PSE activities of nonprofit organizations were less relevant to the labor market than jobs in government agencies. The PSE jobs sponsored by nonprofit agencies less often had a counterpart in private industry. Supervision was alleged to be inadequate, hence less learning occurred. In addition, three-fourths of all respondents thought that the ability of nonprofit organizations to absorb PSE enrollees as part of their regular staffs was more limited than government agencies because of their limited resources and job openings.

In about half the areas which reported an increased share of PSE going to nonprofit organizations, local officials said that the larger share was associated with higher enrollment of the more seriously disadvantaged. The causality ran two ways. In some areas, a greater share of PSE positions was contracted to nonprofit organizations because they were more willing than government agencies to employ and work with the seriously disadvantaged. In instances where government agencies found it difficult or were less willing to create low-wage jobs, a large share of the PSE program went to nonprofit organizations which, in turn, were more likely to enroll the seriously disadvantaged.

Public officials in a large majority of the study areas found it difficult to compare the usefulness of PSE services provided by nonprofit organizations with those provided by government agencies. However, the consensus was that although the kinds of services differed, the greater use of nonprofit organizations did not have an appreciable effect on the overall usefulness of the PSE services.

The shift of a greater share of PSE to nonprofit agencies was expected to affect the types of services. PSE sponsored by government agencies was perceived as more likely to provide "basic" services such as maintenance of public facilities, police, fire protection, and educational services to the broad public, whereas nonprofit organizations were more likely to provide social services to a more limited disadvantaged population. This is consistent with the findings of earlier studies on the PSE activities of government agencies and nonprofit organizations.[9]

## Effects on Usefulness of PSE

### Basis for Determining PSE Services

More often than not, decisions on which public services to provide through PSE were based on administrative considerations rather than on their advantage to the community. A plurality of areas (36 percent) ranked the wage rates per-

---

9. Mirengoff et al., *CETA: Assessment,* pp. 145-51.

mitted for PSE as the most important factor. PSE slots went to government agencies or nonprofit organizations that could establish jobs for enrollees at low-wage levels even if it resulted in less useful services. Positive considerations—community need for the services and the likelihood that the PSE job experience would lead to a regular job for the enrollee—ranked second and third in importance. The skills available among PSE applicants also influenced the types of services provided. They were, however, most frequently mentioned as a secondary factor (table 51).

## Usefulness of Services

PSE continued to provide useful community services to all but one of the areas in the survey. However, in half of the 28 areas the public services were perceived as less beneficial than those available prior to the 1978 amendments. Officials in one area thought services were more useful, and the remainder reported little change.

Table 51
Basis for Determining PSE Services
Sample Prime Sponsor Areas

| | Importance ranking | | |
|---|---|---|---|
| Factor | 1 | 2 | 3 |
| | (Percent of reporting areas) | | |
| Wage rates permitted for PSE............... | 36 | 14 | 18 |
| Usefulness or community need for the services......................... | 29 | 7 | 11 |
| Likelihood that the work would lead to a permanent job ..................... | 14 | 11 | 29 |
| Skills available among PSE applicants........ | 7 | 43 | 14 |
| Capability of agencies to carry out their proposals........................ | 4 | 4 | 18 |
| Political considerations .................... | 7 | 11 | 7 |
| PSE training requirements................. | 0 | 11 | 4 |
| Other ................................. | 4 | 0 | 0 |

SOURCE: Reports from 28 areas.

NOTE: Detail adds to more than 100 percent because of rounding.

Views on the usefulness of PSE to participants after the 1978 amendments were less frequently negative. Respondents in 39 percent of the survey areas thought the effects of the amendments were adverse, while 29 percent considered them to be beneficial. The remaining one-third perceived little difference (table 52).

**Table 52**
**Effect of Reauthorization Act on Usefulness of PSE Services**
**to the Community and to the Participants**
**Sample Prime Sponsor Areas**

| Effect on usefulness | Percent of reporting areas |
|---|---|
| **To the community:** | |
| More useful | 4 |
| About as useful | 46 |
| Less useful | 50 |
| **To the participants:** | |
| More useful | 29 |
| About as useful | 32 |
| Less useful | 39 |

SOURCE: Reports from 28 areas.

## Effects of Wage Restrictions

A large majority of the CETA directors stated that the wage limits in the 1978 amendments lessened the usefulness of the PSE program to communities and participants (table 53). In a number of areas, the permissible PSE wage was below the established rate even for entry level positions. To avoid violating the prevailing wage requirement, sub-entry jobs were created. However, in the view of many prime sponsors, these jobs did not provide the kinds of services most needed by the community; nor did the PSE enrollees receive the kinds of job experience that would substantially improve their opportunities for unsubsidized employment.

**Table 53**
**Effect of PSE Reauthorization Act Provisions on the Usefulness**
**of Services to the Community and to the Participants**
**Sample Prime Sponsor Areas**

| Factor | Effect on usefulness | | | |
| --- | --- | --- | --- | --- |
| | Less useful | About as useful | More useful | Don't know |
| | (Percent of reporting areas) | | | |
| **Affecting community services:** | | | | |
| Wage limits ............... | 82 | 18 | 0 | 0 |
| More restrictive eligibility requirements ............... | 64 | 32 | 4 | 0 |
| PSE/training requirements .... | 32 | 18 | 39 | 11 |
| 18-month limit on enrollee participation ......... | 32 | 50 | 14 | 4 |
| Smaller size PSE program ..... | 71 | 21 | 4 | 4 |
| **Affecting services to participants:** | | | | |
| Wage limits ............... | 64 | 32 | 4 | 0 |
| More restrictive eligibility requirements ............... | 32 | 43 | 25 | 0 |
| PSE/training requirements .... | 18 | 0 | 75 | 7 |
| 18-month limit on enrollee participation ......... | 18 | 43 | 39 | 0 |
| Smaller size PSE program ..... | 43 | 36 | 7 | 14 |

SOURCE: Reports from 28 areas.

## Effects of Eligibility Criteria

The usefulness to the community of the services provided by PSE was also diminished by the more restrictive participant eligibility criteria according to 64 percent of the CETA directors. The tighter eligibility rules had the intended effect of limiting PSE jobs to seriously disadvantaged workers, but the trade off was lower quality and reduced output of services. This was reflected in comments by local officials such as, "A more needy client population is now being served . . . skill levels are lower and quality of services has declined." Another said, "As a result of higher unemployment, many persons with skills were looking for work but did not qualify for CETA because of the strict eligibility requirements.''

Perceptions of the job performance of PSE workers were less favorable after the 1978 amendments. In 1977, when local officials were asked to compare the work of PSE enrollees with that of non-CETA employees in similar jobs, about 70 percent said that performance was about the same. Only one in six of the officials judged PSE workers to be below average and almost as high a proportion said they were better than the regular workers. In mid-1979, after the more restrictive eligibility requirements had been in effect for about nine months and new wage limitations for about three months, about a third of the officials rated PSE workers "below average," and none reported them to be superior to regular workers. Some additional deterioration in the perception of PSE worker performance had occurred by the time of the latest survey in late 1980 (table 54).

**Table 54**
**Job Performance Rating of PSE Workers**
**Sample Prime Sponsor Areas**
**1977, 1979, and 1980**

| | Rating | | |
|---|---|---|---|
| Survey year | Below average | About average | Above average |
| | (Percent of replies) | | |
| 1977[a] .............. | 16 | 71 | 13 |
| 1979[b] .............. | 32 | 68 | 0 |
| 1980[c] .............. | 39 | 59 | 2 |

a. Reports from 117 respondents in 27 areas.
b. Reports from 78 respondents in 26 areas.
c. Reports from 105 respondents in 28 areas.

## Effects of Training Requirement

Recognizing that the effect of the eligibility and wage changes would be to enroll persons with greater employability development needs, the reauthorization act mandated that PSE participants receive off-the-job training in addition to their work assignments. Officials in 75 percent of the study areas reported that the training requirement made the program more useful to participants, and in 18 percent of the areas they expressed negative views. In the few remaining areas, respondents felt that the training was only marginally effective or that it was too early to assess its impact.

PSE training was also presumed to enhance the usefulness of community services. The beneficial effects—improved skill levels—were viewed as long-run advantages. The proportion (39 percent) of CETA administrators who held this view was slightly larger than those who believed community services would be adversely affected (32 percent). The latter group ascribed this effect to such short-run considerations as the disruptive effect on work output. Some also believed that the training provided was not pertinent to the PSE job. (Chapter 5 discusses training activities more extensively.)

### Effects of the 18-Month Limitation

In about half the study areas, the 18-month limit on enrollee participation had little effect on the usefulness of the PSE services to the community or to the enrollee. Administrators in the other areas, however, thought it was more likely to help the enrollee and hurt the public services. The limit on participation was perceived as helping the PSE enrollee in two ways: (a) the employing agency was forced to make a decision on whether to hire the worker for its regular staff or lose him/her, and (b) faced with a firm termination date, the worker was motivated to actively seek unsubsidized employment.

Where the limit on duration of enrollment reduced the effectiveness of the PSE services, it was attributed to higher turnover and the more frequent need to train new participants for ongoing PSE services. In a few areas the productivity of the enrollees and their commitment to the PSE job had fallen off because of the temporary character of the job.

A few areas had established their own tighter limits on participation—usually 12 months—in order to encourage transition and to serve more people.

### Effect of Reduction in PSE Program

The effect of the 40 percent reduction in the number of PSE participants from 555,000 in September 1979 to 328,000 a year later was predictable. Most CETA directors pointed out that the smaller size of the program meant that useful services were discontinued and fewer enrollment opportunities were available for needy applicants.

In areas where the program was cut by at least 20 percent, two-thirds of the respondents said that the reduced size of the program had very little independent effect on the types of jobs and services that were eliminated. High-wage jobs were dropped because of the need to reach a lower average wage. The reduction in program size merely made unnecessary the establishment of low-wage replacements.

Where the smaller program size did influence the mix of jobs and services it was usually due to a decision by the prime sponsor to maintain PSE slots with government agencies even though that required relatively deep cuts for nonprofit organizations. The social service and arts programs provided by the nonprofit organizations were deemed less essential than the assistance PSE had been giving government agencies.

One indication of the usefulness of PSE services is the extent to which they were continued after federal support was withdrawn. In 25 of the 28 study areas, PSE enrollment declined by more than 20 percent between fiscal years 1978 and 1980. In 64 percent of these areas, some of the services were continued with local funding and in 16 percent, more than one-fourth of the activities were picked up with local funds (table 55).

**Table 55**
**Percent of Activities Discontinued by PSE**
**Which Were Continued with Local Funding**
**Sample Prime Sponsor Areas**

| Percent of former PSE activities which were continued | Percent of reporting areas |
| --- | --- |
| Zero ........................................... | 36 |
| Less than 10................................... | 24 |
| 10 to 25 ...................................... | 24 |
| More than 25.................................. | 16 |

SOURCE: Reports from 25 areas.

Most frequently, those retained were associated with police work—community service officers, parapolice and police technicians. Various other activities were also continued—energy conservation, transportation services for the elderly, administration, planning, public works, and social case work in nonprofit organizations. In four-fifths of the areas where services were continued with local funding, most PSE enrollees were retained; the remaining areas retained some PSE workers.

## Factors Having Greatest Impact on Usefulness

Of all the changes in the reauthorization act affecting the usefulness of PSE, the wage limits were the most influential. They were the dominant—and adverse—factor with respect to community services in over 60 percent of the reporting areas according to local officials. Thirty-seven percent cited their adverse effect on participants. Only one of the 1978 amendments—training requirements—exercised a predominantly positive influence, for both participants and community services (table 56).

**Table 56**
**Factors Having the Greatest Impact on the Usefulness**
**of PSE Services to the Community and to the Participants**
**Sample Prime Sponsor Areas**

| Factor | Percent of reporting areas |
|---|---|
| **Affecting community services:** | |
| **Total** ..................................... | **100** |
| Adverse effect | |
|    Wage limits ............................. | 61 |
|    Eligibility requirements ..................... | 21 |
|    Smaller size PSE program .................. | 11 |
|    18-month limit on participation ............. | 0 |
| Favorable effect | |
|    PSE training requirements ................. | 7 |
| **Affecting services to participants:** | |
| **Total** ..................................... | **100** |
| Adverse effect | |
|    Wage limits ............................. | 37 |
|    Eligibility requirements ..................... | 15 |
|    Smaller size PSE program .................. | 4 |
| Favorable effect | |
|    PSE training requirements ................. | 33 |
|    18-month limit on participation ............. | 11 |

SOURCE: Reports from 28 areas.

The adverse effects of lower wages cited by local officials in some areas seem extreme in relation to the size of the reduction in the permitted average wage from $7,800 to $7,200 or 9 percent. However, the reduction came at a time when wages for regular employees were increasing. The $7,800 average was already scraping the bottom of the local government wage scale for a number of areas. An earlier report found that in large northern and western cities the PSE wages permitted under the 1978 amendments were generally below the entry wage level for such lower skills jobs as Class B typists, refuse collectors, janitors, and laborers.[10] In addition, the flexibility that the prime sponsors had to supplement PSE wages was cut back in the 1978 amendments.

## Summary

The restrictive wage provisions of the 1978 amendments accomplished their objective of focusing the PSE programs more sharply on those most in need of employment assistance. There were, however, adverse consequences: difficulties in establishing PSE positions and reduced usefulness of PSE activities.

### Adjustments to 1978 Reauthorization

The 1978 wage provisions reduced the national annual average wage for PSE jobs from about $7,820 per year in the first half of fiscal 1979 to $7,360 in the last half. In many areas the permissible PSE wages had slipped below the prevailing wages for jobs previously used for PSE. Agencies were compelled to discontinue many higher wage PSE positions, restructure others, or create new low-wage jobs. Many shifted PSE slots to nonprofit organizations that were better able to accommodate the lower wage requirements.

The effect of these strategies was to decrease the proportion of PSE jobs requiring specialized skills and increase the share of minimal skill jobs. As a result, the opportunities and incentives for "creaming" among eligible applicants were much reduced, and the occupational composition of PSE jobs was then more like the pattern of jobs last held by the long term unemployed.

---

10. Mirengoff et al., *The New CETA*, p. 80.

Supplementation of the CETA wage, which was fairly extensive prior to the 1978 amendments, was almost entirely eliminated in over three-fourths of the study areas. PSE employers, unable under the new wage provisions to establish the kinds of skilled positions they most preferred, were unwilling to use their own funds to support the low level jobs permitted under the amendments.

Persons who applied for PSE jobs after the 1978 amendments had fewer job skills than earlier applicants. The more restrictive eligibility requirements screened out many of the better qualified workers, and the lower wages made the PSE jobs less attractive to eligible workers who had alternative opportunities.

Nonprofit organizations increased their share of PSE jobs substantially after the 1978 amendments from 24 percent of total in 1977 to 38 percent in 1980. The shift to nonprofits was due primarily to the imposition of wage limits in the 1978 amendments. It was harder for government agencies than for nonprofit organizations to set up low-wage PSE jobs that paid the prevailing rate for similar jobs. However, in about one-third of the study areas the share of PSE going to nonprofits declined. These areas preferred to reserve a larger share of a smaller PSE program to continue important public services provided by government agencies.

The increased share of PSE by nonprofit organizations was believed to reduce the likelihood that enrollees would move from PSE to unsubsidized jobs. A majority of local officials believed that the skills learned in a nonprofit organization were not readily transferable to private industry and that nonprofit organizations had fewer openings in their regular staffs than government agencies.

The price paid for achieving the targeting objectives of the 1978 amendments was reduced usefulness of PSE activities.

In half of the study areas, local officials said PSE was less useful than previously to the community, and in 39 percent of the areas the program was believed to be less useful to participants. The major factor was the requirement for lower PSE wages. The kinds of jobs created to conform to lower PSE wages did not provide services as useful as those previously supplied and the new low-wage jobs often did not provide the participants with the kinds of job experience that would improve their employability.

## Wage Limits and CETA Decentralization

The wage amendments of the reauthorization act accomplished what they set out to do: reserve larger proportions of PSE jobs for the seriously disadvantaged, reduce the tier of high salary positions, and discourage the use of PSE workers in place of locally financed regular employees. However, the wage constraints chipped away at a philosophical pillar of CETA—decentralization of program control from the federal to local governments. The range of PSE jobs that local officials could approve was narrowed and, as a consequence, the services were limited, their usefulness diluted, and some local agencies that considered the tradeoffs to be disadvantageous withdrew from the PSE programs.

The study examined the question of whether the congressional objectives for PSE could have been attained by the eligibility restrictions alone. The survey findings suggest that to achieve the targeting objectives the wage provisions were a necessary supplement to the eligibility restrictions.

# 7 The Role of Organized Labor in CETA

Organized labor has been closely involved with the Comprehensive Employment and Training Act since its inception. Unions generally have been sympathetic to the CETA goals, but they have also sought to ensure that the implementation of CETA programs would not adversely affect the interests of union members. Congress and the Department of Labor sought organized labor's support and involvement because (1) unions are knowledgeable in matters relating to training needs, content, and methods; and (2) union surveillance of prime sponsor planning and operations was expected to forestall activities that would disrupt union-management relations or jeopardize established wages and working conditions. Several provisions in the law and in the regulations provide the framework for union involvement in local CETA programs.

Organized labor has had a national as well as a local role. The CETA principle of decentralization to local and state governments was tempered by providing that national organizations, such as organized labor, with a history of in-

The author of this chapter is Dr. Jack Chernick, Professor Emeritus, Institute of Management and Labor Relations, Rutgers University.

227

volvement in employment and training programs, would continue to be funded directly by the Secretary of Labor. Labor organizations have operated a number of nationally funded CETA training and technical assistance programs.

This chapter examines the participation of labor organizations in CETA activities at both local and national levels. It is introduced by a brief description of organized labor's position on employment and training policy. Data drawn from reports on 28 prime sponsor areas are supplemented by information supplied by the Department of Labor and labor organizations. In each of the survey areas, field research associates discussed issues touching on union participation with at least one labor representative familiar with the activities of the prime sponsor, with the CETA administrator, and with officials in agencies employing CETA participants.

## Organized Labor's Views
## on Employment and Training Policy

Spokesmen for organized labor see employment and training policy as part of a larger set of economic policies designed to maintain high levels of employment. Persistent, high unemployment is taken as evidence that the private sector is unable to provide jobs to employ all those willing and able to work. In light of this, labor maintains that public policy should include measures which increase employment in the public sector through subsidized public service employment, public works, and urban development. In addition to absorbing the unemployed, such activities would supplement the supply of public services. Labor supports training of the disadvantaged provided this can be done in skills and occupational lines for which there is likely to be a demand at the end of training. It also favors the upgrading of workers stuck in low level entry jobs, and retraining workers whose skills have been made obsolete by technological change or international competition. Whatever the program, a major concern is that nothing be done to weaken the standards governing wages and working conditions of regular workers as incorporated in collective bargaining agreements.

The rationale for labor support of employment and training programs was clearly expressed in testimony offered by representatives of the AFL-CIO in the course of hearings in February 1972, which led eventually to enactment of CETA.[1] Against the background of 5.5 million unemployed in January 1972 (without allowance for hidden unemployment), the AFL-CIO spokesman insisted that the 150,000 jobs envisioned in the Emergency Employment Act passed some six months earlier were inadequate. He argued for a substantially larger program of public service employment in the CETA proposal.

> . . . the fundamental concern of the AFL-CIO is with jobs. We want a large-scale public service employment program—to meet the job and income needs of American workers who can't find jobs in the private sector of the economy and also to meet the needs of our society for vastly expanded services in the public sector.[2]

In respect to training, the position of the AFL-CIO was elaborated as follows:

> A manpower program consisting mainly of training is simply not an adequate manpower program. We recognize that disadvantaged workers need training to compete effectively for available jobs and we support such training—but we repeat that

---

1. See statement of Kenneth Young, Assistant Director, Department of Legislation, AFL-CIO, U.S. Congress, House, *Hearings before the Select Subcommittee of Labor of the Committee on Education and Labor,* 92nd Congress, February 17, 1972, p. 736.

2. Ibid., p. 739.

> training without job opportunities for those trained is a con game producing social dynamite. . . .

> . . . in the establishment of manpower programs, in both the private and public sectors, we insist on provision of adequate wage and working standards . . . federal funds should not be used to supplant present payrolls in either the public or private sector.[3]

The AFL-CIO position was reiterated in many forums. In 1978, after the addition and expansion of Title VI, the AFL-CIO called for further increases. The goal proposed by the AFL-CIO Executive Council was 1.1 million PSE job slots in fiscal year 1979 instead of the then authorized level of 750,000 slots.

In hearings on the CETA reauthorization of 1978, AFL-CIO spokesmen opposed a number of the changes proposed by the administration, but took pains to point out that ". . . the AFL-CIO wants to make it clear that it continues to support CETA as the nation's major manpower program."[4] In the same presentation the AFL-CIO took exception to the form of the Title VII Private Sector Initiatives Program as it appeared in the Senate bill and reiterated a central concern of organized labor in all manpower legislation.

> Whatever disposition is made by Congress of the Administration's Private Sector Initiative Program, it is essential that the wage and labor standards and protections and anti-displacement requirements and other requirements of Section 121,

---

3. Ibid.

4. Statement by Kenneth Young, Associate Director of Legislation, AFL-CIO, to the Senate Committee on Human Resources, Subcommittee on Employment, Poverty, and Migratory Labor on S. 2570, *The Comprehensive Employment and Training Amendments of 1978,* March 1, 1978, p. 864.

amended as we have proposed, be applied to the final version of PSIP.[5]

The views on employment and training policy formulated and expressed at the level of the Federation have carried over, in their essential, to the international and local unions that have been called on to participate in the implementation of CETA. But the adaptation at the local level has by no means been uniform. The variety of experience may be glimpsed in the account of union involvement in the 28 prime sponsor areas surveyed.

## Labor Participation in Local CETA Programs

Policy makers in the legislative and executive branches of the federal government sought to ensure that organized labor would have the opportunity to participate in the implementation of and contribute to the accomplishment of its goals. For several years before CETA, the AFL-CIO and several major national unions contracted with the Department of Labor to provide services designed to promote the training and employment objectives of the Manpower Development and Training Act and the Economic Opportunity Act. With the decentralization of employment and training programs, emphasis shifted to inducing participation at the local prime sponsor level.

Organized labor's participation in local CETA activities has dual objectives—ensuring that the training received by CETA participants is effective for obtaining employment, and protecting the rights and working standards of union members.

The chief formal mechanism for organized labor's participation in local CETA programs is the provision in CETA

---

5. Ibid.

(Sec. 109) requiring the prime sponsor to form a planning council composed of representatives of community groups, including labor unions. In addition, Section 104 specifies that the prime sponsor shall submit master and annual plans for review to "labor organizations in the area which represent employees engaged in work similar to that proposed to be funded. . . ." Labor officials also can seek informally to make their opinions and concerns known to the CETA administrator and staff.

With the addition of the Title VII Private Sector Initiative Program in 1978, the requirement for labor representation was extended to the private industry councils (PICs). Moreover, annual CETA plans include a section on proposed activities under Title VII, thus making it available to appropriate labor organizations not directly represented on the PIC.

The regulations require union consultation or concurrence. Prime sponsors must obtain written concurrence from the appropriate union when training or employment activities are proposed that may affect existing collective bargaining agreements. Even where existing contracts are not affected, prime sponsors are to consult with appropriate unions before launching employment or training programs in occupations that are substantially equivalent to these in which employees are represented by unions.

The sections that follow examine the participation and influence of labor organizations in the CETA system, and the effects of the CETA programs on labor standards and collective bargaining agreements.

## Participation in the Planning Process

Organized labor is in a position to influence local CETA plans through membership on the planning council, through a formal review of the prime sponsor's comprehensive plan before it is submitted to the DOL, and by informal exchange of views with the CETA administrator or the staff.

*Representation on the planning council.* The planning councils created by the CETA legislation are to "participate in the development of, and submit recommendations regarding, the comprehensive employment and and training plan." Although the recommendations of the council are to be given special consideration, responsibility for final decisions remains with the prime sponsor.

There were labor representatives on all but one of the CETA councils in the study areas.[6] About half the councils had a single labor member and most of the others had two or three. On the average, labor representatives constituted about 8 percent of the council membership in 1980, but there was considerable variation (table 57).

Table 57
Number of Labor Representatives on CETA Planning Councils
Sample Prime Sponsor Areas, 1980

| Number of labor representatives | Percent of reporting areas | Total membership of planning councils (Range) |
| --- | --- | --- |
| 0................. | 4 | 29 |
| 1................. | 46 | 10-30 |
| 2................. | 18 | 19-27 |
| 3................. | 29 | 21-38 |
| More than 3 ........ | 4 | 64 |

SOURCE: Reports from 28 areas.
NOTE: Detail adds to more than 100 because of rounding.

Members of CETA planning councils are appointed by local elected officials. The labor members were chosen after

6. The one exception was a balance-of-state council where the labor representative had resigned 18 months before the survey but had not been replaced. There were, however, labor representatives on the substate regional CETA advisory boards.

consultation with labor leaders in three-fourths of the 28 study areas. Preponderantly, those selected represented central bodies rather than the local unions or district councils of international unions. In 16 of the areas, the AFL-CIO central labor council was represented on the planning council; additionally, building trade councils or individual unions supplied representatives in almost half of the areas. Staff members of the Human Resources Development Institute (HRDI) served on six planning councils.[7] The American Federation of State, County and Municipal Employees (AFSCME), whose members work alongside PSE enrollees, had members on only three of the councils despite the fact that the large expansion of public service employment impinged very significantly on the interests of that union (table 58). The explanation may well be that the labor representatives were selected at an earlier stage of CETA when public service employment was a relatively minor part of the program. However, in two-thirds of the study areas labor members on the council were from unions which represented workers in jobs similar to those filled by PSE workers.

Organized labor's influence on local CETA plans and operations depends in large part on the interest and effectiveness of the union representatives on the CETA planning council and their initiative in informing individual union locals on matters that affect their interests. Even if a prime sponsor appoints more than the single labor representative required by law,[8] it is seldom possible to appoint representatives from all the unions that might have an interest in CETA. In 19 of 28 survey areas, union representatives

7. HRDI is a research and technical assistance arm of the AFL-CIO which encourages local union participation in CETA, provides technical assistance, and cooperates with local unions in placing CETA enrollees in jobs. Field staff of HRDI are located in a number of metropolitan areas. Its activities in employment and training programs are discussed later in this chapter.

8. The appointment of more than one representative is, in fact, recommended by the DOL. See Field Memorandum No. 134-80, February 27, 980, p. 6.

reported to a labor organization on CETA activities. In some cases the reporting was irregular and informal, suggesting that unless some major issue came up at a planning council meeting, very little information would be transmitted to other local union officials. In other areas, however, the representation function was taken seriously and apparently worked to give labor organizations the kind of voice in CETA decision making that was contemplated in the legislation.

**Table 58**
**Organized Labor Representation on CETA Planning Councils**
**Sample Prime Sponsor Areas, 1980**

| Type of labor organization | Percent of reporting areas |
|---|---|
| AFL-CIO central council .............. | 57 |
| Construction trades .................... | 46 |
| HRDI .............................. | 21 |
| AFSCME .......................... | 11 |
| Other ............................... | 46 |

SOURCE: Reports from 28 areas.
NOTE: Detail adds to more than 100 percent because many councils had more than one union member.

Organized labor's role in the Ramsey County, Minnesota planning council where unions had three labor representatives out of a total of 21 members illustrates this kind of active relationship. One of the labor members was drawn from the local Building and Trades Assembly, a central labor organization; the second came from a Teamsters' local that represented municipal workers; and the third was a staff member of HRDI. The Building and Trades representative was chairman of the CETA planning council as well as secretary of the Building and Trades Assembly. The Assembly regularly received reports on general CETA activities, supplemented by ad hoc reports on union-related questions. When an issue arose that directly involved a local union, one of the three council labor members notified the union. If, for example, a proposed training program or a PSE position was thought likely to affect an employer whose employees were unionized, the union involved was informed. No other prime sponsor area in the sample reported so ample a transmission line between the planning council and the local labor organizations.

Some labor representatives who served on one or more planning council committees used them as an avenue for raising questions of concern to them and, on occasion, of influencing planning decisions of prime sponsors. Ten prime sponsors in the sample either had no committee structure or had committees without labor representation. In the remaining areas, labor representatives most often served on youth committees (10 areas); evaluation and monitoring committees (5 areas); and in four areas they served on executive committees. In several instances, union representatives—most commonly HRDI or central labor body members—were chairpersons of these committees.

*Organized labor's response to prime sponsors' plans.* CETA regulations require that labor organizations (and other groups) be given 30 days to review and comment on the prime sponsors' master and annual plans before they are submitted to the Department of Labor. Most prime sponsors complied with this requirement; in 26 out of the 28 areas labor organizations were invited to comment. In the other two, the practice appears to have fallen into disuse because labor organizations were disinterested and prime sponsors did not pursue the matter. The regulations also require that the complete plan be sent to "appropriate labor organizations," defined as those that represent employees in jobs that are the same or substantially equivalent to those for which the prime sponsor provides, or proposes to provide, employment and training under the Act.[9] The prime sponsor is thus faced with the decision as to which organizations to include in a mailing of the plan. In the majority of areas, Central Labor Councils and HRDI representatives serve as the channel through which the prime sponsor makes these plans available to potentially interested unions.

Reactions of labor organizations to the opportunity to comment on prime sponsor plans were mixed. In 12 prime sponsor areas no comments were offered or the plans were approved without accompanying comment; in 13 areas union representatives did submit responses and in three others union officials had influenced the plan during its preparation. Some union representatives complained that the role given labor unions in the development of CETA plans was too limited; others, that insufficient time had been allowed for a careful review of the plans. In several areas, unions urged increased labor representation on the planning council. Beyond these procedural matters, concern about the substance of planned activity ran in two basic directions: (a) protecting the wage and employment conditions of the regular employees in government and private industry, and (b) ensuring that the employment and training design and operation would enhance the employability of CETA participants.

Unions attempted to protect the status of their members in a number of ways:

- They sought to prevent the use of PSE workers to perform work that otherwise would be done by regular employees.
- They objected to training in occupations for which a surplus of labor existed. To this end, they sought ad-

9. U.S. Department of Labor, Employment and Training Administration, "CETA Regulations," *Federal Register,* Part IX, May 20, 1980, 675.4. In the grant application sent to the regional office of DOL, the prime sponsor is required to list the labor organizations to which the plan was mailed.

vance consultation, as provided for in the CETA regulations, on the types of skill training to be offered.

- In some areas, they objected to proposed PSE jobs that were below the prevailing rate for similar work performed by regular employees.
- In three areas, they requested upgrading programs for regular employees to be funded by CETA in order to equalize benefits with PSE workers who were given release time to participate in training programs.

Local labor officials also sought to improve the quality of CETA training programs:

- They criticized some training programs that, in their view, would not provide adequate skills or lead to unsubsidized employment.
- In a few areas, they tried to tie CETA training to apprenticeship programs.
- In one instance, the local union urged the prime sponsor to make greater use of community colleges, technical institutes, and vocational schools.

Other recommendations on behalf of CETA participants included hiring preference for regular public sector job openings, credit counseling, and a more effective grievance procedure (table 59).

*Influence of labor organizations on planning.* By and large, prime sponsors were meeting the formal requirements for involving organized labor in CETA planning. Yet an overall assessment of the depth and significance of union involvement led to the conclusion that, for the majority of prime sponsor areas in the sample, union participation did not have a substantive impact. In 19 of the 28 survey areas, the involvement of labor organizations in planning activities was described by field research associates as perfunctory and its influence as minimal. In five prime sponsor areas, however, the union presence was very much in evidence and its influence was substantial. Union influence was classified as moderate in three areas, while in the remaining case an AFSCME local exercised great influence, but through program operations, not through planning council activities.

### Table 59
### Organized Labor's Major Concerns with CETA Plans
### Sample Prime Sponsor Areas, 1980

| Concern | Percent of reporting areas |
|---|---|
| Greater participation in the planning process | 39 |
| Substitution of PSE workers for regular employees | 29 |
| Payment of prevailing wage to PSE workers | 21 |
| Training in skills that lead to a job | 21 |
| Quality of the training | 14 |
| Use of OJT to subsidize low-wage firms | 14 |
| More upgrading or retraining opportunities for regular employees | 11 |
| Advance consultation on OJT contracts | 11 |
| Other | 18 |

SOURCE: Reports from 28 areas.

NOTE: Detail adds to more than 100 percent because two or more concerns were expressed in some areas.

The reasons for these differences are complex. In about one-half of the areas where labor exercised little influence, it was by its own choice. Some labor representatives appeared to be uninterested in CETA, seldom attended council meetings, and did not react to the plans proposed by the prime sponsor. Their inaction may have been due in part to satisfaction with the proposed plan, or, alternatively, to the fact that earlier efforts to play a more substantive role had been frustrated. In the other half of the areas where labor's impact was limited, there were two explanations: (a) in some areas, particularly in the Midwest and the South, labor's views, even when expressed, carried little weight because its position in the local community was weak; and (b) in the other areas, labor's views were seriously considered but had little effect on the final plan.

This pattern of involvement may reflect an inherent weakness in the device relied upon to encourage participation. The advisory planning council is the vehicle for conveying to the prime sponsor the wishes and perceptions of community groups interested in employment and training. But this will work only if council members are well informed. In fact, very few members of councils have been able to or willing to devote the time and energy necessary to keep abreast of the constant stream of information, changes in program emphasis, and new programs that have engulfed the local prime sponsor. The influence of the councils varied widely, depending on the relationships of key members with the CETA administrators, elected officials, and the local community.

## Participation in Planning
## Title VII Programs

*Private Sector Initiative Program (PSIP).* Recognition that employment and training efforts had had limited success in opening opportunities in the private sector for the disadvantaged led to the addition of Title VII to the CETA legislation. Title VII established the private sector initiative program as a strategy to engage the cooperation of private firms in meeting the training and employment needs of the CETA target population. To assist prime sponsors in accomplishing these goals, the act called for the establishment of local private industry councils (PICs). Their functions include: serving as an intermediary between the employment and training agency and private business and industry; providing information about private sector needs for employment and training and the facilities available to meet those needs; and, together with the prime sponsor, developing specific employment and training projects. The composition of the PICs is stipulated in the provisions of Title VII and in DOL regulations. A majority of the members and the chairperson are to be drawn from local business and industry organizations (including small business and minority business). However, each PIC is to have at least one representative from organized labor.

Since the PSIP plans are included in the prime sponsor's annual plans they are available for review by appropriate labor organizations. Moreover, as in the development of other CETA training and employment projects, appropriate labor organizations must be consulted in the planning of activities and labor's concurrence must be secured prior to proceeding with programs which may impinge upon existing collective bargaining agreements.

The present survey attempted to determine the extent to which labor organizations participated in the development of PSIP plans, the problems that arose, and the perceptions of labor spokesmen with respect to the prospects for effective implementation of employment and training programs in the private sector. As of December 31, 1979, 448 out of a possible 470 prime sponsors had established private industry councils, and many of the others were well on their way to full PIC establishment.[10] At the time of the survey (October-December 1980), the PICs had been established for approximately one year, but because of funding uncertainties and other start-up problems were not fully operational in all the study areas.

---

10. See U.S. Department of Labor and U.S. Department of Health and Human Services, *1980 Employment and Training Report of the President* (Washington: Government Printing Office, 1980), p. 40. For an analysis of the implementation of Title VII, see Ripley et al., *A Formative Evaluation of the Private Sector Initiative Program,* Report 6, June 1981.

*Representation on private industry councils.* The number of labor representatives on the PICs ranged from one to five members, but half of the PICs in the sample of 28 had the minimum required single member (table 60). On the average, union representatives constituted 8 percent of the PIC membership; nearly two-thirds consisted of business and industry representatives.[11] In areas with a single union member, it is quite possible that many meetings of the council occurred without representation from organized labor. There is some evidence, too, that appointees to the PIC were often chosen from among labor representatives who were also serving on the planning council.

**Table 60**
**Number of Labor Representatives**
**on Private Industry Councils**
**Sample Prime Sponsor Areas, 1980**

| Number of labor representatives | Percent of reporting areas | Total PIC membership (Range) |
|---|---|---|
| 0[a] | 4 | 22 |
| 1 | 50 | 9-28 |
| 2 | 29 | 16-40 |
| 3 | 7 | 20-57 |
| More than 3 | 11 | 25-38 |

SOURCE: Reports from 28 areas.

NOTE: Detail adds to more than 100 percent due to rounding.

a. In one prime sponsor area the original appointee resigned; no replacement had been named by the date of the survey.

The regulations state that, in appointing labor members, the prime sponsor should consult with state or central labor bodies, building and construction trade councils, the Human Resources Development Institute, "as well as unions representing major occupations in the area." Most of the

---

11. *1980 Employment and Training Report of the President,* p. 40.

l̃abor representatives who served on the PICs did, in fact, represent central councils or HRDI. Among the international unions, United Automobile Workers' local supplied the largest number of representatives on PICs (table 61).

Table 61
Organized Labor Representation on Private Industry Councils
Sample Prime Sponsor Areas, 1980

| Type of labor organization | Percent of reporting areas |
|---|---|
| AFL-CIO central council ................ | 40 |
| Construction trades .................... | 36 |
| HRDI ............................... | 32 |
| UAW................................ | 14 |
| Other ............................... | 39 |

SOURCE: Reports from 28 areas.
NOTE: Detail adds to more than 100 percent because almost half the councils had more than one union member.

*Role of organized labor in Title VII plan development.* Representation on the PICs presents an opportunity for participation in planning private sector training activities, but does not ensure it. When asked whether organized labor had been involved in the development of proposals for private sector programs, the respondents in the study areas were about equally divided between those that reported substantive involvement and those that did not. In three areas, union representatives were described by field research associates as very active and influential in the organization and work of the private sector program. In one of these, the labor representative chaired the PIC and influenced the funding and content of proposals. Efforts were made to secure the participation of unions likely to have an interest in programs that were ultimately developed. In a second area, the union representative was vice-chairman of the PIC, and also chairman of the planning council. The PICs in 10 areas were described as having union representatives who participated somewhat actively, made suggestions in council meetings, and offered advice based on their knowledge of the labor market and the training required for skill development. In 12 cases, unions participated in the work of private industry councils, but with minimal interest and little influence. In several councils, the union representatives regarded their roles as limited to matters of direct interest to local unions, and they became involved only as programs appeared to affect collective bargaining agreements. In this regard, they were not unlike other council members who are protective of their institutional interests. In the remaining three areas, the PICs were not well enough established to permit judgments on the role of organized labor (table 62).

**Table 62**
**Participation of Organized Labor**
**in the Private Sector Initiative Program**
**Sample Prime Sponsor Areas**

| Extent of participation | Number of reporting areas |
| --- | :---: |
| Major role in program development . . . . . . . | 3 |
| Active participation in PIC deliberations . . . | 10 |
| Perfunctory or minimal participation . . . . . . | 12 |
| Too early to judge . . . . . . . . . . . . . . . . . . . . . | 3 |

SOURCE: Reports from 28 areas.

## Views of Organized Labor
## on Title VII

The predominant sentiment among union spokesmen was that the increased emphasis on the role of the private sector in training and employment programs is a desirable development in CETA. When union respondents were asked: "What is organized labor's view of the usefulness of the private sector initiative program (PSIP) in aiding disadvantaged workers in obtaining employment," almost two-thirds of those who replied saw private industry programs as a useful and productive means for reaching CETA goals.

|  | Number of prime sponsor areas |
|---|:---:|
| Very good, useful, best CETA program .... | 9 |
| Good, useful tool ...................... | 8 |
| May be useful, but not clearly evident ...... | 5 |
| Not useful ............................ | 4 |
| No response .......................... | 2 |
| Total ............................ | 28 |

Many who took this position saw greater job placement opportunities available in the private sector OJT programs in contrast to the limited job openings in the public sector or in nonprofit organizations. One respondent commented, "The jobs are in the private sector; that is where the disadvantaged are most likely to find openings, and that is what they should be trained for." When asked about the possible role for unions in this effort, a majority of respondents expected unions to have a substantive to major role in planning and operating such programs. These union spokesmen expressed an interest in playing a greater role in PIC deliberations and programs than they have in other CETA efforts.

What role does organized labor see for itself in PSIP?

|  | Number of prime sponsor areas |
|---|:---:|
| A large, important role ................. | 8 |
| Some substantive input ................. | 7 |
| Some input, but major role is to protect labor's interest .............. | 4 |
| Only role is to protect labor's interest ...... | 2 |
| No role at present ..................... | 5 |
| No response ......................... | 2 |
| Total ............................ | 28 |

Respondents who saw a large role for organized labor in PSIP tended to be those who consider that the new private sector approach in CETA is desirable. They also saw themselves as being able to provide expert assistance in defining future job prospects, designing training programs, and specifying the qualifications of instructors. Some added that employer and union representatives on the PIC are more likely to "talk the same language" than is true with the prime sponsor or other members of the planning council. As in many other aspects of CETA, the interests of labor representatives on the PICs were twofold: (a) the use of CETA to assist those most in need to participate successfully in the labor market; and (b) to ensure that this is done in ways that do not threaten the position of regular employees, union members, or collective bargaining arrangements.

## Organized Labor's Participation in Program Operations

Preceding sections have been concerned with the role of organized labor in the planning of CETA programs through the deliberations of the planning council and the PIC. Once a plan is approved by the regional office of DOL, its elements must be implemented by prime sponsor staff and subrecipients. The implementation process opens a number of potential avenues for participation by labor organizations, some of which are mandated by law. This section describes the manner in which unions handled their consultation and concurrence responsibilities and explores the character of union involvement in the operations phase of CETA.

### Consultation and Concurrence

Prime sponsors are obligated "to provide for the participation of organized labor in the design of programs and activities, and coordination in the subsequent operation of programs." Under this broad mandate, they must:

1. Consult with appropriate labor organizations . . . in the planning, design, and content of

the training, work experience, and public service employment . . . with respect to job descriptions, wage rates, training standards and arrangements, and occupations planned;

2.  Obtain written concurrence from the appropriate bargaining agent where a collective bargaining agreement exists with the participating employer covering occupations in which training or subsidized employment is proposed. . . .[12]

The important distinction between the two requirements lies in the relation of the proposed training to collective bargaining contracts: consultation, when there is general interest of a labor organization in an occupation for which training is proposed; and written concurrence when the proposed training programs, such as on-the-job training or a pre-apprentice program, are for jobs that are covered by a collective bargaining agreement. If the request for concurrence is not responded to in writing within 30 days of notification, the program may proceed.

Written requests for concurrence had gone to appropriate labor organizations in 16 of the study areas; in 11 areas no request for concurrence had been sent, while in one case, information was not available. Reasons for not requesting concurrence were either that no collective bargaining agreements were involved in any of the proposed training or PSE activities, or that formal procedures were unnecessary since the prime sponsors and union representatives were in sufficiently close contact to resolve any issues surrounding the proposed activities. There were some instances in which unions had so little interest in any CETA proceedings as to make formal attempts at consultation purposeless.

In 7 of the 16 prime sponsor areas where concurrence was requested, union objections had been raised to some of the

---

12. *Federal Register,* Part IX, May 20, 1980, 676.24(b).

proposed programs. The grounds for objection varied: three involved proposed PSE projects, and in every case the proposal was withdrawn. In one of these, a hospital union complained that the proposed program would use PSE enrollees in one part of the hospital while regular employees in another part would be laid off. A second involved a project in a county welfare agency. The union argued that the project would have overtaxed the supervisor to whom the enrollees were to be assigned. The third PSE proposal was challenged by a building trades council on the grounds that the painting to be done in a public building should instead be put up for bidding. In the remaining instances, union objections were to specific training programs, usually in building crafts. Most were resolved in discussions with prime sponsors. One training proposal for welding was withdrawn when the union representative (HRDI) pointed to the absence of jobs in that occupation.

In addition to those instances in which union objection to a proposed program was asserted in writing, there were six areas where the objections were handled through consultation.The objections centered on training programs which union officials thought were unnecessary or poorly designed. In some cases, the issues were resolved through modifications in the program; others were cancelled or were still pending at the time of the survey. In a few cases, the unions helped prepare an acceptable modification.

Apart from the involvement stemming from objections to proposed training programs, unions participated more broadly in CETA activities. In answer to a specific query, respondents in 15 areas replied that representatives of organized labor contributed to the design or operation of specific training programs other than PSE. They provided information on labor market needs, training content, and particularly on the possibilities for pre-apprentice and apprentice training.

Are there opportunities for union participation in the design and operation of programs that have not yet been exploited? A majority of prime sponsor and union representatives think there are; but when asked to specify what could be done, and to suggest why such opportunities had not been used more fully, the responses tended to be very general. One did propose that, "Labor could be involved more in the design phase of activities, could suggest programs, rather than just review those proposed by the prime sponsor." "However," he added, "the prime sponsor has never solicited this kind of involvement."

Some union representatives ascribed their limited participation to the inadequacy of union representation on councils and the difficulty of attending CETA meetings when they are held during the day.

### Delivery of Program Services

Unions may participate directly in the work of CETA by contracting to deliver services, and a number have done so. But these activities at the local level were dwarfed by the efforts undertaken by the national AFL-CIO and by international unions under Title III contracts. These instances of direct involvement of labor organizations in the employment and training system will be discussed in turn.

*Local contracts.* In almost half of the survey areas, prime sponsors contracted with labor organizations for delivery of some training or other services. Three prime sponsors awarded contracts to the United Automobile Workers: two for training in technical skills or OJT, and one for special job development and placement of CETA clients in auto plants. The International Brotherhood of Electrical Workers had one contract for training in a Skill Training Improvement Program.

In the remainder of the survey areas in which such contracts were noted, the contracting organization was a central labor body—either a local council, a state AFL-CIO federation, or in one case, the local office of HRDI. These organizations located openings in unionized plants, facilitated entry of CETA participants, and promoted apprenticeship opportunities. There were a number of instances in which training was provided, some of which was conducted in a classroom setting.

*National agreements.* While the bulk of CETA funds are allocated to local and state prime sponsors, Title III reserved a portion[13] to be administered directly by the Department of Labor in programs that serve groups considered to be particularly disadvantaged in the labor market. As it had for many years prior to CETA, the Department of Labor contracted with many national unions and other organizations to supply employment and training services under Title III.[14] The rationale for such activity was elaborated in a joint statement in 1967 by AFL-CIO President George Meany and Secretary of Labor Willard Wirtz: "To mobilize and utilize the vast resources of skilled talent and experience available within the labor movement to plan, develop, coordinate, and operate manpower programs for the hardcore unemployed."[15] The Department of Labor contracted with

---

13. Outlays for all Title III programs, including programs for native Americans, migrants, and other special groups, amounted to $0.5 billion or 6 percent of total CETA outlays in FY 1979. See *1980 Employment and Training Report of the President*, p. 25.

14. It is worth noting that in the discussions that preceded the enactment of CETA there was some concern on the part of AFL-CIO spokesmen that decentralization implied the end of the national programs which constituent unions were then operating. William H. Kolberg, then Assistant Secretary of Labor, describes a meeting with Kenneth Young of the AFL-CIO in which these concerns were voiced. Kolberg writes: "I assured him that we had no intention of taking this action with respect to union training programs and that as long as I was Assistant Secretary no such decentralization would take place." See William H. Kolberg, *Developing Manpower Legislation: A Personal Chronicle* (Washington: National Academy of Sciences, 1978), p. 38.

15. "Tenth Anniversary Report to the HRDI Board of Trustees" (Washington: AFL-CIO Human Resources Development Institute, 1978).

labor organizations for an additional reason: it was expected to influence firms and unions to provide greater access to major industries and occupational areas for minorities and other disadvantaged persons.

Under CETA Title III, organized labor has provided several services: operational, promotional, and technical assistance. The first included a variety of programs designed to foster the training and employment of persons eligible under CETA rules. The second grew out of the decentralization of CETA and entailed the use of union staff members to disseminate information about CETA and to encourage local union officials to become involved in the work of prime sponsor councils as well as the PICs. Under the third, union men and women have been trained to serve effectively at the local level.

The most extensive operational projects have been the Targeted Outreach Program (TOP) and the National OJT Program. TOP has sought to secure openings for minorities and women in apprenticeable jobs in the construction and other highly skilled occupations. Among the five organizations which contracted with the Department of Labor to sponsor such projects on a multiregional basis, three were union-related: the Human Resources Development Institute, the United Automobile Workers, and the International Association of Firefighters. The TOP projects have done no training; the aim has been to recruit "fairly qualified job seekers from the target groups, provide them with a relatively modest level of counseling, tutoring, and supportive services, and develop appropriate job opportunities to which they can be referred.[16]

TOP has operated in approximately 100 cities. In 22 of these, the projects have been coordinated by HRDI and in another 20, by locally based organizations, most of which

16. *1980 Employment and Training Report of the President,* p. 29.

are union affiliates. As indicated, TOP concentrates on apprenticeable jobs in the skilled construction trades. Although a high proportion of all apprenticeship programs registered with the Bureau of Apprenticeship and Training are in the construction trades, the persistent high rate of unemployed in the industry has kept down the number of openings for apprentices. Nevertheless, it is estimated by the DOL that TOP placed approximately 50,000 persons in skilled trade positions from 1967 to the end of FY 1976.[17] In FY 1979, half of the 14,000 placements made through TOP were in the skilled construction trades, while 6,500 individuals were placed in other skilled occupations and 800 went into nonskilled jobs.[18]

The national OJT program, like TOP, was established in the late 1960s. It has sought to open employment opportunities through the intervention of groups which have better access to job markets than do prime sponsors. Most of the 20 separate training projects have been operated by national labor organizations, and some employer associations also have participated. Training on the job, supplemented in some cases by classroom training, helps participants acquire the skills needed to function successfully in the labor market. Because participants in the projects immediately become part of the employer's workforce, their retention upon completion of the project is high—on the order of 70 percent. In 1979, some 17,000 persons received training under the program. Of those placed in unsubsidized jobs, approximately 24 percent were women and 46 percent were from minority groups.[19]

The second category of national agreements in which organized labor has had an important role has been pro-

---

17. Ibid.

18. Ibid. It should be noted also that TOP operations were substantially reduced following budget reductions for fiscal 1981 and 1982.

19. Ibid., pp. 29-30.

grams to promote effective union participation in the decentralized CETA system. As we have seen, the act opens opportunities for union participation, but this does not ensure that local labor organizations will take advantage of them. Under a national agreement with the Department of Labor to provide information to unions on the purpose, functions, and usefulness of employment and training programs, the HRDI has conducted leadership education and training programs to increase the effectiveness of union members who serve on planning councils, youth councils, and PICs. In addition, HRDI representatives, operating through a national network of 59 offices, have examined prime sponsor plans to identify problems relating to union involvement and try to resolve them either at the planning stage or in the design of specific training activities. Following the CETA amendments of 1978, the increased emphasis on prime sponsor consultation with labor organizations and the requirement of concurrence in certain circumstances enlarged the scope of technical assistance activities.

HRDI, like its counterpart in the business community, the National Alliance of Business, had the additional task of promoting the establishment of private industry councils through its own participation and by facilitating the participation of other labor organizations. The agreement between the DOL and HRDI for services in 1980 called on the organization to continue its activities in support of the private sector initiative program (PSIP):[20]

- through publications and education programs to continue the work of making labor more aware of the opportunities for participation in PSIP;
- to foster labor participation in program planning both through PICs and planning councils and through CETA review and comment procedures;

20. *Human Resources Development Institute: Scope of Work,*. Based on contract between the HRDI and U.S. Department of Labor for the period January 12, 1980 through January 10, 1981. No date. (Processed.)

- to make use of its union and employer contacts in business and industry to develop new job placement opportunities in support of PSIP; and
- to assist labor organizations to develop worthwhile job and training programs with private employers.

A similar effort to provide technical assistance designed to smooth the operation of Titles IID and VI of CETA was envisioned in the national agreement with AFSCME Career Development, Inc. The Employment and Training Administration (ETA) enlisted the help of AFSCME to minimize the PSE problems that were expected to arise from the 1978 amendments to CETA. Under the agreement, AFSCME Career Development, Inc. assigned seven persons to provide technical assistance to prime sponsors when called upon. These trained union representatives were to "work with prime sponsors to discuss and resolve problems that may arise from hiring, promoting, or terminating CETA workers in terms of impact on regular public sector employees." The agreement focused particularly on the potential impact on regular employees of waiver requests by prime sponsors to allow temporary extensions of PSE tenure.

Promotional activities similar to those of HRDI have been performed by the AFL-CIO Great Lakes Regional Council in DOL Region V (Minnesota, Wisconsin, Illinois, Indiana, Ohio, and Michigan). Created with the support of the six state AFL-CIO federations, the council has seen itself as a technical resource for ETA, CETA prime sponsor staff, and labor unions. Under the Title III agreement with the DOL, it has operated in areas that have been serviced neither by HRDI nor a state AFL-CIO program.

The continuation of national programs after the decentralization of the employment and training system was based on the judgment that there are special advantages in using the various national networks of service delivery which most prime sponsors could not be expected to duplicate in the early years of CETA. With respect to the role of organized labor in CETA, the national agreements represent an alternative means of enlisting the more vigorous participation of local labor organizations.[21]

## Organized Labor
## and Public Service Employment

As indicated earlier in this chapter, the AFL-CIO and its affiliates regard public service employment legislation as desirable economic and social policy. This position is based on the premise that a federal subsidy to employ jobless people in local and state government in periods of recession moderates high levels of unemployment and increases the supply of public services. However, support for such programs is conditioned on enforcement of rules that prevent local administrators from substituting federally subsidized workers for regular employees or using the program to undermine existing standards of wages and working conditions.

The AFL-CIO was successful in incorporating such safeguards in legislation authorizing public employment programs. Organized labor supported the passage of the Emergency Employment Act of 1971 that provided employment for approximately 150,000 unemployed persons in public sector jobs but proposed a number of safeguards that became part of the statute. Regular workers were not to be displaced, wages were not to be below the legal minimum nor the prevailing rate, employees under the act were to receive the same benefits as other workers, and labor organizations were to get a chance to comment on the local official's application for funds.

---

21. At the time this report was being completed, the Reagan Administration had proposed a sharp reduction for fiscal 1982 in the Title III funds available for national agreements such as those with organized labor.

The Comprehensive Employment and Training Act of 1973, also warmly endorsed by organized labor, carried forward most of these protective provisions. The large and rapid increase in PSE enrollment, the difficult fiscal situation confronting many local governments, and the growth of union organization among public employees combined to complicate the administration of public service employment programs. These administrative difficulties were aggravated by the 1978 amendments to CETA. The wage, eligibility, and monitoring provisions that were enacted to bring the local programs into closer conformity with national policies and to control program abuses were especially difficult to administer. This section examines problems encountered in the implementation of PSE, with particular emphasis on the problems that arose as local governments and labor organizations sought to adjust to the strains created by the 1978 amendments and, subsequently, to the sharp decline in the size of the PSE programs. The findings are derived mainly from the experiences of the prime sponsors in the sample, but information from other sources has been taken into account with respect to some of the issues.

## Extent of Employee Organization

Employee organization membership and collective bargaining in the public sector increased greatly in the 1960s and 1970s. In 1978, just over 4.7 million full-time state and local government employees in approximately 30,000 bargaining units belonged to an employee organization. They represented 37 percent of all state and local government employees. Among state employees, coverage was 29 percent; in local government, 40 percent.[22]

In four out of five of the study areas PSE enrollees were employed in local governments, some of whose regular

---

22. U.S. Department of Commerce, Bureau of the Census, *Labor Management Relations in State and Local Governments,* vol. 3, Public Employment No. 3, October 1979, p. 1.

employees were covered by a collective bargaining agreement. Coverage was not as great in state agencies that enrolled PSE participants (54 percent). Nonprofit organizations employing PSE workers had labor contracts in less
than a fifth of the areas (table 63). The proliferation of state
laws requiring public employers to recognize and bargain
collectively with organizations supported by a majority of
the workforce was undoubtedly the most important factor in
explaining the rapid expansion. Whatever the reason, prime
sponsors had to take into account the presence of organizations alert to the interests of their members and ready to take
issue when those interests appear to be jeopardized.

**Table 63**
**Percent of Areas in Which Any PSE Employers**
**Have Collective Bargaining Agreements**
**With a Labor Organization**
**Sample Prime Sponsor Areas, 1980**

| Type of PSE employer | Percent of reporting areas |
|---|---|
| Local government | 79 |
| State government | 54 |
| Nonprofit organization | 18 |
| No agreements with PSE employers | 21 |

SOURCE: Reports from 28 areas.

Despite the high proportion of areas in which some agencies employing PSE workers had collective bargaining contracts, relatively few PSE workers were covered by such
agreements. In more than 80 percent of the survey areas,
fewer than half of the PSE enrollees were in agencies that
had labor contracts (table 64).

In almost two-thirds of the prime sponsor areas, PSE
workers assigned to agencies covered by agreements were ad-
mitted to membership in labor organizations or were
represented by them even if they did not become members.
The most frequently identified labor organization which

enrolled and/or represented PSE participants was AFSCME; others mentioned were local independent unions, or teacher associations affiliated with state bodies.

**Table 64**
**Proportion of PSE Workers in Agencies**
**With Collective Bargaining Agreements**
**Sample Prime Sponsor Areas, 1980**

| Proportion of PSE workers | Percent of reporting areas |
| --- | --- |
| More than half ......................... | 18 |
| One-fourth to one-half ................. | 36 |
| Up to one-fourth ...................... | 25 |
| None ................................. | 21 |

SOURCE: Reports from 28 areas.

## Prime Sponsor-Labor Organization Issues

The assignment of public service employment participants to employing agencies in which wages and working conditions have been incorporated in a bargaining agreement constituted a potential source of conflict between prime sponsors or employing agencies and labor organizations. The new PSE wage provisions of the 1978 reauthorization act enlarged the grounds for differences. This section reviews the issues that arose in the administration of PSE and presents organized labor's perceptions of the 1978 changes.

*Substitution.* The use of federally financed PSE workers to supplant rather than to supplement the regular workforce was a continuing concern of labor organizations. Even though CETA regulations prohibit this practice, some unions feared that public employers might use this means to undermine their bargaining position. On the other hand, some employing agencies charged labor organizations with raising this issue only to improve their bargaining position.

In 8 of the 28 study areas, organized labor objected to the use of some PSE enrollees in positions that labor believed should be filled by regular employees. In some instances the PSE workers had been put in jobs vacated by regular employees. In others, the effect on regular workers was less direct—hiring PSE workers for a project in one department of a hospital while regular workers in another department were laid off; and in another instance, using PSE workers in new positions that the union believed would have been funded from local budgets in the absence of PSE.

The unions were successful in changing the situation in seven of the eight areas. Several approaches were used: eliminating the questioned positions, changing the nature of the PSE jobs, and transferring PSE workers to the regular payroll. Attrition solved the problem in one case, and in another the union reluctantly went along with the proposed PSE jobs because of the city's severe financial problems.

*Job restructuring.* Actions taken to adjust to lower wages were regarded by labor organizations as a threat to the labor standards of the regular workforce or, in some cases, as unfair to CETA participants. The combined effect of the limitations on average wages and supplementation increased labor's apprehensions. In some jurisdictions the prevailing entry level salary for some occupations in which PSE participants had previously been placed was above the salary the prime sponsor could pay and stay within the limits imposed by the amendments. A Labor Department suggestion for overcoming this problem was to restructure jobs by retaining only the lesser tasks of the original positions; that is, to pitch the new job at a somewhat lower skill level.

PSE jobs were restructured in about two-thirds of the survey areas. Labor organizations were consulted in about half of these areas. Some unions charged that the low wage "restructured" jobs were, in fact, the same as, or very little different from, the previous higher paying jobs and tended to undermine existing wage structures. In Philadelphia, the union refused to go along with restructuring the lowest level laboring and clerical jobs, and PSE hiring for city agencies was temporarily frozen. There were a few instances where unions reluctantly went along with the lower wage "restructured" jobs even though they believed them to be simply the old jobs with new titles. In other areas, the unions worked with the government agencies to create "trainee" positions that they felt would not jeopardize the established wage structure.

*Effects on collective bargaining agreements.* Following the enactment of the 1978 amendments, collective bargaining provisions dealing with PSE were changed in six areas. In half the areas, new PSE job classifications at wages below the previous contract minimum were included in the agreement. Other changes dealt with the transfer of PSE workers to regular positions, prior notification to the union of any changes in CETA staffing, and in one case, raising the wages of regular employees to match a higher CETA wage.

## Labor's Views of the 1978 Amendments

Labor representatives objected strongly to the wage provisions of the 1978 amendments to CETA. Respondents in almost two-thirds of the sample areas thought that the permissible wage levels should be raised; in only 10 percent of the areas did the respondents believe that they should remain unchanged. For the rest, there was either no information, or the opinions expressed were not clear (table 65). The objection to lower wages is based not alone on the fear that it may undermine the prevailing entry level wages. Some respondents made the point that the disadvantaged would not be helped if the wage restrictions forced prime sponsors to place participants in low wage, low skill positions that would not provide the skills necessary to obtain employment in the competitive labor market.

**Table 65**
**Views of Labor Representatives on the 1978 Amendments**
**to CETA Title IID and Title VI**
**Sample Prime Sponsor Areas, 1980**

| Provision | Percent of reporting areas |
|---|---|
| **Eligibility rules** | |
| Should be: | |
| Tightened ......................... | 7 |
| Loosened......................... | 46 |
| Left as they are ................... | 29 |
| Don't know or no answer ........... | 18 |
| **PSE wage rates** | |
| Should be: | |
| Raised ........................... | 64 |
| Lowered ......................... | 0 |
| Left unchanged ................... | 11 |
| Don't know or no answer ........... | 25 |
| **PSE training:** | |
| A good idea...................... | 71 |
| Not a good idea .................. | 4 |
| Don't know or no answer ........... | 25 |

SOURCE: Reports from 28 areas.

Organized labor also reacted to the changes in the PSE eligibility provisions of the 1978 amendments. Labor spokesmen in almost half of the prime sponsor areas favored looser eligibility rules. They believed that PSE should be opened to a wider spectrum of applicants by reducing the required weeks of unemployment or increasing the maximum permissible income. On the other hand, in 36 percent of the areas, union respondents thought the rules should be left as they were or, in two cases, tightened.

Concern for the needs of the disadvantaged was reflected in the strong support by labor respondents of the mandate requiring prime sponsors to spend part of Title IID and Title VI funds for training PSE participants. Some, however, felt that such expenditures would be wasted if they were spent only on job search techniques; they preferred job skill training.

The new limitation on duration of enrollment in PSE jobs created problems for labor organizations which represented PSE participants. They pressed local governments to hire more PSE workers for unsubsidized jobs or at least to give them preference when jobs became open.

## Labor Perceptions of PSE Usefulness

In an attempt to determine organized labor's perception of the PSE program, labor officials were asked if, in their opinion, PSE jobs or projects were useful to the community and beneficial to the participants (table 66). Of those who expressed an opinion, a majority found the program useful to both the community and the disadvantaged participant. But the favorable attitudes were not overwhelming, and some respondents expressed reservations. Some felt, for example, that the community benefits would be greatly enhanced if the maintenance of effort requirements were enforced. Local governments, it was argued, should find other means of dealing with fiscal crises. Although the usefulness of PSE for participants was generally acknowledged, some respondents believed that the benefits are precarious unless the training is geared to prospective job needs and its quality improved.

**Table 66**
**Opinions of Labor Representatives on Usefulness**
**of Public Service Employment to Community and Participants**
**Sample Prime Sponsor Areas, 1980**

| Opinion of labor representatives | For community | For participants |
|---|---|---|
| | (Percent of reporting areas) | |
| Useful ......................... | 25 | 21 |
| Useful, but with reservations ........ | 18 | 25 |
| Not useful ..................... | 36 | 32 |
| No opinion or no information ....... | 21 | 21 |

SOURCE: Reports from 28 areas.
NOTE: Details may not add to 100 percent due to rounding.

When asked about their views on the size of the PSE program, about half of those who expressed an opinion would increase it. In the main, they believed PSE to be an effective means of helping at least some of the jobless in periods of high unemployment. About one-third would reduce the program because they thought other types of training were superior. The remainder would keep it at the size it was in December 1980.

# Summary

- Organized labor has consistently supported employment and training legislation as sound economic and social policy. It has, however, insisted that such programs must not endanger the employment and wage standards of the regular labor force.

- Framers of CETA provided a role for organized labor in the planning and conduct of CETA programs and, in the main, prime sponsors have observed the requirements of the statute. Labor is represented on advisory committees in all the areas surveyed, they are consulted on program content and design, and where necessary, their concurrence is solicited.

- In the decentralized CETA system however, organized labor has not had a major role in planning CETA programs except in a relatively few places. In two-thirds of the areas surveyed, labor's role has been described as perfunctory. This reflected an absence of union effort in some places and a lack of influence in others. In 18 percent of the areas, labor's role was active and its influence, significant. It played a moderate role in an additional 11 percent of the areas.

- Organized labor's interest in CETA ran in two directions: (a) protection of the established standards for wage and working conditions, and (b) improvement of the quality of training programs and their relevance to the needs of the labor market. With respect to safeguarding its interests, organized labor was concerned over limited participation in the planning process, the substitution of PSE workers for regular employees, and the level of wages paid to PSE workers. The use of some PSE enrollees in jobs that otherwise would have been filled by regular workers was a labor-management issue in 8 of the 28 study areas. In all but one instance the union position prevailed or the problem was solved by attrition. Unions were consulted in less than one-third of the areas where PSE positions were restructured to meet the mandated lower wage levels. In most areas, the unions cooperated with the employing agency to establish "trainee" positions and to formulate a new set of duties that would justify a lower wage.

- Organized labor generally viewed PSE programs as useful and favored increasing their size or maintaining December 1980 levels. About a third of the labor respondents, however, did not share this view. Many union spokesmen supported the use of PSE funds for training provided that the quality could be improved and the training more closely geared to meeting the needs of the job market.

- With respect to labor's position on the 1978 amendments, most respondents favored loosening the eligibility requirements to permit wider participation in CETA programs, raising the level of PSE wage rates, and placing greater emphasis on training.

- In about 80 percent of the survey areas, one or more of the agencies that employ PSE participants had a collective bargaining agreement with a labor organization, and in 18 of the 28 areas, the unions enrolled and represented CETA enrollees.

- Following passage of the 1978 reauthorization act, provisions of collective bargaining agreements dealing with PSE issues were modified in one quarter of the areas where such contracts were in effect. Most of the modifications were the result of the new wage provisions and involved the establishment of new positions and the protection of the existing wage structures.

- The introduction of the Private Sector Initiative Program was supported by organized labor, and in a majority of the study areas union officials expected to assist in the development of the program.

- In addition to participating in local employment and training activities, organized labor was involved in nationwide programs funded under Title III. These were direct arrangements between the Department of Labor and specific national unions and operated outside the local prime sponsor system. In this respect, they were a departure from the decentralized mode of CETA. In the main, these arrangements predate CETA and were intended to meet special needs that could not be accommodated through the local prime sponsor system.

- Many nationwide contracts consisted chiefly of programs to recruit and place minority members and women in skilled and apprenticeable occupations and to arrange for OJT placements in firms where unions had collective bargaining agreements. The purpose of some of the contracts, such as those with HRDI and AFSCME, was to foster union interest in local prime sponsor activities and to supply educational assistance to accomplish this.

# 8 Finding Jobs for CETA Participants

The placement of participants in suitable unsubsidized employment—transition—has long been a major objective of employment and training progams. This objective was reaffirmed in the CETA legislation which declared that the purpose of the programs was to assure "that training and other services lead to maximum employment opportunities and enhance self-sufficiency. . . ." The reauthorization of 1978 expanded the objective to include increasing "earned income." Thus, the goal became not merely a job, but stable employment at a higher level of compensation.

Although CETA is charged with many objectives, its success generally is measured by the number of enrollees who enter unsubsidized employment and the level of their post-CETA earnings. These outcomes reflect the policies, emphasis, and management practices of CETA administrators as well as labor market conditions. The kinds of training and services provided to enrollees and the efforts to place them have much to do with their ability to obtain suitable employment.

This chapter is concerned with the organization and procedures used by prime sponsors to arrange for the placement of CETA enrollees in unsubsidized jobs and the effect of the 1978 CETA amendments on these efforts. It also reviews the

267

effect of CETA on the postprogram employment adjustment and earnings of participants.

## Legislative and Administrative Developments

While the job placement objective has been central in CETA, emphasis has fluctuated with changes in economic conditions. Early Department of Labor (DOL) regulations called for a discussion of placement goals in the CETA plans and a description of mechanisms and procedures to be used. Prime sponsors were to place Title I (later Title IIB) enrollees in training only if there was a reasonable expectation of employment in the occupation for which they were being trained. In the case of public service employment programs (PSE) one of the following conditions was to be met: one-half of the PSE enrollees were to be placed in unsubsidized jobs; or agencies employing PSE workers were to fill one-half of the vacancies occurring in their regular workforce with CETA enrollees. These PSE goals, however, were soon watered down by congressional action and DOL regulations.

As early as 1974, in legislation establishing the Title VI countercyclical public service employment programs, Congress made clear that, although the Department of Labor could establish "goals" for placement of Title VI participants, these were not to be treated as "conditions" for receipt of funds. A further weakening occurred in 1977 when DOL regulations relaxed placement goals for "project" participants.[1] This revision was made during the 1977-1978 build-up of CETA public service employment as part of President Carter's economic stimulus program. During that period there was pressure to increase enrollment levels rapidly, and the placement emphasis was a casualty in the process, although still acknowledged as an objective.

---

1. The Emergency Jobs Programs Extension Act of 1976, Pub. L. 94-444, October 1976, provided that all new Title VI public service employment positions above existing levels must be in short duration "projects."

Although placement goals and performance against goals were routinely reviewed by DOL representatives as part of the annual performance assessments, the first major initiative by the Department to stress the transition objective was a field directive issued in May 1978.[2] The national unemployment rate at that time had fallen to 6 percent from a 1976 peak of about 8 percent, and emphasis shifted from building up to phasing down PSE enrollments. The directive urged prime sponsors to prepare an employability development plan for each enrollee, register all job-ready participants with the employment service, and enforce a seldom used regulation which permits terminating enrollees who fail to accept a bona fide job offer. It also required employment service offices to refer PSE participants to job openings and to use their contacts with employers for job development.

## Reauthorization Act Reinforces Job Placement Objectives

The reauthorization act of 1978 underscored the importance of moving participants into unsubsidized jobs and increasing their earned income. The act:

- Required the Secretary of Labor to assess the adequacy of sponsors' accomplishments in accordance with performance standards;
- Required sponsors to provide CETA enrollees with job search assistance;
- Required sponsors to set aside funds for training PSE enrollees to enhance their employment potential;
- Mandated the preparation of an employability plan for all Title II and some Title VI enrollees;[3]

---

2. Field Memorandum 307-78, *Emphasis on Transition of CETA PSE Participants into Unsubsidized Employment,* May 22, 1978.

3. Title II of the reauthorization act provides for comprehensive training services (Title IIB), upgrading and retraining programs (Title IIC), and public service employment programs for the structurally unemployed (Title IID).

- Lowered PSE wages to encourage enrollees to seek unsubsidized jobs;
- Limited the tenure of enrollees to 18 months in PSE programs and 30 months in all CETA programs; and
- Established a private sector initiative program under Title VII to assist in placing CETA participants.

Taken together these provisions created conditions which were expected to improve the likelihood of CETA participants obtaining unsubsidized employment. On the other hand, the more stringent eligibility requirements and the low skill jobs necessary to meet the new wage provisions were likely to make the placement task more difficult.

## Effect of the Reauthorization Act on Placement Rates

The reauthorization act's provisions affected the organization of prime sponsors' placement mechanism and the processes used but did not necessarily produce better results.

The most common indicator of short run outcomes is the rate of entry into unsubsidized employment of persons who leave CETA programs. It is important to note, however, that immediate job entry rates are not always the most appropriate measure of program effectiveness. For some programs the aim is to keep youth in school and to provide useful experience. Others, such as adult basic education, are designed mainly to enhance long range employability and self-sufficiency. Work experience programs for older workers are intended mainly to provide income supplements through useful employment. Nevertheless, changes in the job entry rate (i.e., the number of terminees who enter employment immediately after leaving a CETA program expressed as a percent of the total number of terminees) are still the most convenient barometer for determining the extent and direction of change in program effectiveness.

## Job Entry Rates 1978-1980

Between 1978 and 1979, the combined job entry rate for CETA Titles IIB/C, IID, and VI edged up slightly, while in 1980 the composite rate fell sharply:[4]

| Fiscal year | Combined job entry rate | Title I (IIB/C) | Title II (IID) | Title VI |
|---|---|---|---|---|
| | | (Percent) | | |
| 1978 . . . . . . . . . . | 43 | 48 | 45 | 33 |
| 1979 . . . . . . . . . . | 44 | 47 | 47 | 36 |
| 1980 . . . . . . . . . . | 38 | 41 | 35 | 35 |

SOURCE: Based on Table 67.

The drop in 1980 was concentrated in Title IIB/C and in Title IID, while the job entry rate for Title VI, which had been lower than the other titles in 1978, remained relatively stable (table 67). The "indirect" placement rate is the most critical measure since it reflects efforts made by CETA sponsors or program operators to find employment for enrollees who have left a training or employment program. The indirect placement rate dropped sharply between 1978 and 1980 in Title IIB/C. The decline in Title IIB/C may be related to the changing characteristics of enrollees, as discussed more fully below. Job entry rate trends in the BSSR sample areas were consistent with those for the United States. Placement rates for PSE rose in most areas between 1978 and 1979 but declined between 1979 and 1980 (table 68). The trend was more variable among areas for Title VI and for Title IID. Rates in Title IIB/C declined in a plurality of areas in both years. On the whole, rates were lower in 1980 than before the reauthorization in 1978.

4. These rates are based on Department of Labor Management Information System (MIS) reports. They were calculated by excluding persons who transfer from one CETA title to another from the termination figures which are the denominator of the job entry rate formula. Data from the DOL *Continuous Longitudinal Manpower Survey* (CLMS) show higher employment rates. The reasons for differences are discussed later in this chapter.

## Table 67
### Individuals Served, Terminations, and Job Entries
### CETA Title IIB/C, Title IID, and Title VI, Fiscal 1978-1980
(numbers in thousands)

| Termination status | Title IIB/C | | | Title IID | | | Title VI | | |
|---|---|---|---|---|---|---|---|---|---|
| | 1978[a] | 1979 | 1980 | 1978[b] | 1979 | 1980 | 1978 | 1979 | 1980 |
| Total individuals served | 1,332 | 1,194 | 1,114 | 210 | 460 | 486 | 1,017 | 791 | 410 |
| Total terminations[c] | 931 | 772 | 707 | 87 | 184 | 248 | 512 | 368 | 249 |
| Total entered employment | 450 | 366 | 288 | 39 | 86 | 88 | 167 | 131 | 86 |
| | (Percent of terminations) | | | | | | | | |
| Terminations | 100 | 100 | 100 | 100 | 100 | 100 | 100 | 100 | 100 |
| Entered employment[d] | 48 | 47 | 41 | 45 | 47 | 35 | 33 | 36 | 35 |
| Direct placement[e] | 10 | 9 | 7 | 1 | f | f | f | f | 1 |
| Indirect placement[g] | 26 | 26 | 23 | 27 | 30 | 22 | 16 | 20 | 21 |
| Self-placement and other | 12 | 13 | 11 | 17 | 17 | 13 | 16 | 15 | 13 |
| Other positive terminations[h] | 21 | 22 | 25 | 7 | 10 | 9 | 8 | 12 | 9 |
| Nonpositive terminations | 31 | 30 | 35 | 49 | 44 | 55 | 60 | 53 | 57 |

SOURCE: Employment and Training Administration, U.S. Department of Labor data.

NOTE: Details may not add to 100 percent due to rounding.

a. Title I in fiscal 1978.

b. Title II in fiscal 1978.

c. Excludes transfers to other titles.

d. The job entry rate is defined as the ratio of the number of terminees who obtained employment to the total number of terminations.

e. Individuals placed in unsubsidized employment after receiving only outreach, intake, assessment, referral and/or supportive services from CETA.

f. Less than 0.5 percent.

g. Individuals placed in unsubsidized employment after participating in CETA training, employment programs, or supportive services.

h. Individuals terminated from CETA who enrolled in school, the armed services, or a non-CETA training program.

**Table 68**
**Changes in Job Entry Rates**
**Sample Prime Sponsor Areas, Fiscal 1978-1980**

| Direction of change in job entry ratio 1978-1980 | Title I (IIB/C) | Title II (IID) | Title VI |
|---|---|---|---|
| | (Percent of areas) | | |
| Increase.................. | 16 | 28 | 36 |
| Little change[a] .............. | 8 | 12 | 32 |
| Decrease ................. | 76 | 60 | 32 |

SOURCE: Program data for 25 prime sponsor areas with comparable jurisdictions in all 3 years.

a. Less than 5 percentage points change between 1978 and 1980.

## Reasons for Decline in Placement Rates

The decline in placement rates in 1980 as compared with those of 1978 is attributable to a combination of economic and programmatic factors.

- A rise in the nation's unemployment rate from 6.1 percent in 1978 and 5.8 percent in 1979 to 6.8 percent in 1980 suggests that the decline in job entry rates may be at least partly due to generally looser labor market conditions. A number of prime sponsors cited changes in local employment conditions, especially widespread layoffs in industry.
- The changed socioeconomic profile of CETA enrollees since the reauthorization act and the accompanying increase in the hard-to-employ were also frequently cited by prime sponsors.

Earlier studies suggest that management practices, including the amount of emphasis placed on transition and the resources and strategies employed to support the placement objective, can be a significant factor in transition.[5] In late fiscal 1979, prime sponsors, facing the prospect of large-scale terminations of participants who reached the newly imposed 18-month limit of enrollment, geared up for placement of enrollees. By 1980, the emphasis had diminished, and lower PSE placement rates may have been due to lessening pressure on prime sponsors to find jobs for laid off PSE enrollees.[6]

Declining opportunities in the public sector may also have affected job prospects for PSE enrollees. In fiscal 1980, 60 percent of the PSE enrollees who terminated and found jobs were absorbed in the public sector. But the rate of growth of state and local government employment has been declining in recent years. In the first half of the 1970s, it grew at an annual rate of 4.3 percent, but in the second half the rate slowed to 2.3 percent, and between 1978 and 1980, to less than 1.5 percent.[7]

## Job Entry Rates
## by Characteristics of Enrollees

Between 1978 (prior to the reauthorization) and 1980 the proportion of hard-to-employ terminees rose in all three titles, but particularly in Title IID, the PSE title specifically designed for the structurally unemployed (table 69). The pro-

---

5. Mirengoff and Rindler, *CETA: Under Local Control,* pp. 232-33; Ripley et al., *CETA Prime Sponsor Management Decisions,* pp. 21-25; Mirengoff et al., *The New CETA,* pp. 112-16.

6. Under the reauthorization act, CETA PSE enrollees who had been in the program for more than six months as of October 1978 could continue for another 12 months. This created a "cliff" problem in September 1979 when some 200,000 to 250,000 enrollees reached their 18-month tenure limit and had to be terminated. See Mirengoff et al., *The New CETA,* pp. 30-31.

7. Without CETA public sector jobs, the growth rate in the late 1970s would have been even smaller. CETA PSE enrollees comprised a significant part of the growth in state and local public service employment during the period 1975-1980. At the peak month of March 1978, the Title II and VI enrollees in governmental agencies accounted for about 4.3 percent of the 13 million state and local government employees.

Table 69

Selected Characteristics of Terminees of CETA Title IIB/C, Title IID, and Title VI
Fiscal 1978-1980

| Selected characteristic | Title IIB/C | | | Title IID | | | Title VI | | |
|---|---|---|---|---|---|---|---|---|---|
| | 1978[a] | 1979 | 1980 | 1978[b] | 1979 | 1980 | 1978 | 1979 | 1980 |
| | | | | (Percent of total) | | | | | |
| Education: Less than 12 grades........ | 48 | 48 | 49 | 21 | 26 | 33 | 29 | 28 | 31 |
| Race: Black........................ | 33 | 33 | 34 | 22 | 26 | 32 | 26 | 28 | 33 |
| AFDC recipient .................... | 15 | 17 | 20 | 8 | 12 | 18 | 11 | 11 | 15 |
| Other public assistance recipient...... | 9 | 7 | 6 | 6 | 7 | 7 | 8 | 6 | 6 |
| Economically disadvantaged........... | 79 | 88 | 98 | 63 | 83 | 94 | 83 | 85 | 90 |
| Handicapped....................... | 5 | 6 | 8 | 4 | 5 | 6 | 4 | 5 | 5 |

SOURCE: Employment and Training Administration, U.S. Department of Labor data.

a. Title I in fiscal 1978.

b. Title II in fiscal 1978.

portion of terminees in Title IID who were welfare recipients, for example, nearly doubled from 14 to 25 percent.

The differential job entry rates among client groups tend to support the view that the decline between 1978 and 1980 was due in part to a change in characteristics and qualifications of terminees. Rates were significantly lower for school dropouts, AFDC recipients, and blacks than for other groups (table 70). They were higher for persons in prime working ages, those with high school or post-high school education, and white persons. Unemployment insurance recipients, who generally have stable labor force attachments, had the highest ratio. Placement rates of the low income group were about average because nearly all participants were in the low income category in fiscal 1980.

Table 70
Job Entry Rates by Selected Characteristics
CETA Title IIB/C, Title IID, and Title VI
Fiscal 1980[a]

| Selected characteristic | Title IIB/C | Title IID | Title VI |
|---|---|---|---|
| | (Percent) | | |
| U.S. Total ................. | 37 | 31 | 31 |
| School dropout............. | 37 | 24 | 22 |
| AFDC recipient ........... | 27 | 26 | 23 |
| Low income .............. | 37 | 31 | 30 |
| Black .................... | 31 | 25 | 24 |
| Age 22-44 ................ | 47 | 33 | 33 |
| High school and post-high school .......... | 48 | 35 | 34 |
| White (not Hispanic) ........ | 40 | 36 | 35 |
| Unemployment insurance recipient ............... | 51 | 39 | 35 |

SOURCE: Employment and Training Administration, U.S. Department of Labor data.
a. Job entry rates calculated for this table with individuals who transferred from one CETA title to another included in the termination figures. This accounts for lower U.S. rates than those shown in table 67.

# Management Practices Affecting Transition

In 1978, the General Accounting Office examined the systems used by five prime sponsors for moving PSE participants into unsubsidized employment and identified five major problems:[8] (1) Although CETA jobs were supposed to be temporary, many participants had held these positions for a long time—some for over three years. (2) Of the participants who found jobs, a high proportion went into public sector rather than private sector jobs. (3) Sponsors had not developed systematic approaches to transition. Only a small proportion of enrollees were assessed to help them achieve their employment goals, and formal, job related training was not being provided to those most in need of training. (4) Job-ready participants were not identified, referred to the employment service, or given placement assistance or job search training. (5) Participants were not encouraged to look for unsubsidized jobs. Where PSE wages were higher than the wages in prospective unsubsidized employment or where the participants expected to be absorbed by the PSE employers, the incentives were to remain in the PSE program. These GAO criticisms applied only to PSE participants, who were generally considered to be more job-ready than those enrolled in other CETA programs.

The reauthorization act did not deal directly with placement mechanisms. However, several of its provisions have strengthened management practices that are conducive to the placement of enrollees in unsubsidized employment. The following section explores the extent to which management practices have changed and assesses the effects of such changes on program outcomes.

---

8. General Accounting Office, *Moving Participants from Public Service Employment Programs into Unsubsidized Jobs Needs More Attention,* HRD 79-101, October 1979, pp. 15-26. The study was conducted in five sites between July and November 1978.

*Department of Labor*
*Emphasis on Placement*

The Department of Labor relies on regulations, instructions for preparing the plans and grant applications, review of plans, and performance assessments to discharge its responsibility for the oversight of placement activities.

The DOL regulations to implement the new provisions of the reauthorization act—employability development plans, job search assistance, PSE training, and establishment of private industry councils—were expected, indirectly, to help achieve the job placement goal. However, the regulations that deal directly with placement activities and systems appear to be weaker and less specific than the rules in effect prior to the reauthorization, at least for PSE. Earlier regulations stated clearly that each prime sponsor, program agent, or subgrantee was responsible for placing all PSE participants in unsubsidized private or public sector jobs, and placement "goals" were set at one-half of participants.[9] Revised regulations do not contain explicit transition goals except for participants whose tenure has expired and who are held over on waivers. Instead, they call for a description in the master plan of job development and placement services and contain a lengthy section dealing with tenure restrictions and the conditions for obtaining waivers of these limits.[10]

Revised instructions for grant applications are more specific than formerly. Prior to the reauthorization, prime sponsors were asked to describe placement and followup procedures and to indicate how placements are verified. Revised instructions call for a description of how

9. U.S. Department of Labor, "CETA: Compilation of Current Regulations for Titles I, II, and VI," *Federal Register,* Part III, October 18, 1977, 96.33(c), p. 55758.

10. U.S. Department of Labor, Employment and Training Administration, "CETA Regulations; Final Rule and Proposed Rule," *Federal Register,* Part IX, May 20, 1980, 676.10-4(c) (4) and 676.30, pp. 33865 and 33878.

employability development plans are developed and used as well as the institutional arrangements for job search assistance, job development, and placement.

A third point at which the federal government may intervene in providing guidance to sponsors is in the review of plans. The authorization in the act to set "performance standards" gave the Department of Labor more authority to establish individualized placement rate standards for each prime sponsor, taking into account the local area's economic situation, mix of programs, and clientele. This system gives the Department a more formal and objective means of testing the adequacy of the prime sponsor's transition plans than it had previously.

Finally, the Department is responsible for assessing the sponsors' placement systems and their progress in meeting placement goals. Emphasis in the formal assessment varies from year to year, but placement rates and costs continue to be key elements.

On the whole, the reauthorization act has strengthened the Department's authority to monitor placement activities. The results of the revised approach, however, depend on the manner in which performance standards are implemented. Because of time involved in developing regulations, the performance standards system was not fully implemented by fiscal year 1981.

The DOL role has become more forceful with the decision to drop the PSE programs in fiscal year 1981. Over 300,000 PSE enrollees were to be terminated beginning in March 1981. The DOL urged prime sponsors to accelerate the placement of enrollees in unsubsidized private sector jobs and encouraged local governments and other employing agencies to absorb them into their agencies. All programs administered by the Employment and Training Administration were required to make the employment of laid off PSE enrollees their first priority.[11] (See chapter 2.)

## Local Perceptions of the Effect of Reauthorization on Placement

In the survey conducted immediately after the reauthorization amendments went into effect (1979), prime sponsors reported that they expected the limits on the duration of program participation to be the key factor in encouraging transition.[12] The lower wages for PSE participants and tighter eligibility requirements were considered likely to decrease transition.

The followup study in October 1980 showed a change in some of these views. The coupling of training with PSE, not the limit on duration of enrollment in CETA, was viewed as exerting the greatest positive influence on transition among Title IID and Title VI participants. The tighter eligibility requirements for PSE enrollees and the limits placed on PSE wages were again identified by most respondents as hindering transition. But the tenure limitation provisions and the introduction of employability development plans were considered by most respondents as having little effect (table 71). Two reasons were offered for this conclusion: some sponsors had already established limits for participation; others felt that providing waivers for enrollees who had reached their tenure limits had the effect of extending the enrollment period so that there was little actual difference in participants' length of stay in CETA programs.

The coupling of training with PSE was seen as a transition related improvement. Respondents reported that employers

---

11. Field Memorandum 133-81, *Management of the Phaseout of Programs Funded Under Titles IID and VI of the Comprehensive Employment and Training Act by September 30, 1981,* March 13, 1981.

12. Mirengoff et al., *The New CETA,* pp. 104-105.

Table 71
Perception of Effects of Legislative Changes on Participants' Transition
to Unsubsidized Jobs, Sample Prime Sponsor Areas

| Perceived effect | 18-month limit in PSE | 30-month limit- any CETA program | Tighter eligibility for PSE | Limits on PSE wages | Introduction of employability development plan | Coupling training with PSE |
|---|---|---|---|---|---|---|
| | | | Legislative change | | | |
| | | | (Percent of all reports) | | | |
| Number of areas reporting.......... | 23 | 24 | 23 | 22 | 25 | 20 |
| Increased transition........ | 35 | 21 | 0 | 23 | 32 | 70 |
| Decreased transition........ | 4 | 0 | 74 | 59 | 0 | 5 |
| No effect on transition..... | 61 | 79 | 26 | 18 | 68 | 25 |

SOURCE: Reports from sample areas.

are interested in the skills enrollees acquire and in their certification of program completion and competence. Enrollees who had received training were viewed as more marketable than those who had not. Moreover, the efforts of the training agencies to place their enrollees were expected to improve transition outcomes. In addition, experience of training by enrollees was viewed as evidence of motivation—a characteristic that made them easier to place.

The reauthorization act's tighter eligibility and wage restrictions were seen as depressing placement prospects for several reasons. PSE enrollees, subject to these reauthorization provisions, were considered to be less job-ready and therefore less appealing to local governments which have been prime placement sources. For many of the least qualified enrollees, the 18-month limit on PSE participation did not provide sufficient time to acquire the skills and experience necessary to obtain unsubsidized employment. Similarly, the wage provisions were regarded as diminishing transition prospects, since only workers with limited skills were willing to accept the low wage offers, and many prospective firms saw such enrollees as risky acquisitions. In addition, the lower wage provisions have led to assignments in nongovernmental agencies that were less able to absorb participants.

## Effect of Reauthorization on Organization of Placement Responsibility

Prime sponsors respond to legislative and regulatory imperatives in ways they view as most appropriate for their jurisdictions. The survey demonstrated several approaches sponsors had taken to organize the job placement functions (table 72). Changes were made in the job search and job development processes, and staff was added to "beef up" these activities. A few major changes in institutional arrangements for placing enrollees have also occurred since

Table 72

Assignment of Major Responsibility for Participant Placement
by Type of Prime Sponsor, Sample Prime Sponsor Areas

| Type of sponsor | Number | Major placement responsibility | | | |
|---|---|---|---|---|---|
| | | Prime sponsor | Employment service | Employers or program operators | Shared responsibility |
| Total | 28 | 9 | 5 | 10 | 4 |
| City | 8 | 5 | 1 | 2 | 0 |
| County | 8 | 2 | 1 | 5 | 0 |
| Consortium | 8 | 2 | 2 | 3 | 1 |
| Balance-of-state | 4 | 0 | 1 | 0 | 3 |

SOURCE: Reports from 28 areas.

reauthorization, and in most of these cases they were not attributed to the reauthorization provisions.

The most common approach to handling placement, and the one adopted by over one-third (36 percent) of the sample sponsors, was to delegate the responsibility to employers or program operators. This decision was based on the belief that they were familiar with the enrollees and were likely to know of employment opportunities. A nearly equal number of sponsors (32 percent) assumed the responsibility for placement themselves, often through a central placement unit. The remaining sponsors either delegated the function to the employment service, or used more than one approach. Most urban sponsors preferred to handle the placement function "in house," while counties and consortia relied frequently on employers and program operators. In the balance of states, several organizations shared the responsibility.

The operations of the St. Paul sponsor illustrate the centralized approach:

> The CETA prime sponsor is a single-center delivery system in which all enrollees under all titles receive like services. The counselor, with the employability development plan team, develops a specific EDP for each enrollee. The head of this team is a counselor who is responsible for the placement of a given enrollee. Job developers will seek jobs by making contact through the various businesses and organizations within the community. These jobs are made available to the counselor who is in charge of specific enrollees. As the enrollees are made job-ready, their names appear on a job-ready list. It is at this point that the counselor will meet with the enrollee and determine with him the jobs that are available that he might qualify for. The cards are made out for the enrollee and he is sent to the employer for an initial inter-

view. If he is not accepted, he has another meeting with the counselor and the search for suitable employment continues.

The North Carolina balance-of-state placement program, on the other hand, is highly decentralized and relies on program operators and the employment service:

> Throughout the BOS areas, placement functions are handled independently by CETA contractors for the programs they operate. In some counties, the same operator may be responsible for all CETA activities and for placement of all participants; in others, however, programs and placement responsibilities may be parcelled out to a half-dozen or more operators. In one county for example, the local ES handles placement for Title IIB classroom and individual referral training, the state DOL handles OJT placements, and the community action agency is responsible for IIB work experience, Title IV youth programs, and all PSE placements.

In an effort to improve placement performance, five sponsors in the survey shifted the responsibility for the placement function after 1978, either by developing their own placement units or by placing the responsibilities directly on their subcontractors. A BSSR field research associate described the reasons for the changeover by an urban sponsor:

> The main effect that the reauthorization act has had on the prime's placement system has been to lead the prime to take over this responsibility itself, rather than, as before, subcontracting it to the ES. This change stemmed from the prime's decision to take over assessment and referral from ES following the elimination of the hold harmless clause for ES eligibility determination. Once assessment and referral were brought "in house," the prime felt it,

rather than the ES, was in a better position to handle placement.

In other areas where changes in the placement system occurred, they involved such internal organization or procedural shifts as an increase in the number of job developers, greater alliance with local PICs, and an expansion of job search workshops and job clubs. These changes, however, were not entirely attributable to the reauthorization act's emphasis on transition. One field associate noted that:

> Although the most effective parts of the prime's placement system occurred at about the same time as reauthorization, it is hard to attribute specific actions to the act itself. Most likely the act provided increased emphasis and stimulated the internal organization and procedures the prime had installed. Thus, the effects of the act on placement are much like those on employability development planning: the act encouraged progress and accelerated progress in areas in which the prime was already operating.

### Placement Strategies Since Reauthorization

There are several prerequisites to the placement of enrollees in unsubsidized jobs. First, a supply consideration: enrollees must possess the basic qualifications and specific skills appropriate for the needs of local labor markets. Second, a demand consideration: openings must exist to which enrollees can apply. Third, intermediary institutions such as the training agencies, PSE employers, public employment services, community based organizations and prime sponsor placement units must perform the labor exchange function of bringing the supply and demand together and, of course, the participant must actively seek employment. This survey examined each of these factors.

*Skill acquisition.* Occupational skill training was the principal form of training for PSE enrollees who participated in training programs. (See chapter 5 for a fuller discussion.) It was also the major training activity of Title IIB enrollees. Although critical of specific training provisions of the reauthorization act and of the manner in which they were being implemented, most respondents indicated that, on balance, the training provided PSE enrollees did enhance their ability to obtain unsubsidized employment.

*Labor market conditions.* The second condition, availability of suitable openings, is a function of the labor market. During the period 1978 to 1980, 19 of the 28 areas experienced increased unemployment rates. However, the overall unemployment rate in an area is an imperfect indicator of placement possibilities for a particular program. Because labor markets are segmented in terms of occupations, industry, and geography, it may be possible to place enrollees in the interstices of these job markets, even when overall unemployment rates are high. Layoffs in manufacturing establishments, for example, may co-exist with shortages in service industries. Similarly, there may be few openings in a declining inner city while nearby suburban communities may be experiencing employment growth. Moreover, the presence of a trained labor force may encourage economic development and, with it, employment opportunities. Further, job openings due to turnover—workers retiring or leaving for other reasons—provide job opportunities in many occupations during periods of both good and bad business conditions.

*Use of intermediaries.* The third condition—reliance on PSE employers, training agencies, and other intermediaries to assist enrollees—is particularly significant. Respondents in most areas acknowledged that PSE employers have a responsibility either to hire participants or to assist in placing them in unsubsidized private sector jobs where employment possibilities exist. However, in most cases the execution of this obligation depended entirely on an understanding that good faith efforts would be made.

Only six prime sponsors—one-fourth of those in the sample—specified placement goals in the PSE employer contracts, and only two made the absorption of some enrollees within the PSE employing agency a contractual requirement. In two of the largest cities, New York and Philadelphia, obligations to meet placement goals were specified in contracts with some nonprofit organizations, but not with municipal agencies. In late 1980, however, the mayor of New York issued an executive order encouraging city agencies to hire PSE workers when possible. Philadelphia, too, planned to give qualified PSE workers preference in hiring for permanent city jobs in 1981. In Orange County (California) and the Balance of Arizona, goals were specified in contracts based on prior placement experience, while in Kansas City (Kansas) and Phoenix, contracts stipulate that the employer must place 50 percent of the participants in unsubsidized jobs with their own organizations or with other employers.

Some sponsors were reluctant to set placement goals for PSE employers because of the low skill levels of the enrollees and because "it smacks of coercion." They preferred to encourage employers to hire or assist in placing the most job-ready enrollees where feasible and rewarded those who did so by replacing the vacated PSE positions with other enrollees.

Sponsors were more prone to use training agencies for placement. About 40 percent of those surveyed had established placement goals for some of the agencies providing skill training, and these were specified in contracts. These goals, ranging from 70 to 100 percent of enrollees, were somewhat higher than those set for PSE employers. In Chester County, for example, a weatherization training program had a 75 percent placement goal. The major training contractors in Middlesex County also had to meet a 75 percent placement goal. Union County, New Jersey required that skill centers place 70 percent of their CETA enrollees. In their contract with the New Jersey Department of Labor for pre-apprentice machine craft training, 30 percent of the contract payment was prorated according to placements.

There were several reasons why some prime sponsors had not insisted upon placement goals for training agencies. Some handled placements themselves. In other instances, the training agencies were not equipped to handle placements, and to force them into placement activities might divert resources from skill training. Finally, where skill training services were only available outside the sponsors' areas, it was considered unrealistic to require placement performance from agencies unfamiliar with the job market in the sponsor's area.

Whether placement goals were stated in contracts or agreed on informally, sponsors were faced with the problem of dealing with the minority of training agencies and employers who did not meet their placement commitments. Forty percent of the sample sponsors imposed sanctions on PSE employers, and 50 percent applied sanctions on training agencies. The primary forms these measures took were nonrenewal of training contracts and refusal to provide PSE employers with additional participants. Several sponsors rated placement performance and then tied dollar allocations and PSE enrollment to the ratings. In most cases, however, the threat of nonrenewal or reduction in contracts was sufficient. This strategy was especially effective with nonprofit organizations and private training agencies. It was not so effective with government organizations who were less dependent upon PSE resources.

*Use of employment service.* Local employment service offices are another resource for CETA placement assistance. In 1980, most sponsors (65 percent for PSE, and 69 percent for Title IIB/C) used this capability. Placement assistance was among the activities most frequently provided to prime sponsors by the employment service (see chapter 3). However, the assistance was generally limited to requiring CETA participants to register with ES placement units.

Sixty-one percent of the sponsors rated the employment srvice record of placing CETA enrollees as poor, and a number stopped referring enrollees to the employment service for placement.[13] Only three sponsors included the employment service in their list of organizations successful in placing enrollees. Several respondents attributed this record to the fact that the post-reauthorization enrollees are less marketable than their predecessors.

*Participant efforts.* While sponsors viewed participants' efforts as an important element of the transition process, few requirements were actually placed on enrollees other than registration for jobs. Our 1979 survey found 65 percent of sponsors requiring all of their Title IID and VI enrollees to register with the employment service. In 1980, the figure fell to 57 percent. Only one-half of the survey sponsors imposed this requirement on their Title IIB enrollees.

Some sponsors insisted upon more active participant efforts. Chester County required its Title IIB work experience enrollees to interview two employers per month on 10 hours of paid time. Those who did not were terminated. All Title VI enrollees in Cook County were given release time to seek unsubsidized employment during the final months of their enrollment. In Mid-Counties, Michigan all Title IIB and PSE enrollees were sent letters at regular intervals reminding them of their responsibility to seek employment. Although sponsors imposing these requirements did not uniformly exhibit the highest job entry rates, respondents felt that such practices did enhance participants' employment possibilities.

13. In FY 1979 the employment service placed 20 percent of all applicants in unsubsidized jobs. See *1980 Employment and Training Report of the President,* p. 58.

However, a majority of the sample sponsors did not require their PSE enrollees to do more than register with the ES where they were provided with information on available jobs and encouraged to apply for them. Many sponsors relied on the 18-month PSE limitation to motivate participants to seek unsubsidized employment.

In sum, a number of changes in job placement strategies occurred following reauthorization. Increasingly employers and program operators were given placement responsibilities, while the employment service continued to play a limited role. A number of sponsors began specifying placement goals for employers and skill training contractors, and some imposed sanctions on those who failed to meet goals. Most sponsors continued to place only minimal requirements on participants. On balance, sponsors increased their emphasis on placement activities; but these changes were not the direct result of the reauthorization act. Rather, they reflected a refinement of strategies and operations as program administrators gained experience.

### Transition Directed Practices

There are a host of factors that are likely to affect transition performance. Some are well within the control of sponsors and subcontractors, others less so, and some not at all (Chart 4).[14]

Local labor market conditions and funding levels are among the constraints within which sponsors must operate. In 1980, unemployment rates in the survey areas ranged from 3.7 percent in Capital Area, Texas to 13 percent in Lorain, Ohio. Funding levels determine the number of persons that can be enrolled and, subsequently, the placement effort that must be made on their behalf.

---

14. For a list of factors used in analyzing sponsor program performance, see Ripley et al., *CETA Prime Sponsor Management Decisions,* p. 74.

## Chart 4
### Factors Affecting Transition Performance

**Factors Over Which Sponsors Have Little or No Control**

1. Labor market conditions
2. Job entry requirements
3. Legislative mandates, e.g., eligibility criteria
4. National program priorities
5. Level of funding

**Factors Over Which Sponsors Have Some Control**

1. Community attitudes toward CETA program
2. Characteristics of program participants
3. Attitudes of program participants
4. Mix of programs and activities
5. Duration of participant enrollment

**Factors Over Which Sponsors Have a High Degree of Control**

1. Location of the placement function
2. Selection of staff
3. Selection of PSE employers
4. Selection of training agencies
5. Use of the labor market intermediaries
6. Establishment and enforcement of transition goals
7. Staff and resources assigned to placement
8. Development of strategies and processes to facilitate placement in unsubsidized employment

Legislative provisions and national program priorities represent a second set of factors over which sponsors cannot exercise control. The limits placed on PSE wages, eligibility criteria, and the coupling of training and PSE employment, as well as other provisions of the act, affect transition probabilities.

Sponsors, through their public relations activities, recruitment practices, and counseling and training activities, can exert a modicum of control over such transition-related factors as community attitudes toward their program and the characteristics and attitudes of the enrollees. Considerably more discretion, however, can be exercised by program administrators in their selection of PSE employers and training agencies, and in the strategic and administrative devices to facilitate transition. This section examines the practices over which the sponsor has significant control.

All sponsors were asked to review their placement experience, and the responses of those with above average job entry rates were examined. The key to their success appears to be the strategies they developed in working wih PSE employers, training agencies, and program participants.

Most frequently, these sponsors attributed their placement results to their close working relationships with employers. Employers were encouraged to provide PSE enrollees with release time to seek employment, and participants were assigned only to employers who had previously absorbed enrollees. The second most frequently mentioned strategy was to approve training only in high demand occupations and give training agencies a major role in placement. The third approach focused on participants. Respondents underscored the importance of reminding participants of the temporary nature of their assignment and cited the importance of counseling and followup. One sponsor deliberately selected only highly motivated program applicants.

Asked to identify elements which impede transition, the same group of sponsors mentioned factors over which they have little or no control: economic downturns, the lower qualifications of enrollees, and the poor image of CETA in the eyes of employers.

# Trends in CETA Program Outcomes

To assess more fully the outcomes of the CETA employment and training programs, it is necessary to disaggregate the job entry rates, examine program outcomes other than placements, and track long term trends. This section examines the components of placement data and looks at CETA outcomes from fiscal 1975 through fiscal 1980. It also discusses the intermediate term effect of the program on labor force adjustment and earnings of participants.

## *Job Entry Rates*
### *by Program Activity*

Job entry rates of CETA enrollees are associated with kinds of program activities as well as with the characteristics of enrollees (table 73). Highest rates were reported for those enrolled in on-the-job training and for Title IIB/C enrollees who received only "services," such as counseling or job market information. On-the-job trainees are in an advantageous position since they are already part of the employer's workforce. Persons receiving "services" only are generally job-ready and can be placed with minimal effort.

Occupational skill trainees are more successful in obtaining immediate employment (44 percent in 1980), than enrollees in courses such as adult basic education or English as a second language (34 percent) which enhance the person's basic qualifications rather than prepare him for a specific occupation.

Job entry rates for public service employment participants in 1980 were virtually the same for Title IID and Title VI (36 and 35 percent). Three-fifths of these placements were in public sector jobs, which indicates that CETA has been successful in accomplishing a social objective—chanelling disadvantaged persons into public employment.

The lower job entry rate for PSE enrollees compared with those in Title IIB/C may be due to the "direct placements" under Title IIB/C (see discussion below). There is also a possibility that the expectation of being absorbed into the regular workforce of the employing agency may deter job seeking efforts on the part of PSE enrollees.[15]

### Components of Job Entry Rates

*Direct, indirect and self-placements.* Job entry rates are a composite of placements made with the assistance of prime sponsors or subagents and of jobs found by enrollees themselves. Those made by CETA sponsors or subagents may be "direct" or "indirect." Direct placements are those which are made with limited services to the participant (i.e., intake, assessment, counseling, job market information, job referrals or supportive services). Indirect placements are those made after an individual has been enrolled in a substantive training or employment program. The indirect placement rate is a more critical measure of program outcomes, since it reflects the result of the training or experience offered to clients as well as placement efforts.

The major difference between job entry rates for Title IIB/C and for PSE is the proportion (17 percent) of Title IIB/C placements classified as direct. Direct placements do not generally apply to PSE participants since they are enrolled in programs. Without direct placements, rates for all

---

15. General Accounting Office, *Moving Participants,* pp. 20-21.

Table 73

## Job Entry Rates by Activity, CETA Title IIB/C, Title IID, and Title VI, Fiscal 1980
(percent of terminations)

| Termination status | Classroom training | | On-the-job training | Public service employment | Work experience | | |
|---|---|---|---|---|---|---|---|
| | Occupational skill | Other | | | In school | Other | Service only[a] |
| **Title IIB/C** | | | | | | | |
| Total: Number[b] | 156,754 | 58,536 | 68,860 | c | 104,096 | 83,924 | 73,744 |
| Percent | 100 | 100 | 100 | - | 100 | 100 | 100 |
| Entered employment | 44 | 34 | 63 | - | 5 | 36 | 58 |
| Private sector | 36 | 29 | 57 | - | 4 | 23 | 51 |
| Public sector | 8 | 5 | 6 | - | 1 | 13 | 7 |
| Other positive terminations | 16 | 25 | 4 | - | 76 | 21 | 13 |
| Nonpositive terminations | 40 | 41 | 33 | - | 19 | 43 | 29 |
| **Title IID** | | | | | | | |
| Total: Number[b] | 6,774 | 2,684 | c | 197,816 | 2,104 | 5,400 | 5,465 |
| Percent | 100 | 100 | - | 100 | 100 | 100 | 100 |
| Entered employment | 34 | 23 | - | 36 | 9 | 24 | 30 |
| Private sector | 27 | 19 | - | 14 | 2 | 16 | 25 |
| Public sector | 7 | 4 | - | 22 | 7 | 8 | 5 |
| Other positive terminations | 20 | 29 | - | 8 | 50 | 29 | 16 |
| Nonpositive terminations | 46 | 48 | - | 56 | 41 | 47 | 54 |
| **Title VI** | | | | | | | |
| Total: Number[b] | 2,054 | c | c | 188,567 | c | 3,732 | 2,136 |
| Percent | 100 | - | - | 100 | - | 100 | 100 |

| | | | | | | | |
|---|---|---|---|---|---|---|---|
| Entered employment........ | 48 | – | 35 | – | 7 | – | 40 |
| Private sector.............. | 42 | – | 14 | – | 4 | – | 30 |
| Public sector .............. | 6 | – | 21 | – | 3 | – | 10 |
| Other positive terminations .... | 12 | – | 6 | – | 68 | – | 15 |
| Nonpositive terminations ...... | 40 | – | 59 | – | 25 | – | 45 |

SOURCE: U.S. Department of Labor, Employment and Training Administration, based on annual CETA program activity summary reports.

a. Includes employment services such as intake, counseling, referral to employers, and/or supportive services such as health care, transportation, child care, etc.

b. Excludes transfers to other CETA titles.

c. Number of terminations 2,000 or fewer.

three titles would be more similar. A second difference is a higher proportion of self-placements among PSE enrollees.

| | Fiscal year 1980 job entries | | |
|---|---|---|---|
| Type of job entry | Title IIB/C | Title IID | Title VI |
| | | (Percent) | |
| Total .................... | 100 | 100 | 100 |
| Made by sponsor | | | |
| or subagent .............. | 73 | 64 | 64 |
| Direct................... | 17 | 1 | 2 |
| Indirect ................ | 56 | 63 | 61 |
| Self-placements and other .... | 28 | 36 | 36 |

SOURCE: Based on table 67.

*Other positive and nonpositive terminations.* Participants who do not enter unsubsidized employment are classified either as "other positive"—those who return to school or join the armed forces—or "nonpositive." Since more than one-third of the Title IIB/C enrollees are 19 years of age or younger, and more than half of that age group are still in school, the rate of other positive terminations is higher for Title IIB/C (25 percent in 1980) than for PSE titles (9 percent).

The other side of the placement coin, "nonpositive terminations," also bears examination. One of the most striking facts shown by table 67 is the large proportion of such terminees, those who were not known to have obtained jobs, returned to school, or entered the armed forces. More than one-half of the fiscal 1980 terminees from public service employment programs and more than one-third of Title IIB/C terminees were classified as nonpositive.

A longitudinal study of persons enrolled in CETA in fiscal year 1976 who terminated by the end of that year sheds some light on reasons for nonpositive terminations. Twelve percent of the nonpositive terminees left for personal reasons—health, family care, transportation, or removal from the area. Seventeen percent were either laid off because of completion of a CETA project, lack of funds, or refusal to continue in their CETA program. And 10 percent were "administratively separated" for other reasons. This left 61 percent whose reason for terminating was not ascertained.[16]

The large proportion in the "unknown" category may include some persons who left CETA and were not able to obtain jobs immediately or those who withdrew from the labor force. On the other hand, it may include some who actually entered employment but failed to notify the prime sponsor. Nonpositive terminations may also reflect programmatic problems—selection of enrollees not able to benefit from training or jobs, mismatch between CETA programs and clients' needs, lack of counseling or supportive services, or failure to stress the job finding objectives.

## Intermediate Term Outcomes of CETA Programs

While the immediate postprogram employment experience of enrollees is useful for comparative purposes and as a measure of short range program outcomes, a longer term view of the impact of CETA programs is more meaningful.

The multiple objectives of CETA make it extremely difficult to develop suitable quantitative measures to evaluate results. Reports of the Department of Labor's management information system and the Continuous Longitudinal Manpower Survey of CETA enrollees and terminees provide the best data to analyze postprogram labor market experience. But even this information does not convey the full range of benefits associated with CETA activities.

---

16. Derived from data in Westat, Inc., "Impact on 1977 Earnings of New FY 1976 CETA Enrollees in Selected Program Activities," *Continuous Longitudinal Manpower Survey,* Net Impact Report I, prepared for Office of Program Evaluation, Employment and Training Administration (Rockville, MD: Westat, Inc., March 1981), pp. 3-36.

During the first six years of CETA, close to 10 million persons were enrolled in the major locally administered CETA programs, according to DOL reports (table 74). Nearly two-thirds of these were in Title IIB/C. Of the 10 million, about 9 million left the program, and slightly more than one-third of these got jobs immediately either through the assistance of CETA sponsors or subcontractors or through their own efforts. Job entry rates over the years were higher for persons in training programs (Title IIB/C), than for PSE enrollees (37 vs. 28 percent average for 1975-1980) (table 75).

On the whole, job entry rates, even for Title IIB/C programs, have been lower than in the pre-CETA manpower programs. But this may be due in part to inclusion in CETA of activities not specifically intended to lead to job placement, such as work experience programs for in-school youth.[17]

### Changes in Labor Force Status

CLMS reports indicate that the employment experience of CETA terminees improves over time. A followup study of terminees who entered CETA adult-oriented programs in 1976 shows that 50 percent were employed immediately after leaving CETA and 60 percent a year later (table 76).[18] The study indicates that those with the most stable pre-entry employment histories had relatively good post-termination

---

17. Mirengoff and Rindler, *CETA: Under Local Control*, pp. 225-6. Job entry rates averaged 57 percent in selected DOL training programs in fiscal 1974 compared with an average of 37 percent for CETA Title IIB/C from 1975 to 1980. However, CETA figures include in-school youth not included in the selected pre-CETA manpower programs.

18. The higher placement rates shown in the CLMS reports (table 76) compared with DOL's management information system (MIS) (table 75) may be due to differences in the programs included or in the method of gathering the data: (a) CLMS reports are for adult-oriented programs while DOL reports include some programs for in-school youth; (b) CLMS reports, based on interviews with a sample of enrollees, may have more complete information on persons who obtained employment on their own than MIS reports, derived from prime sponsor records.

Table 74

New Enrollees, Terminations, and Job Entries, CETA Title I (IIB/C), Title II (IID), and Title VI, Fiscal 1975-1980

(thousands)

| Fiscal Year | New Enrollees[a] | | | | Terminations[b] | | | | Job Entries | | | |
|---|---|---|---|---|---|---|---|---|---|---|---|---|
| | Title I (IIB/C) | Title II (IID) | Title VI | Total | Title I (IIB/C) | Title II (IID) | Title VI | Total | Title I (IIB/C) | Title II (IID) | Title VI | Total |
| Total......... | 6,449 | 1,397 | 2,025 | 9,871 | 5,931 | 1,150 | 1,999 | 9,080 | 2,216 | 331 | 553 | 3,100 |
| 1975.......... | 1,126 | 227 | 157 | 1,510 | 553 | 71 | 34 | 658 | 176 | 17 | 10 | 203 |
| 1976[c]........ | 1,553 | 324 | 381 | 2,258 | 1,670 | 216 | 469 | 2,355 | 505 | 49 | 94 | 648 |
| 1977.......... | 1,119 | 165 | 432 | 1,716 | 1,049 | 261 | 162 | 1,472 | 409 | 46 | 55 | 510 |
| 1978.......... | 965 | 101 | 556 | 1,622 | 1,007 | 100 | 531 | 1,638 | 450 | 38 | 162 | 650 |
| 1979.......... | 891 | 348 | 346 | 1,585 | 875 | 220 | 521 | 1,616 | 388 | 93 | 146 | 627 |
| 1980.......... | 795 | 232 | 153 | 1,180 | 777 | 282 | 282 | 1,341 | 288 | 88 | 86 | 462 |

SOURCE: Employment and Training Administration, U.S. Department of Labor data.

a. First time enrollments for each title. Includes transfers from other titles.

b. Includes transfers to other titles of CETA.

c. Includes transition quarter (July-Sept. 1976).

employment. However, those with little employment before CETA did not attain a high employment level afterward, but they had greater average gains in employment status.[19]

Table 75
Job Entry Rates
CETA Title I (IIB/C), Title II (IID), and Title VI,
Fiscal 1975-1980[a]

| Fiscal year | Combined rate | Title I (IIB/C) | Title II (IID) | Title VI |
|---|---|---|---|---|
| | (Percent of terminations) | | | |
| 1975 .......... | 31 | 32 | 24 | 29 |
| 1976 .......... | 28 | 30 | 23 | 20 |
| 1977 .......... | 35 | 39 | 18 | 34 |
| 1978 .......... | 40 (43) | 45 (48) | 38 (45) | 31 (33) |
| 1979 .......... | 39 (44) | 44 (47) | 42 (47) | 28 (36) |
| 1980 .......... | 35 (38) | 37 (41) | 31 (35) | 31 (35) |
| Average 1975-80 ..... | 34 | 37 | 29 | 28 |

SOURCE: Employment and Training Administration, U.S. Department of Labor data.
a. Ratio of job entries to terminations. Actual job entry rates for Title II and VI may be higher than the rates shown because intertitle transfers are included in termination figures. Figures in parentheses show job entry rates for fiscal 1978-1980 with intertitle transfers excluded.

It is striking that one-fourth of those enrolled in CETA were not in the labor force prior to enrollment, and one-fifth were not, after termination. According to the CLMS study, a large proportion—25 percent—of those not in the labor force for a considerable part of the year prior to CETA enrollment returned to a not-in-the-labor force status after CETA termination. Enrollees classified as not in the labor force after leaving CETA were persons whose principal activity was school or training, who were in an institution, or

19. Westat, Inc., "Postprogram Experiences and Pre/Post Comparisons for Terminees Who Entered CETA During Fiscal Year 1976," *Continuous Longitudinal Manpower Survey,* Followup Report 2, prepared for Office of Program Evaluation, Employment and Training Administration (Rockville, MD: Westat, Inc., March 1979), pp. 1-2, 1-7, 1-9.

who were not seeking work because of ill health, family responsibilities, or for other reasons.

### Table 76
### Labor Force Status of CETA Terminees
### Prior to CETA Enrollment and Subsequent to Termination[a]

| Point of time | Labor force status | | |
|---|---|---|---|
| | Employed | Unemployed | Not in labor force |
| | (Percent of terminees) | | |
| **Prior to entry** | | | |
| 1 month.............. | 26 | 48 | 26 |
| 1 day ................ | 24 | 51 | 25 |
| **Post-termination** | | | |
| 1 day ................ | 50 | 21 | 29 |
| 1 month.............. | 50 | 28 | 22 |
| 3 months ............ | 53 | 26 | 21 |
| 6 months ............ | 55 | 24 | 21 |
| 12 months ........... | 60 | 21 | 19 |

SOURCE: Westat, Inc., *Continuous Longitudinal Manpower Survey, CLMS,* Followup Report 2, March 1979, app. D, table 42.

a. Persons who entered adult-oriented CETA programs during fiscal year 1976 and who had been out of CETA at least 12 months.

Terminees from on-the-job training and public service employment had better employment records than persons leaving other program activities, according to the CLMS (table 77).[20] About one-half of the PSE terminees who were employed three months after termination were working for public employers.

---

20. According to the DOL management information system data (table 73), PSE terminees had lower placement rates than those terminating from other activities immediately after termination while CLMS data show them as having better employment records than those in classroom training or in adult work experience.

## Table 77
## Labor Force Status of CETA Terminees by Program Activity
## 3 and 12 Months After Termination[a]

| Labor force status | All activities | Program activity | | | | |
| --- | --- | --- | --- | --- | --- | --- |
| | | Classroom training | On-the-job training | Adult work experience | Public service employment | Multiple activities |
| | | (Percent of terminees) | | | | |
| **3 months post-CETA** | | | | | | |
| Total .................. | 100 | 100 | 100 | 100 | 100 | 100 |
| Employed ............. | 52 | 46 | 64 | 52 | 54 | 44 |
| Unemployed .......... | 26 | 32 | 21 | 26 | 23 | 30 |
| Not in labor force .... | 21 | 22 | 16 | 22 | 23 | 26 |
| **12 months post-CETA** | | | | | | |
| Total .................. | 100 | 100 | 100 | 100 | 100 | 100 |
| Employed ............. | 60 | 54 | 68 | 56 | 64 | 57 |
| Unemployed .......... | 21 | 25 | 20 | 22 | 16 | 24 |
| Not in labor force..... | 19 | 21 | 12 | 22 | 20 | 19 |

SOURCE: Westat, Inc., *Continuous Longitudinal Manpower Survey*, Followup Report 2, March 1979, table 5-8, pp. 5-14.

a. Persons who entered adult-oriented CETA programs during fiscal year 1976 and who had been out of CETA at least 12 months.

## Earnings Changes

The 1978 reauthorization act, for the first time since CETA was enacted, recognized a change of earnings as an explicit objective. For the most part, enrollees had higher earnings after leaving the program than they had before entering. CLMS studies found that annualized earnings of those out of CETA for 12 months averaged $4,990 compared with $2,850 in the fourth quarter before entry, a gain of 75 percent.[21] Enrollees who had the poorest employment records before enrollment in CETA made the greatest earnings gains after termination, while those employed before their participation in CETA, on the average, did not return to their pre-CETA earnings levels. Annualized earnings gains after one year, in absolute terms, were highest for those who had been enrolled in on-the-job training programs. Public service employment program enrollees registered the second highest increases. Classroom training enrollees ranked third, while adult work experience enrollees had the lowest post-CETA earnings gains. The percentage gain over pre-CETA earnings was greatest for classroom training enrollees, however.

The earnings gains of CETA enrollees take on more meaning when compared with the experience of a matched group of persons not enrolled in CETA. To compare the change in earnings of the two groups, the CLMS project used the Current Population Survey (CPS) files to identify a comparison group and social security earnings records to measure the income of both groups.[22] The study supports the conclusion that CETA enrollees on the average, had higher earnings

---

21. Westat, Inc., Followup Report 2, pp. 1-2, 1-12, and appendix table 57.

22. Westat, Inc., Net Impact Report 1, Chapter 3. The CETA group includes persons enrolled in CETA in fiscal 1976 and terminated by December 31, 1976. Direct referrals to jobs, those not assigned to a CETA activity, and youth in summer jobs were omitted. For a discussion of methods of selecting the comparison group, techniques used to adjust for differences between the comparison group and the treatment group, and methodological problems, see chapters 3 and 4 of the CLMS study.

gains than comparable nonparticipants, and that those enrollees with poor earnings or employment histories gained most. The overall net earnings impact is relatively small, however.

CETA 1976 enrollees who terminated before 1977 had 1977 earnings gains above pre-CETA levels averaging $300 or about 8 percent more than the gains of the comparison group (table 78). The increase among the low pre-CETA earners averaged $550 more than earnings gains of persons in the comparison group. The gains of high pre-CETA earners, however, were $50 less than those of their counterparts in the control groups. Outcomes varied by sex: females, who generally had lower pre-CETA earnings, scored greater gains compared with their matched group than did males.

Those CETA enrollees who were placed by the prime sponsor on termination gained more than the matched group (an average of $1,250 more). The CETA enrollees who terminated and were not placed by the prime sponsor did not show significant earnings gains compared to their matched group.

When compared with their matched counterparts, the largest earnings gains were registered by on-the-job trainees; participants in classroom training (rather than PSE) were second. The lower gains recorded for PSE enrollees were believed to understate their true gains, since a proportion entered state or local government employment after termination and may not have had their earnings covered by social security. The earnings of work experience participants in 1977 were not significantly different from those of the comparison group.

## Table 78
## 1977 Earnings Gains of CETA Terminees in Excess of Earnings Gains of Comparison Group by Level of Preprogram Earnings and by CETA Program Activity

| Preprogram earnings group | Program activities | | | | | |
|---|---|---|---|---|---|---|
| | All | Classroom training | On-the-job training | Public service employment | Work experience | Multiple activities |
| All groups............ | $300[a] | $350[a] | $ 850[a] | $250[b] | $-150 | $350[c] |
| Low earners........... | 550[a] | 600[a] | 1,300[a] | 900[a] | 0 | 550[b] |
| Intermediate earners.... | 50 | 0 | 450[a] | 0 | -200 | 250 |
| High earners.......... | -50 | 250 | 300 | -250 | -800[c] | 100 |

SOURCE: Westat, Inc., *Continuous Longitudinal Manpower Survey*, Net Impact Report 1, March 1981, pp. 3-29.

NOTE: This table covers fiscal 1976 CETA enrollees who terminated before December 1976 excluding direct referrals to jobs, persons not assigned to a program activity, and summer youth enrollees. Figures not adjusted for Social Security noncoverage.

Level of significance:

  a = significant at the 0.01 level.
  b = significant at the 0.05 level.
  c = significant at the 0.10 level.

# Summary

Several provisions of the reauthorization act help to provide conditions which are more conducive than the original CETA legislation to placing CETA enrollees in unsubsidized employment; others tend to hinder placement. Respondents in the BSSR sample noted particularly the salutary effect in enhancing employability of new training provisions for public service enrollees. On the other hand, the stricter eligibility requirements and lower wages have tended to enroll persons with fewer job qualifications, dampening opportunities for transfer to either public or private sector jobs. The 18-month limit on tenure in public service jobs programs and the 30-month limit for all CETA titles were believed to have little effect on placement outcomes during the second year after the reauthorization act.

The reauthorization amendments created a greater awareness of the transition objective but did not result in higher job entry rates upon termination. The combined job entry rate for CETA Titles IIB/C, IID, and VI, rose slightly from 43 percent in 1978 to 44 percent in 1979, but dropped sharply to 38 percent in 1980. Local officials attributed the decline to a softer labor market (the U.S. unemployment rate rose from 5.8 in 1979 to 6.8 percent in 1980), but lower skilled, less marketable enrollees were also believed to be a factor in the decline. The biggest drops occurred in Title IIB/C and Title IID; Title VI placement rates, which were lower than those of other titles in 1978, remained stable.

Immediate placement outcomes depended, to a considerable degree, on management practices, and emphasis given to the placement objectives. Several of the sponsors in the BSSR sample have intensified placement efforts by assuming responsibility themselves or placing more responsibility on subcontractors. Others have made changes in internal organization and procedures. On the whole, sponsors are placing more emphasis on placement activities, but changes are not due entirely to the reauthorization act.

While the short range placement outcomes are significant, the longer term trends add perspectives. Between 1975 and 1980, over one-third of the 9 million CETA terminees were placed immediately after termination either through their own efforts or through a CETA intermediary. Longitudinal studies, however, show improved labor force status over time. A followup study of 1976 terminees from adult programs showed 60 percent employed after one year.

The impact of CETA is reflected in improved earnings as well as labor force status. The CLMS national sample survey found that average annualized earnings of 1976 terminees were $4,990 for the fourth quarter after leaving CETA—$2,140 more than their earnings in the fourth quarter before entry. Largest gains were made by those who were unemployed or out of the labor force before entry, while some who had been employed before CETA averaged lower post-CETA earnings. A comparison of CETA enrollees with a group of non-enrollees with like characteristics showed estimated 1977 earnings gains after preprogram earnings averaging about 8 percent higher ($300) for the CETA group. Those who were placed by CETA sponsors at termination averaged better earnings gains over their nonparticipant counterparts than those who obtained employment on their own or by some other means.

The intermediate labor force and earnings gains of CETA enrollees support the view that programs targeted to persons with poorest employment histories are most effective and that management practices can contribute significantly to placement results and earnings.

# Appendix

Table A-1
## Changes in Characteristics of Public Service Employment Participants
### U.S. Total and Survey Areas, Fiscal 1978 and 1980
(percent of all participants)

| Characteristic | U.S. total 1978 | U.S. total 1980 | Study areas 1978 | Study areas 1980 | Changes 1978 to 1980 U.S. total | Changes 1978 to 1980 Study areas |
|---|---|---|---|---|---|---|
| Female ............ | 39 | 48 | 41 | 49 | +9 | +8 |
| Youth, 16 to 21 ..... | 21 | 25 | 22 | 25 | +4 | +3 |
| Less than high school education ... | 26 | 32 | 23 | 26 | +6 | +3 |
| Public Assistance recipient ......... | 19 | 25 | 20 | 26 | +6 | +6 |

SOURCE: U.S. Department of Labor, Employment and Training Administration, Management Information System.

## Table B-1
### Characteristics of Populations Eligible for Public Service Employment Programs Before and After the Reauthorization Act

| Characteristic | Before Reauthorization | | | After Reauthorization | | | | | |
| --- | --- | --- | --- | --- | --- | --- | --- | --- | --- |
| | Population 1 | | | Population 2 | | | Population 3 | | |
| | Total | Unemployed 30 days or more | Under-employed | Total | AFDC | Other | Total | AFDC | Other |
| Total eligible (thousands) | 18,291 | 13,000 | 5,291 | 5,685 | 2,142 | 3,543 | 3,870 | 2,142 | 1,728 |
| | (Percent of total) | | | (Percent of total) | | | (Percent of total) | | |
| Sex: Male | 53 | 56 | 44 | 49 | 24 | 64 | 42 | 24 | 63 |
| Female | 47 | 44 | 56 | 51 | 76 | 36 | 58 | 76 | 37 |
| Age: 21 and under | 25 | 25 | 25 | 17 | 14 | 20 | 16 | 14 | 19 |
| 22-44 | 54 | 55 | 51 | 62 | 73 | 56 | 64 | 73 | 53 |
| 45 and over | 21 | 20 | 24 | 20 | 13 | 25 | 20 | 13 | 28 |
| Race/Ethnic Group: | | | | | | | | | |
| White, Non-Hispanic | 70 | 72 | 65 | 61 | 46 | 69 | 56 | 46 | 68 |
| Black, Non-Hispanic | 20 | 19 | 24 | 29 | 40 | 22 | 33 | 40 | 24 |
| Hispanic | 7 | 7 | 9 | 9 | 12 | 7 | 9 | 12 | 7 |
| Other | 2 | 2 | 2 | 2 | 2 | 2 | 2 | 2 | 2 |
| Education: 0-11 years | 40 | 36 | 48 | 47 | 58 | 40 | 51 | 58 | 43 |
| 12 years | 37 | 40 | 31 | 35 | 34 | 36 | 33 | 34 | 33 |
| 13 years and over | 23 | 23 | 21 | 18 | 9 | 24 | 15 | 9 | 24 |
| Economic Status: | | | | | | | | | |
| AFDC recipient | 12 | 10 | 16 | 38 | 100 | 0 | 55 | 100 | 0 |
| Economically disadvantaged | 55 | 37 | 100 | 82 | 100 | 70 | 100 | 100 | 100 |
| Unemployment Insurance Claimant | 19 | 26 | 2 | 17 | 0 | 27 | 11 | 0 | 25 |

SOURCE: Unpublished data from the March 1979 Current Population Survey, the Bureau of Labor Statistics; and Table 30, "Characteristics of WIN Registrants," WIN office of Employment and Training Administration, U.S. Department of Labor.

Definitions:

Population 1 - Population eligible for Title II and for Title VI sustainment, before the reauthorization act—population includes persons unemployed 5 weeks or more in 1978 and persons employed 48 weeks or more with family income below the OMB poverty level.

Population 2 - Population eligible under Title VI of the reauthorization act—population includes persons unemployed 10 weeks or more with family income no greater than 100 percent of the BLS low-income standard in 1978 and persons registered with WIN in fiscal 1979.

Population 3 - Population eligible under Title IID of the reauthorization act—population includes persons unemployed 15 weeks or more with family income no greater than 70 percent of the BLS low-income standard in 1978 and persons registered with WIN in fiscal 1979.

NOTE: Eligible populations overlap; persons eligible in one population may also be part of one or both of the other two populations.

The estimates of the population eligible for PSE before and after the reauthorization are rough approximations based on special tabulations of Current Population Survey (CPS) data. The CPS data cannot be tabulated to conform fully to the PSE eligibility criteria. In particular, eligibility is based on a period of unemployment immediately before application for PSE (30 days before application, 10 of the 12 weeks and 15 of the 20 weeks before application). It was possible to tabulate the annual CPS data only for the total weeks unemployed during the entire previous year. Thus persons who were unemployed for more than one stretch during the year may have been included in the estimated number of eligibles even though none of the stretches of unemployment was long enough for eligibility. This results in overestimates of the number of eligibles. About 40 percent of Population 1, and 45 percent of Population 2 and 3 had two or more stretches of unemployment between March 1977 and March 1978.

The treatment of income data acts in the opposite direction—to underestimate the number eligible. The income criteria for PSE eligibility refer to periods of less than a year (3 months for Title VI and 6 months for Title IID). The CPS income data could be tabulated only for the full year. More individuals will meet the low-income criteria for a 3- or 6-month period than will meet it for a whole year.

Prior to the reauthorization, eligibility for the nonproject portion of Title VI was open to persons who had been unemployed as little as 15 days if they lived in areas where the unemployment rate was over 7 percent. This group is not included in the estimate of the number of eligibles in the prereauthorization period because it could not be tabulated separately for areas with over 7 percent unemployment. For the country as a whole, over 4 million persons had between 2 and 4 weeks of unemployment in the March 1977 to March 1978 period.

# Survey Areas
# and
# Field Research Associates

Arizona:
Phoenix
> John S. Hall, Associate Professor and Director of Research, Center for Public Affairs, Arizona State University

Balance of Arizona
> Constance M. LaMonica, Director of State Affairs, Samaritan Health Service, Phoenix

California:
Long Beach
> Pamela S. Tolbert, Research Associate, Institute for Social Science Research, University of California at Los Angeles

Orange County Consortium
> Lynne G. Zucker, Assistant Professor, Department of Sociology, University of California at Los Angeles

San Joaquin Consortium
> C. Daniel Vencill, Associate Professor, Economics Department, San Francisco State University, and Vice President, Center for Applied Manpower Research, Berkeley

Stanislaus County
> Linda Gruber, Research Associate, Center for Applied Manpower Research, Berkeley

Florida:
Pasco County
Pinellas County-St. Petersburg Consortium
> Emil Bie, former Deputy Director, Office of Technical Support, U.S. Employment Service

Illinois:
  Cook County
    Marilyn D. Jacobson, Assistant Professor, School of
    Education, Northwestern University

Indiana:
  Gary
    Roger L. Pulliam, Director, Center for Urban Studies,
    University of Illinois at Chicago

Kansas:
  Kansas City-Wyandotte County Consortium
    Anthony L. Redwood, Associate Professor, School of
    Business, University of Kansas
  Topeka-Shawnee County Consortium
    Charles E. Krider, Associate Professor, School of
    Business, University of Kansas

Maine:
  Balance of Maine
    Roderick A. Forsgren, Professor of Management, Col-
    lege of Business, University of Maine

Michigan:
  Mid-Counties Employment and Training Consortium
    E. Earl Wright, Director, W.E. Upjohn Institute for
    Employment Research, assisted by Jo Bentley Reece
  Lansing Tri-County Regional Manpower Consortium
    H. Allan Hunt, Research Economist, W.E. Upjohn
    Institute for Employment Research, assisted by Jo
    Bentley Reece

Minnesota:
  St. Paul
  Ramsey County
    David Thompson, Great Lakes Research, Minneapolis

New Jersey:
  Middlesex County
  Union County
    Jack Chernick, Professor, Institute of Management and
    Labor Relations, Rutgers University

New York:
  New York City
    Barbara R. McIntosh, Assistant Professor, Institute of
    Management and Labor Relations, Rutgers University

North Carolina:
  City of Raleigh
    Charles L. Usher, Policy Analyst, Center for the Study
    of Social Behavior, Research Triangle Institute
  Balance of North Carolina
    Edward F. Dement, Research Project Director, MDC,
    Inc.

Ohio:
  City of Cleveland
    Lance M. Smith, Research Associate, Mershon Center,
    Ohio State University
  Lorain County
    Henry H. Hixson, Adjunct Professor, The Gill Center
    of Business and Economic Education, Ashland College

Pennsylvania:
  Chester County
    Harry Greenspan, Research Associate, Bureau of Social
    Science Research
  Philadelphia
    Albert L. Shostack, former Chief, Division of Residen-
    tial Living, Job Corps, U.S. Department of Labor

Texas:
  Capital Area Consortium
    Robert E. McPherson, Director, Human Resources Professionals Program, University of Texas at Austin, assisted by Richard Mackay
  Balance of Texas
    Robert W. Glover, Acting Director, The Center for the Study of Human Resources, University of Texas at Austin, assisted by Hubert Smith

# Reports of the Employment and Training Evaluation Project

The Comprehensive Employment and Training Act: Impact on People, Places, and Programs, National Academy of Sciences, Washington, D.C. (1976)

Transition to Decentralized Manpower Programs: Eight Area Studies, National Academy of Sciences, Washington, D.C. (1976)

The Comprehensive Employment and Training Act: Abstracts of Selected Studies, National Academy of Sciences, Washington, D.C. (1976)

CETA: Manpower Programs Under Local Control, National Academy of Sciences, Washington, D.C. (1978)

Employment and Training Programs: The Local View, National Academy of Sciences, Washington, D.C. (1978)

CETA: Assessment and Recommendations, National Academy of Sciences, Washington, D.C. (1978)

Developing Manpower Legislation: A Personal Chronicle, National Academy of Sciences, Washington, D.C. (1978)

CETA: Assessment of Public Service Employment Programs, National Academy of Sciences, Washington, D.C. (1980)

The New CETA: Effect on Public Service Employment Programs, National Academy of Sciences, Washington, D.C. (1980)